MY PARENTS

MY PARENTS

A Differing View

James Roosevelt

with Bill Libby

ΡℽΡ

A Playboy Press Book

Design by Tere LoPrete

Library of Congress Cataloging in Publication Data

Roosevelt, James, 1907–
  My parents.

  Includes index.
  1. Roosevelt, Franklin Delano, Pres. U.S.,
1882–1945. 2. Roosevelt, Eleanor Roosevelt, 1884–
1962. 3. Roosevelt, James, 1907– 4. Presidents—
United States—Biography. 5. Presidents—
United States—Wives—Biography. 6. Legislators—
United States—Biography. I. Libby, Bill, joint
author. II. Title.
E807.R658   973.917′092′2 [B]   76–43994
ISBN 0–87223–476–2

For the Rebel

Preface

My parents probably were the most important pair of personalities in the two-hundred-year history of this country. Franklin Delano Roosevelt served as president for more than thirteen years, longer than any other president has served. And he served during a period that was as critical as any in our history. Eleanor Roosevelt pioneered the participation of women in public life. Lately, their private affairs have been made public property. A case can be made for the Kennedys, but John F. Kennedy served as president less than three years, while Jacqueline Kennedy is, unfortunately, better known for her private than for her public affairs. Washington, Jefferson, Lincoln and our other presidential immortals did not have wives who made any real public impact.

More than ninety years after the birth of my father and mother, almost forty-five years after he was elected to the presidency, more than thirty years after his death, and more than fifteen years after hers, there has been a reawakening of interest in them. There have been television and stage plays based on their lives, and, of course, many books have been written about them. Why, then, another book? Partly because many of these works are by people who never knew them and so cannot present them properly. Others, of course, are by those who knew them, but even many of these do not present them in human terms. We see them as politicians, not as people. At best there are many inaccuracies in these works. At worst there is dishonesty. Words are put into my parents' mouths that others never heard. Scenes are imagined. A distorted picture of my parents emerges; they are mistaken for the actors who portray them, rather than emerging as the people they were. Conclusions are drawn—some of them by my brother, Elliott, in his books—with which I disagree. I take a differing view of so much that has been presented to the public about my parents that I feel I should now speak out in print. And speak only of that which I know to be true.

Also, there is more to a family than a father and mother. Our parents had six children—one son died in infancy. And my father's mother, Sara Roosevelt, was influential in our family life. When others speak of the Roosevelts they speak primarily of Franklin, Eleanor and Sara. When I speak of them I speak also of myself, my sister Anna and my brothers Elliott, Franklin, Jr., and John—eight individuals who formed the family unit which up until now has never been portrayed accurately and in detail.

Finally, the pressures of prominence and the weight of responsibilities placed upon my father and his successors— Harry Truman, Dwight Eisenhower, John Kennedy, Lyndon Johnson, Richard Nixon and Gerald Ford—and their families altered them and those close to them. I want to say something about this from the standpoint of the Roosevelts. Most of these presidents aged terribly in the office. Three died naturally, but before their wives. One was assassinated, another resigned. Some gave in to the temptations of power, others suffered torment over decisions that decided life and death for millions. Some have been soiled by scandals, stains that will not wipe out. Clearly, whatever else they were, they were men with weaknesses as well as strengths. Demands were made on them which would have tried gods and saints. And more has been expected of their wives and children than many of them had to give.

While I do not plan to carry it beyond reason, interesting

comparisons can be drawn among these presidents and their families of the last forty to fifty years, between the Roosevelts and Kennedys, for instance. Sons and brothers, some of us were supposed to contribute to presidential dynasties, to cite one circumstance. But we did not—or could not. Things are being divulged now about the Kennedys that are reminiscent of those past probings into the privacy of the Roosevelts. Did my father have mistresses? How close were he and my mother? Or was there an agreement to maintain a marriage in name only?

I do not seek to sensationalize the lives of the Roosevelts, nor any other presidential family. I want to present as accurate a portrait as possible. And I want to show the famous people of my day as I saw them. I worry what my children will think, but I owe it to my small place in history to tell it "like it is."

Facing the facts may hurt. The five Roosevelt children have had seventeen marriages. Obviously, most ended in divorce. Two of those we married eventually took their own lives. We cannot take this lightly. How many of these marriages and lives were bent and perhaps broken by the pressures of prominence? Or were we merely betrayed by our own weaknesses? We have had our ups and downs in both our public and private lives. We have had successes and failures in both politics and business. I, for one, have had four marriages. Three ended in divorce. My political life has included losing the races for mayor of Los Angeles and for governor of California. In business, I've been associated with Bernie Cornfeld, Bob Vesco and IOS, all in disrepute now. On the other hand, I was elected six times to Congress, and I served with the United Nations.

My brothers have had their troubles, too, but Franklin also was elected to Congress and served with John Kennedy. Elliott was mayor of Miami Beach.

Circumstances thrust my father into power at a time when he probably had a greater and more enduring effect on the lives of more people of this country than any other man of our time. The day does not go by that I do not see some reference to him, as well as some examples of the way his work has lasted. Dramatically overcoming the crippling curse of polio, he remains an inspiration to many. In the wake of Watergate, we may never again trust a leader as most of the people of this country trusted him. But it is important that we do. Yet, he was a man of immense ego, and pure politician. No woman has done more for this country in general and for women in particular than my mother. Yet, she had to be pushed to play a prominent part in public life.

They were more successful as politicians than as parents. It is as admirable, but imperfect, people that I see my parents. Well, which of us is perfect? I am not, certainly. Nor are my brothers and my sister. But there are things to be said for us, as well as against us.

As the eldest son of Franklin and Eleanor Roosevelt, the eldest survivor among their children and the one who worked the most frequently with my father during his presidential days, I feel that I have had a unique view of the family. Serving him, I was cursed by critics on charges of nepotism. I am, however, proud to have served him. I saw him crawl across the floor—a cripple practicing his escape from a fire which never came. I helped him hobble up to platforms of power. And I laid him on the floor of a private railway car to rest at a time when his illness kept him from making the sort of public appearance expected of him.

Only I know that my father was prepared to drop an atom bomb on Japan. Only I know why he left in his will so much to a woman not his wife. Those secrets I have nursed I now set free in order to set the record straight. Now is the time, before it is too late.

I remember my father's rage when he was accused of seeing his sons safely through a war in which we all faced fire. I remember my brother Elliott saying it would be best if one of us was killed in action in order to clear his record. I remember that my mother did not cry when he died. Do not believe for a moment that she did not care. Understand, instead, that she had forgotten how to cry.

Understand, also, that for every sad memory, there is a happy one. That there has been laughter as well as tears in our lives. That there were moments important to us which may have been unimportant to the historians. Thus I propose a personal memoir. I am concerned with the moments of historic significance only as they affected the Roosevelts personally. I am more concerned with the anecdotes, amusing or sad, that best illustrate the personalities of the Roosevelts and those many and often prominent people who surrounded them than I am with delving into the presidential decisions that shaped a world. This, then, will not be a politically profound work, shot through with pretensions. I will speak as plainly as possible. I have a story to tell, so I will tell it.

James Roosevelt
SPRING 1976.

ACKNOWLEDGMENTS

The authors wish to thank Playboy Press; their editor, Jody Ward; and the producer of the project, Bill Adler, without whose work this book would not be a reality. They wish to thank all who have written and spoken of the family of Franklin and Eleanor Roosevelt so helpfully, as well as Jim's brothers, Elliott, Franklin and John, and their late sister Anna, who have been so deeply a part of his life for so long. They wish to thank all of the photographers who contributed to the pictorial spreads within. And they wish, finally, to thank the faithful transcribers of the tapes, Jackie Sommers, La Juana Rogers and Cheryl Thibault.

MY PARENTS

I

Contrary to popular belief, the Roosevelts never were rich as the Rockefellers, but we were born blue bloods, or so Sara Roosevelt kept telling us. Granny, or Mama, as my father called her, never let us forget for a moment that we were special people, inheritors of a grand name and proud tradition, and a part of high society. We were expected to act accordingly. We certainly were not poor, though many of us encountered financial troubles later in life. We were reared primarily on country estates, either along the Hudson River in upstate New York, or on Oyster Bay on Long Island. We had, for the most part, whatever we wanted. We had tutors and went to private schools. We mingled with the wealthy and famous.

The family was so large and complex that many of us married within the family—one distant cousin marrying another, as was the case with my father and mother. Her father was his godfather, for that matter. When we went outside the family, we did not stray far from "the 400," as the socially prominent were known. My brother married a du Pont. I married a Cushing, daughter of the most famous surgeon of his day. These were the people we knew. There has been so much inmarriage, so many branches that bore the Roosevelt name, so many leaves that bore the given names of Franklin,

James, Elliott, Theodore and Anna, that one easily can get lost climbing through the family tree. I will lead you through it only to identify the central characters of my story and to indicate where our roots are buried. Along with a few family skeletons.

The web is so tangled that the Roosevelt name is pronounced differently by the various branches. Granny always said the Oyster Bay branch was wrong in pronouncing it "Roo-ze-velt," but then she stemmed from the Hudson River branch, which preferred "Rose-eh-velt." The original name, van Rosenvelt, is translated from the Dutch as "field of roses," so perhaps she was right.

Claes Martenszen van Rosenvelt was the first member of the family to come to this country. He arrived from Holland in 1649 when New York was Nieuw Amsterdam. It was a small settlement of less than a thousand people living in fewer than a hundred houses in what we now know as lower Manhattan. By the Revolutionary War, the population had swollen to twenty-five thousand and the Roosevelt family had expanded to fifty branches.

Originally, the Roosevelts were merchants and traders, from which my father's fond feeling for the sea may have sprung. The Roosevelts went into business when Jacobus and Johannes—the grandsons of Claes, and the sons of Nicholas, who was the first American-born Roosevelt in 1658—ventured into real estate with the purchase of the Beekman Swamp. The development of the Beekman Swamp had an enduring impact on the development of New York City. However, much as the Indians sold Manhattan, Jacobus sold Beekman cheap. He then moved to Dutchess County. It was Jacobus and Johannes who created the two divisions of the family, establishing the Hyde Park and Oyster Bay branches, respectively.

Jacobus came to call himself James, a name passed on to many, including me. Johannes called himself John, which was passed on to my youngest brother, among others. The son of James was named Isaac and he became the president of New

York's first bank. His son was named James, who called his
son Isaac. He could be considered an eccentric; he became a
doctor who did not practice medicine because he could not
stand the sight of blood. Isaac's son was named, naturally,
James. This James was born in 1828 and he was my father's
father. James was the eighth-generation Roosevelt born in
this country. I don't know how he escaped being named Isaac,
but father was named after an uncle of his mother's and given
her family name, Delano, as a middle name.

My father's father had two marriages. First he married
Rebecca Howland at midcentury. They had a son named
James. Apparently proud of their ancestry, they gave him the
middle name as well as the last name of Roosevelt. James
Roosevelt Roosevelt came to be known as "Rosy." Although
he was my father's half brother, they never were close. Rosy
was in his late twenties and had his own son at the time my
father was born. Uncle Rosy was married to and divorced
from an Astor. Then, while with the American Embassy in
London, he met and married an English barmaid named
Betty. This created a scandal, because she was unacceptable
to many in the family, but Betty was a sweet person and
father was fond of her. She was our next-door neighbor for
a while and he saw to it that she was invited to family functions. Uncle Rosy's son, James, was a rebel too. He got involved with some "Sadie of the Tenderloin" and was disowned when he married her. It did not work out as well as
his father's later marriage to a "commoner." His mother did
leave him part of the Astor fortune in trust, but money meant
nothing to him. He wound up a recluse, living in a garage in
the Bronx. When the keepers of the trust asked him how he
wished to use his annual income of $60,000 or so, he'd tell
them not to bother him. Knowing of his wealth, some members of the family did try to keep in touch with him, but he
told them, too, to go away. When he died they went to quite
a bit of expense to give him a fancy funeral, so it came as quite
a shock when he left his several millions to the Salvation
Army.

Rebecca Roosevelt died in 1876 at age forty-five. Four years later, on October 7, 1880, her widower, James, married Sara Delano. He was fifty-two and she was twenty-six. She was not only half his age, she was the same age as his first son. Less than two years later she presented him with his second son, my father. They had no more children. Sara felt that her husband was too old. Also, she preferred traveling to being tied down. She took her son to Europe eight times during his first fourteen years. She also lavished so much affection on him she would have had little left for any others. This one child more than satisfied her.

Sara's father and mother had been less restrained. They were the parents of eleven children, of which she was their seventh. Warren Delano made two fortunes in trade with the Orient. When he lost the first one, he simply returned to make another. The second time he invested wisely. Warren, because he was rich, dominated his wife, and with her inheritance of more than a million dollars his daughter Sara would dominate her husband, her son and his family for many years.

The Delanos had been merchant captains, another peg on which father hung his passion for the sea. The first of this Flemish line arrived in the Massachusetts Bay Colony in 1621. Sara liked to point out that this was well before her husband's family reached these shores. Warren Delano had retired to a Victorian mansion in Newburgh, overlooking the Hudson, when Sara married James Roosevelt and moved the twenty miles to Hyde Park to become mistress of the mansion there. Warren Delano liked James Roosevelt and said of him, "He is the first person who made me feel a Democrat can be a gentleman." But Warren thought James too old for Sara. Sara admired her father's strength, but she was not afraid of defying him, and although she went out of her way to treat her husband well, she always had her way. She called him "a kind man," and he was. But he was not strong. She, however, was strong. She gave birth to her son at home in Hyde Park, almost dying of an overdose of chloroform during the delivery, and she, rather than her husband, reared their son. Proud of her heritage, she is supposed to have said, "Franklin is a Delano, not a Roosevelt," though I found her respectful of the Roosevelt tradition.

James Roosevelt had attended Union College and Harvard Law School. He was the president of a railroad, among other things. Between his marriages, the Hyde Park home that had been passed on to him burned down. He moved a few miles north and built another. Here my father and his children grew up.

James Roosevelt traveled about the country in a private railroad car. At home he bred trotting horses and prize-winning livestock. He loved sports and the outdoors and he sailed a yacht off his summer home on Campobello Island. James introduced his son to a love of the outdoors, of sailing and of sports. Virtually an only child, Franklin found friendship in the creatures of the forest. He requested and received a rifle so he could kill one of each kind and he amassed the most complete collection of stuffed and mounted birds in the county. The collection remains on display at Hyde Park. When he asked for a horse, he was given one. Alone a lot, he was started on his famous stamp collection by his mother. What he wanted he was given. Loving the life, he once said, "All that is in me goes back to the Hudson." It was his inheritance and he passed it on to us. He had governesses and tutors, so he wanted us to have them. He prepped at the private Groton and attended exclusive Harvard, so he wanted his sons to follow in his footsteps.

His mother wanted to protect him, but he wanted to be a real boy. He loved sports but was small and unskilled. He played for the football team and managed the baseball team at Groton. Later he was an ardent supporter of his university teams. Unable to excel in athletics, he sang in the choir, joined the debating society, became active in school politics and delved into journalism at Harvard.

My father grew up sailing his father's boats. When his relative Teddy Roosevelt took a leading role in the Spanish-American War of 1898, father wanted to fight, too, to become a man. But the sixteen-year-old lad came down with scarlet fever just when he was going to enlist in the navy and was dissuaded from such a drastic alteration of his life's course.

Father was an eighteen-year-old freshman at Harvard when his father died at the age of seventy-two. He was a junior at Harvard when he began to date Eleanor Roosevelt. In order to be near her, he went to law school at Columbia University. He was twenty-three and she was twenty when they were married in 1905.

My parents' paternal great-great-great-great grandfathers were brothers. My mother's family tree was tangled, too. While my father stemmed from that strain of Roosevelts introduced by Jacobus "James" Roosevelt, my mother stemmed from the strain headed by his brother, Johannes "John" Roosevelt. On the other side she was a descendant of the Livingstons, who played an important role in the early history of this country. John Roosevelt had a son, Jacobus, who had a son, James. His son, Cornelius, had a son, Theodore. He married Martha Bulloch, and they had four children—two daughters, Anna and Corinne, and two sons, Theodore, Jr., and Elliott. Teddy, born in 1858, became assistant secretary of the navy in 1897, governor of New York in 1898 and president of the United States in 1901. Approximately thirty years later, my father followed in his footsteps in each of these posts.

Teddy's brother, Elliott, married Anna Hall in 1883. On the eleventh of October the following year, their daughter was born, my mother, Anna Eleanor. She used her middle name most of her life. Five years later a brother, Elliott, Jr., and two years after that another, Hall, joined her.

Philip Livingston was one of the signers of the Declaration of Independence in 1776. Robert Livingston administered the oath of office of the presidency to George Washington in 1789. Philip's grandson, Edward, had a daughter, Elizabeth, who married Edward Ludlow. Their daughter, Mary Livingston Ludlow, married Valentine Hall, Jr. The Halls originally came from England and were granted land in this country by English royalty. Valentine was wealthy through inheritance, not work. Wild as a young man, he later reformed. Like many reformed men, he resented and sought to reform those who had not seen the light. He invited a preacher to live with him in his gloomy mansion named after the nearby town of Tivoli, and together they preached to others.

Valentine was a domineering man who dominated his wife. He asked her only to be beautiful and to bear him children: They had six—Anna, Elizabeth, Valentine, Edward, Edith and Maude. The first of these, Anna, born in 1863, was my mother's mother. When Valentine died in 1880 at the age of forty-six, his widowed wife was thirty-seven, his eldest daughter, Anna, seventeen. Before she was twenty she married Elliott Roosevelt, who was twenty-one. They announced their engagement at a party hosted by Laura Delano, my grandmother's youngest sister.

Laura, known as Polly, was a lovely lady who never married after her lover jilted her to wed one of her sisters. Polly had a distant cousin and dear friend, Margaret "Daisy" Suckley, who traveled with her wherever she went. It was Daisy who gave father his famous Scottie dog, Fala. Polly and Daisy adored father, who welcomed them wherever he happened to be. They were with him when he died at Warm Springs. Mother had encouraged them to care for him.

"Aunt" Polly, who dyed her hair purple, leaned to the eccentric. I recall once, when she was with us at Campobello, father warned her a solar eclipse was due so she wouldn't worry if it was dark when she came down the next morning. When she descended the next day she was dressed to the teeth and carrying her jewelry box. When father asked her what she was doing, she answered, "Despite what you have said, Franklin, this clearly is the end of the world. I have dressed for the occasion. I have my jewels and I am ready to go to heaven." As she sat down primly, prepared to wait for the end, we collapsed in hysterics, which did not faze her.

Anna Hall Roosevelt's brothers and sisters were rebellious. Her brothers ran with the hard-gambling, heavy-drinking Diamond Jim Brady bunch. Her sisters fell in and out of love with the winking of an eye. Anna was the straight one, so they considered her odd. As her father had, she preached the good life to them, but it was not the life they wanted. Anna's life was cursed by drink. Her brothers, perhaps revolting against the tyrannies of their father, drank to excess. "Uncle Vallie" used to sit drinking in an upstairs window of the family estate and fire a rifle at any stranger who wandered within range. As a boy I was terrified whenever I had to go anywhere near that place. It was a mercy when he died of his dissipations.

When Anna married Elliott Roosevelt, she was charmed by this handsome man and felt that they would have a fine future together. While he had great charm, however, he was flawed. He was never really a well man. Medical science then was not what it is now. What was diagnosed as epilepsy probably was a brain tumor. He suffered from painful headaches and dizzy spells which troubled him to his death. To ease his life he was driven to drink, and drink became his life. At times he worked for relatives who were realtors or brokers, but he cared little for work. He preferred being a playboy and sportsman, and he built a mansion at Hempstead, Long Island, where he gave parties, played polo and "rode to the hounds." At first his wife enjoyed the social whirl, but she tired of it. Anna reprimanded him for wasting his life. When he took to drink, she tore him down and they began to argue a great deal. They had three children—Anna Eleanor, Elliott, Jr., and Gracie Hall, the latter a son despite his name. The children held them together for a time. But Elliott, Jr., died in his fourth year, and, after Hall was born while they were in Europe, Anna broke with Elliott.

Suffering great pain from a broken ankle that had not been set properly and did not heal, Elliott had begun to treat his family badly and to threaten suicide. At one point he simply vanished and spent several months in the South before returning. In those days European resorts had health spas where it was presumed the sick and troubled could find relief. Anna took Elliott on several such trips. After Hall's birth in June of 1891, on the last trip, she had her husband committed

to a hospital for the mentally ill in Paris and she sailed for
home with her children. Less than $200,000 remained from
Elliott's inheritance. With his brother Teddy's help, Anna
sought to gain control of the money by having Elliott declared legally insane in U.S. courts. Claiming he had been
kidnaped and was being victimized by his family, Elliott
wrote the courts in protest. He was freed while the case was
being considered and took up with a woman in Paris. He
claimed she gave him love instead of lectures. Years later my
mother confessed her father probably was right in believing
he deserved more than he had been given by his wife.

In any event, Teddy went to Paris and persuaded Elliott to
return home and submit to treatment for alcoholism, on the
condition the court case be dropped if he agreed to place the
remains of his inheritance in trust for his family. Elliott returned home, but lasted only a few weeks at a clinic. When
Anna refused to take him back, he went to Virginia to manage
a brother-in-law's estate, while she took her children and
moved into a house in midtown Manhattan.

Anna was vain about her beauty. She liked to tell how, in
Switzerland, Robert Burns was so struck by her looks that he
read poetry to her while she had her portrait painted. She felt
she could have had a better marriage than the one she made
to a wastrel. She was annoyed that the daughter she bore was
not a beauty. She repeatedly reminded the child that she was
plain, with the result that Eleanor retreated into a shell, a shy,
sad soul. Believing her old-fashioned, Anna nicknamed her
"Granny."

It is unfortunate that society places so much importance on
physical appearance that it could alter a mother's love for her
daughter. My mother was haunted by being homely almost
from the day she was born. But she was not without beauty.
She had beautiful hair, beautiful eyes. More important, she
had a beautiful spirit. Sadly, it was stifled most of her early
life. My mother never forgave her mother for this mistreat-
ment. She was more forgiving of her father, though he seldom
was there when she needed him. He adored her, but betrayed

her adoration of him with his dissipations and departures and disappearances.

Life with Elliott had taken a heavy toll on Anna's health. She seemed an old woman before she was thirty. Though Eleanor was but a child and had lost any feeling for her mother, she slept in her mother's bed and cared for her after they moved to Manhattan. After several months of illness, Anna died of diphtheria in 1892. It was less than a year after her husband's return and she refused to see him during her dying days. He was a broken man who blamed himself for his wife's death, and consequently he believed that any hope for his redemption was lost. Seeing this, Eleanor later said that on her mother's death she cried not for her mother but for her father. She said that the death of her mother meant nothing to her except that she hoped it would bring her father back to her.

It did not. He told her he loved her, but could not care for her. He suggested that someday when she was older they could make a home together and she could care for him. She was eight and did not wish to wait, but she had no choice. He left and later wrote her from time to time, pledging a love he could not give, making promises he would not keep. She wrote him often, promising to become the woman he wanted her to be, pleading for permission to live with him. He died of injuries suffered in a fall, presumably when he was drunk, just two years after his wife's death. Their daughter was just ten years old, an orphan and already hurt by life.

Early in life, my mother developed a fear of the sea which never left her, much to the distress of that old salt who became my father. When she was two years old her parents took her on a trip. They sailed from New York for Europe on the *Brittanica* and on the first day out their ship was rammed by the *Celtics*. Some people lost their lives, but she and her parents made it into lifeboats, transferred to another ship and returned safely. Clearly, my story came close to ending before it began. When her parents resumed their journey, she remained in New York with relatives. As her parents sparred, she frequently passed from relative to relative. After her mother died, Eleanor went to live with her mother's mother. She lived in many places, none of which was home to her.

As a child, my mother spent a lot of time in the care of her mother's cousin Susan and her husband, Henry Parish. While they were good people, their home was troubled. They had a son who was mentally retarded as a result of a fall from a bicycle, and he lived at home for many years. I can recall Sunday dinners when he would blabber incoherently and have to be taken away. It terrified me, but mother would try to explain his problem to me. Eventually he had to be confined in an institution until his death.

Another relative with whom my mother spent some of her growing-up years was her father's sister, Anna, known as "Auntie Bye." Crippled by curvature of the spine, she could have been considered a hunchback. She eventually married, though the last of her brothers and sisters to do so. She was sensitive and wise and many of the family, including my mother, often sought her out for advice. She made many of the decisions concerning the course to be taken by young Anna Eleanor, who had been named for her. Later in life, Auntie Bye was the closest to a confidante mother had. Mother kept in touch with her until Auntie Bye died, at the age of seventy-six, one year before my father was elected president.

After Teddy's first wife died in childbirth and until he married a second time, Anna took care of Alice, too. The child's stepmother, Edith Carow, tolerated rather than loved Alice, who grew rebellious and independent. Mother was a lonely child, and Alice, who was the same age, was the best friend she had. However, Alice was everything mother was not—beautiful, personable, outgoing—and her father was successful and important. Eleanor admitted she "admired her" and was "afraid of her." Alice teased her unmercifully. Later, as Alice Roosevelt Longworth, mother's cousin would become the colorful rebel of Washington society.

The most troubled household my mother shared during her

formative years was that headed by her mother's mother. Grandma Hall was a bitter, biblically strict woman in her later years. She couldn't control her own children, much less take on the responsibility for rearing grandchildren. While her uncles and aunts carried on, mother became more mother than sister to her young brother Hall.

Mother attended private schools and studied hard, striving to make up in scholarship what she lacked in a social life. At fifteen she was sent to Allenswood, a finishing school outside of London, mainly to get her away from the destructive influence of her hard-drinking uncles. When she returned, almost eighteen, in the summer of 1902, Teddy was president, and Alice, nicknamed "The Princess," was dancing delightedly in the limelight.

Life was less glamorous for Eleanor, who found herself depressed by the dissipations of her uncles and by exposure to high society. Mother was never meant to be a debutante. To the distaste of her family, she turned to social work in the East Side tenements. She belonged to the rich, but joined the Junior League so she could contribute to the poor. Along the way, she met, by chance, her distant cousin Franklin. They started seeing one another, grew serious and, over his mother's objections, eventually married.

Father tried to help her with Hall. But just as Teddy had been unable to help his brother Elliott, so, too, was father unable to help his brother-in-law. For a while father and Hall were fast friends. Hall followed in father's footsteps at Groton and Harvard, was a superior scholar and seemed to be on the road to great things. Then he lost his way. He married and divorced, and drank heavily. He used to take me and my brothers on the town in New York. We were at the age where we thought it was fun. He was past it, but never grew up. One day at mother's Hyde Park refuge, Val-Kill, Hall hurled his young son, Danny, to the ground. A doctor found the boy's collarbone broken. Hall insisted on driving his son to the hospital himself, though drunk, and drove them right into a ditch. A state trooper took over. Mother, thinking her friend,

Marion Dickerman, had been driving, telephoned Marion in a fury. Mother would blame anyone but Hall. Father apologized to Marion for mother.

For a while Danny seemed likely to grow up to be all his father might have been, but he was killed in a plane crash while still young. Hall's drinking increased. He died in 1941 at fifty, a failure, to the despair of my mother, who said sadly, "He was not what he should have been."

Alcohol has been a family problem, more so for some than others. Mother worried about it as had her mother before her, and father's mother, too. Mother drank only an occasional cocktail at parties when it seemed impolite to refuse. Father drank more, but not a lot. He delighted in defying his wife and mother, who could not conceal their concern.

Champagne flowed at my parents' wedding. It was the social sensation of that spring in Manhattan because the president was there. Teddy had become president with the assassination of William McKinley in 1901. Later he was elected on his own in 1904. Franklin and Eleanor Roosevelt attended his inauguration the following March, and he attended their wedding later in the month, on the seventeenth, Saint Patrick's Day, at the adjacent houses of Cousin Susie and her mother, Mrs. Ludlow, on Seventy-sixth Street in Manhattan. Alice, too, was at the wedding. When Alice heard of Eleanor's engagement to Franklin, she wrote mother: "It is simply too nice to be true . . . you old fox, not to tell me before." Accepting Eleanor's invitation to be a bridesmaid, Alice wrote, "It will be too much fun." But privately she put father down. She said, "Franklin was the sort of boy you invited to the dance, but not to the dinner."

Though she denies it, and even has taped a denial to be played after her death, Alice is believed to have been jealous of Eleanor's catch. Years later, when Eleanor came to Washington as the First Lady, Alice clearly regretted being relegated to a lesser position as a secondary Roosevelt. "As far as I am concerned, my father is the only Roosevelt who really belonged in the White House," she said. She contrasted her father's physically robust body to my father's crippled one and suggested Franklin wanted to pull the country into the wheelchair with him. She married a Republican, Nicholas Longworth, later Speaker of the House of Representatives.

At parties Alice delighted in demeaning mother with clever but cruel impersonations of her. At one party, mother asked to see the act she'd heard about. Alice did it defiantly, delightedly. Mother hid her hurt and kept the peace, occasionally seeing Alice socially. However, when father came home late from a party, it was Alice who first told mother about it and hinted he might be straying. And father was not as forgiving of Alice's acts as was mother. He broke with the Oyster Bay bunch and refused to invite Alice to White House parties. Years later he relented.

But she had been at his wedding with her father, who overshadowed both the wedding and my parents. Many people left the parade to gather around the Ludlow place in hopes of catching a glimpse of the president and his daughter. Inside, once the vows were said, the newly wedded couple found themselves alone while the guests gathered around Teddy and Alice in another room.

I was told this story by my parents when, after I was married for the first time, my bride and I found ourselves alone while the guests gathered around another president, my father. I suppose when one follows in the footsteps of presidents, one must expect to be overshadowed, even on what should be one's day in the sun.

II

It is difficult to determine what drew my mother and father together. Anyone who pretends to know is not telling the truth. She was a private person, and even her letters to him do not tell us much. He was less private, but she destroyed his letters to her. Neither of them confided much to family or friends. During the early years of their marriage, we children were too young to ask questions. As the years went by, the questions became embarrassing and remained unasked and, therefore, unanswered.

He was tall, slender, handsome. She was too tall, too thin, homely. He was confident, personable and extroverted. She was unsure of herself, colorless and introverted. He was something of a ladies' man, a passion he passed on to his sons, for better or worse. She showed little interest in men, perhaps because they showed little interest in her. He dressed with style, loved to dance and dated more than was usual in those days. He observed, "Nothing is more pleasing to the eye than a good-looking lady, nothing more refreshing to the spirit than the company of one, nothing more flattering to the ego than the affection of one." Writing home, he shocked his mother with a tale of flirtations with three young ladies at one party: ". . . and ended up by jollying the hostess herself all by her lonesome." Mother, on the other hand, avoided parties, seldom dated and rarely if ever privately expressed an interest in any man. I'm not saying that she would not have married if she had not married father. She had a few suitors, including some young men who were involved in charity work with her. But she could not give herself to these men easily. She had been beaten down by her mother, and she was too aware of her plain appearance, buck teeth and a curved spine which compelled her to wear a brace when she was young.

He, meanwhile, nearly married Frances Dana, whose grandfathers were the novelist Richard Dana, of *Two Years Before the Mast* fame, and the poet Henry Wadsworth Longfellow. Reportedly, Sara Roosevelt talked her son out of this marriage because Miss Dana was a Catholic and as such was unacceptable to the Protestant Roosevelts. When Miss Dana married another man, father became a friend to both of them. Father never forgot an old flame. He remained friendly with Mary Newbold, Evelyn Carter and Alice Parker long after he stopped dating them and they married others. And of course, years later, long after his affair with Lucy Mercer had ended and she had become Lucy Mercer Rutherfurd, then was widowed, he resumed seeing her.

While father had set out on a path of public service at the time he and mother became interested in one another, she would have preferred a private sort of life. While mother had a difficult early life, father had an easy one. And while mother suffered rejections from her mother, father was babied by his. When father was a boy, his mother spent a great deal of time with him. When he had scarlet fever and she was not permitted in his room, Sara scaled a rickety ladder so she could sit and talk to him through his upstairs window. It was not until he was in his teens and at Groton that he could strike out on his own.

For the most part, father's father left the rearing of his son to Sara. James Roosevelt was an old friend of Grover Cleveland and took Franklin to visit the White House when he was seven. Reportedly the weary executive advised the lad, "I hope you'll never be president." It was something to think about, however, since uncle Theodore Roosevelt had moved up in politics until he became president.

My father was fourteen and in his first year at Groton when old grad Teddy returned for a visit. Teddy inspired him, saying, "If a man has courage, goodness and brains, no limit can be placed on the greatness of the work he may accomplish. He is the man needed today in politics. . . ." Father shared the warmth of the spotlight which shone on his uncle and made the lad a class celebrity. He found that he loved the spotlight, but it seldom shone on him at Groton. Starting two years late, he was left out of friendships already formed within his class, and he was left alone a lot. He coveted the position of prefect, but was not elected. Nevertheless, the school had a positive influence on father. The Reverend Endicott Peabody, the headmaster, preached political service to the public. Responding to the call, father joined the Missionary Society and was assigned to visit and run errands for the aged widow of a Civil War drummer boy. Proudly he wrote his mama of these visits to "the old colored lady." I hate to think of what granny thought of her son's visits to the slums.

He was a good, but not outstanding, student. He won a prize for Latin—a set of Shakespeare's works—but did not graduate with honors. Because his father was sick, his parents did not attend his graduation ceremonies. A year later his father died and Sara was willed control of her son's $120,000 trust fund. With it she sought to control him.

Following family tradition, father enrolled in Harvard in September of 1900. Here, reversals continued. He ran for class marshal, but was not elected. It was some time before he began to win elections. Still, he became a member of the Harvard Republican Club so that he could better support Teddy. Father aspired to membership in the Porcellian Club, which consisted of "the best young men." That he was not accepted he called the greatest disappointment of his youth. His Oyster Bay relatives later charged that his attacks on the wealthy of Wall Street stemmed from this rejection.

Meanwhile, mother emerged from her shell at the finishing

school, Allenswood. Her inspiration was her headmistress, Marie Souvestre. She did not preach politics but taught her charges to make the most of themselves and to dedicate their lives to helping those who had less than they had. Under the influence of Marie Souvestre, Eleanor began to believe that even an "ugly duckling" might have something to bring to the world. She began to take an interest in her appearance, to participate in the arts, to read in order to see how others saw life and to think for herself. Returning home, she became the first person in her family to do social work in the slums. Later she showed father these areas, which he had not seen. In time she, who was more liberal, loaned him some of her liberalism.

It was shortly after her return from England that she met father on a train, in the summer of 1902. They had known each other all their lives, but had been thrown together only occasionally. This time they talked and were taken with one another. They began to see one another, secretly at first, as though unsure what others would make of this. They began to find excuses to get together at family functions, then to invite one another to parties. Father invited mother to Hyde Park several times that summer, then to Campobello. They sailed, took hayrides, walked the woods, picnicked. Who can explain chemistry? Although opposites, they were drawn to each other as though fated for one another.

As their interest in each other increased, Sara saw it and did not like it. She was not ready to surrender her son. And when she had to do so, she would want more for him than Eleanor. Sara arranged affairs at which other young women were present, but father usually found a way to be with mother.

I doubt that father acted in a conscious, calculating way. He had been dominated by his mother and did not want a wife who would dominate him. He had dated beautiful women, but dating is one thing, marriage another. Mother was family. She was comfortable, she was safe. And no doubt she would be a faithful wife and a devoted mother. She believed in father and encouraged him. Intelligent and thoughtful, she could contribute to him and to his ideas. Working hard, he had graduated from Harvard in three years. Encouraged by Eleanor, he had attained his first school successes in his third year: He was named to head the school newspaper, the *Crimson*, and he was selected permanent chairman of the Senior Class Committee. She encouraged him to return for a fourth year to take advantage of these positions, and she wrote how proud she was to have helped him, how proud she was of him, how much she hoped to help him in the future.

That fall, he invited her to the Yale game at Cambridge in November. She accepted, inviting him also to accompany her to his old school, Groton, to visit her brother, Hall. There father proposed marriage to mother, and she accepted. She is supposed to have said, "Why me? I am plain. I have little to bring you." And he is supposed to have said, "With your help, I will amount to something." In his book, Elliott doubts that they would have said such things. I take a differing view. It sounds like them to me. It is the way I see their romance to have been. For my father, mother was just the sort of girl he wanted to invite to dinner. As for mother, she could not believe her good fortune in landing so eligible a bachelor as father. Still unsure of herself, she wrote him a love letter, quoting a poem: "Unless you can swear for life, for death . . . Oh, never call it loving." Presumably in his reply, he so swore, and she was his.

Still, she feared disapproval, especially from his mother. When Franklin told Sara, she was stunned. She asked him to keep it secret for a while; if it was not visible, it would not be real, and it would disappear. Sara had Franklin bring Eleanor to her and swore her to secrecy, too. "I had a long talk with the dear child," Sara wrote in her journal. Eleanor wrote Sara, saying, "I do so want you to learn to love me a little . . . I have grown to love you very dearly." Sara's reply suggested that Eleanor was taking Franklin too far, too fast. She commanded a private audience with Eleanor and suggested she see less of Franklin for a while. When Eleanor timidly wrote Franklin of this, he wrote her and his mother ("Dear Mummy") that his feelings were not going to change.

Eleanor wrote Franklin: "I would be very glad if I thought she was even the least reconciled to me." She wrote Sara: "My one great wish is to prove worthy of your son." Sara's response was to take her son to see Joseph Choate, the ambassador to England, in the hopes that he would invite Franklin to London as his secretary. She did not succeed.

Sara's last stand was to talk her son into a five-week cruise to the Caribbean in January of 1904. "It will give him time to think things over," she wrote. When Eleanor wondered why he agreed to go, Franklin said he felt it would be a final fling. So he went. And he had a fling with an older woman on board. But when he returned, he returned to Eleanor.

Sara surrendered. She wrote her son: "I am feeling pretty blue. You are gone. The journey is over and I feel as if the time were not likely to come again when I shall take a trip with my dear boy."

Sorry for Sara, Eleanor told Franklin, "We three must take them together in the future."

In June father finished at Harvard. In September he enrolled at Columbia Law School so he could be close to mother. In October, on her twentieth birthday, he presented her with an engagement ring he had purchased at Tiffany's. In December they formally announced their engagement. They planned to be married in the spring.

If his mother was sorry, most of the family were not. Her aunts wrote mother how pleased they were. If Alice was annoyed, her father was not. Teddy wrote Franklin: "I am as fond of Eleanor as if she were my daughter. I like you and trust in you and believe in you." In March of 1905, following his inauguration, Teddy gave the bride away.

Father and mother moved into an apartment in the Hotel Webster to live until he completed his courses at Columbia in June. He had an income from his trust fund of $5000 a year, and she had an income of $7500. Sara gave them money to help them manage and she paid their rent. That summer they took a three-month honeymoon cruise and tour of Europe, courtesy of Sara. When they returned and he went to work for a law firm, they moved into a house at 125 East Thirty-sixth Street in midtown Manhattan. It was only three blocks from Sara's house at 200 Madison Avenue. Sara found the house for them, furnished it, fixed it up and paid for it.

As we children started to arrive and our parents needed more room, Sara announced at Christmas of 1907 that as a present she was going to have a bigger house built for them. While she was at it, she decided to have an adjoining house built for herself. Joined on the lower and upper floors, these residences at 47 and 49 East Sixty-fifth Street were ready in the fall of 1908. Apparently, mother never complained while the houses were being built, but, reportedly, she later confessed to father that she never could consider this her home. She was beginning to squirm under granny's heavy hand. But father wanted the financial help his mother could give him, so he soothed his wife's feelings as best he could. Father never was one for economies in his personal life. He spent freely to improve his collections of stamps, naval prints, books and autographs, which grew as he moved up in the world. He did not care what these expenditures did to the family budget. Instead, he tried to economize by having the children pass their clothing down to the younger ones. He always bought a lot of expensive clothes for himself, though. Ironically, he was especially fond of fancy shoes.

Mother may have felt guilty, as she accepted a lot from Sara. Even as father moved into positions of political importance, mother did not question it when he sent insurance and medical bills to his mother. Sara also paid for their babies. When I had to have an operation at the age of twelve, Sara sent father a check to cover it. He wrote her: "Dearest Mama . . . You are not only an angel, which I already knew, but the kind which comes at the critical moment in life." Mother herself once wrote Sara making pointed reference to an overdue medical bill of $233. Apparently Sara took the hint, for father later wrote her, "You have saved my life, or, rather, the lives of various doctors."

When my parents were first married, mother took walks

with Sara and had lunch with her almost daily. Sara instructed her in the proper operation of a household. By her own admission, my mother never was a success as a house-wife. She never learned to cook or clean, and she always had servants to do those things for her. Unfortunately she didn't know how to instruct the servants to do things as she wanted. After we children started to arrive, grandmother gave mother instructions on how we were to be reared. Having gained no useful knowledge on the subject from her own unhappy years as a child, mother was absolutely terrified to find herself a parent, and, however much she hated being dominated by her mother-in-law, was relieved to let her take over. Sara hired English nannies to "raise us right," but never really let them take over.

I recall an incident in the summer of 1929. Sara had always taken the children on trips, but mother decided she and her friends Marion Dickerman and Nancy Cook would drive Franklin and John through Europe. Sara was opposed to the trip and spoke openly of her opposition one night at dinner at Hyde Park shortly before the departure date. Mother grew angry. Brother, or "Brud" as we called Franklin, wisecracked that mother no doubt would land them in a ditch. Sara nodded. No one laughed. It was no secret mother was a bad driver. Angrily mother announced she would hire chauffeurs. "I will see that your grandsons travel in the way in which you think they should be accustomed," she said to Sara, and stormed from the room. An invalid by then, father remained locked in his wheelchair. He was upset by the incident, but said nothing.

Mother did not back down from her determination to make the trip, but she made it under the heavy pressure of her fear of failure. Everyone survived it, yet she did not enjoy the trip. She later wrote of her return: "On landing, I breathed a sigh of relief and made a vow that never again would I take a trip in which I had to be responsible for the young."

Franklin was fifteen, John thirteen, far from infants. Yet mother's fear of failure as a mother in turn hurt her as a mother. For many years—until it was too late for her to become a real mother—she let our grandmother act as our mother.

My grandmother's Victorian attitudes were reflected in her teachings. Once when I said I was going to wash my hands because they were dirty, she said, "A gentleman's hands may be *soiled*, James, but they are never *dirty.*" Another time, when I said I was sweating, she said, "A gentleman does not *sweat*, he *perspires.*" Granny kept telling Anna, "No lady ever crosses her limbs when seated. A lady sits with her limbs straight in front of her and her knees together." We had limbs, not legs. When one of my brothers got a job in the lingerie department of a department store, Granny all but fainted when she found out he was handling ladies' underwear, even if no ladies were in them. "It is not an occupation for a gentleman," she announced.

Granny referred to us as her children. She told us, "Your mother only bore you." She also said, "I am more your mother than your mother is." It was a cruel thing to say, but we didn't see it then. Instead we saw her as a sort of fairy godmother. She took us on trips to Europe, and she gave us what our parents would not or could not give us. She tried to buy us, of course, and it took us a while to see this, too.

While I was in college I was given permission by my parents to buy a secondhand car from my savings. I did, but left the top down one winter night and a snowstorm ruined the interior. I asked my parents to buy me another car, but they refused on the grounds that I had a lesson to learn about taking care of my property. I simply took my hard-luck story to granny and she bought me a brand-new and better car.

Later, my brother Franklin wrecked a car our parents had given him on his graduation from Groton. Figuring he, too, had a lesson to learn, they refused to replace it. He, too, went to granny, and again she came through, buying him a better car. Our parents protested, but did not make us return these gifts.

When granny wanted to threaten us because we had been

bad or had neglected her, she'd talk of cutting us out of her will. When she was particularly pleased with one of us, she'd say he was nicer than the rest of the children and she thought she would leave her money to him. This put pressure on us until we were old enough to see that we should not sell ourselves. When we became adults, we began to refuse those gifts from our grandmother which would have obligated us to her.

She got around it at times, however. For example, when Anna was expecting her first child, Sara sent father a check for $1000, along with a letter asking him to pass it on to his daughter in his own name, offering to pay her doctor's bill. It was accepted. When Anna later moved into the White House, Sara gave her a new car because she felt that the car her granddaughter was driving was not suitable for her new role. Anna accepted. She was divorced by then and straightening out her financial affairs. There often was a weakening of our resolve.

Sara never wanted her son to enter politics. She never even wanted him to work. Her highest aspiration for him was that he be a country gentleman. She once wrote that she wanted him to grow up to be a fine, upright man like her father and his father, "a beloved member of his family and a useful and respected citizen of his community . . . living quietly and happily along the Hudson as they had." When, however, a passion for politics stirred in him and he pursued it with a bid for the New York State Senate, he persuaded grandma to finance his campaign. Elected in 1911, he and mother picked out their own place in Albany, which mother considered to be their first real home. However, when father went to Washington as assistant secretary of the navy, Sara rented a house for us from her Auntie Bye at 1733 N Street. After she made her first visit there, Sara noted in her journal, "Moved chairs and tables and began to feel at home." Mother wrote, "My mother-in-law, as usual, helped us to get settled."

We later moved into a house at 2133 R Street, where Sara visited us often. When we returned to Albany in 1928 it was to the governor's mansion. And when we returned to Washington in 1932 it was to the White House. Sara never felt at home in these imposing places, both of which had histories which were not hers, but she visited both frequently.

Almost every summer until my father was stricken with infantile paralysis there in 1921, the family visited Campobello Island, a piece of Canada off the coast of Maine. The year after my father was born, his father bought property and built a house on the island. Later, Sara bought the adjoining cottage for her son and his family and we became summer residents. A rugged place, it was more my father's kind of place than it was his wife's or his mother's. When illness struck and he no longer could use it as it was meant to be used, our regular visits stopped. His illness led him to his retreat in Warm Springs, Georgia, which was almost exclusively his. Sara never visited Warm Springs, and mother was there only once or twice. None of us ever lived there. The family home remained at Hyde Park, but it was my grandmother's house more than it was my father's, and my mother never felt more than a guest there.

My father's father originally purchased a house at Hyde Park in 1826, and after it burned down he built the one we lived in nearby. My father was born there, and later, in 1916, supervised, at Sara's expense, the addition of two wings to the main building which made it a mansion. Each wing had large bedrooms on the top floor with bathrooms and fireplaces. Between father's and grandmother's rooms, mother had a small bedroom with no bathroom and no fireplace. At my mother's request, father later had a cottage built a mile and a half from the main house, by the Val-Kill stream after which it was named. It was completed in 1926. Here she lived many months of each year, mostly in the summers, with her friends and business partners, Marion Dickerman and Nancy Cook. My father never lived at Val-Kill, though we did from time to time. My father had Hilltop Cottage built up the hill from mother's retreat. He wanted his own retreat. He spent time in the cottage but never lived there. Sara never saw any need for my father to have his own place. She considered the main mansion his home, though she paid for its upkeep, hired and fired the servants and ran it. He was free to invite his friends and often entertained political people there. She did not always approve of these people, but she, not mother, was father's hostess at these affairs.

Once, Huey Long was father's guest for luncheon. Sara listened to the crude but colorful Kingfish praise himself until she inquired in a stage whisper that could have been heard in the next county, "Who is that dreadful person?" However, when others attacked her son's political cronies, she sprang to their defense, sometimes with surprising wit. At dinner one night, the younger J. P. Morgan, wondering how Sara's son could support such an uncouth character as Al Smith, remarked that Smith chewed tobacco and used spittoons in the governor's mansion. Granny commented that while all that no doubt was true, she understood "he never misses."

Father's mentor, Louis Howe, was a homely, messy man. Until we got to know his sterling qualities, none of us liked him. Sara never took the trouble to know him, she didn't want him in her home. But father did, and his wishes prevailed. She disliked Jim Farley, but I recall that when she complained about him, father flatly told her, "I don't want to hear another word against him."

Sara was bitterly opposed to her son's return to active public life after he was paralyzed, and she fought Louis Howe and mother on this. Sara wanted her son to retire in his wheelchair to his Hyde Park estate, where the world could not hurt him. When he summoned the strength to resume his political career and went to the top without her help, she was beaten. She had bought him and his family everything she could, but in the end she could not buy him or any of us.

The contention that Sara completely controlled her son and his family is a fatal flaw in most biographies of my parents, in my view. She may have shaped him some in his youth, as all parents do, but in the end, like most children, he grew up and away from her. How often are our children exactly as we would want them? She controlled mother and us children for a long time, but in the end she lost control. Once this occurred, mother went her own way. Regretting her neglect of her early children, she paid greater attention to her later children. Father permitted his mother to dominate his wife. He cared more about his life than he did his wife. He did not want to be bothered. It was only when mother found the strength to lead her own life that she became an individual apart from her husband and her mother-in-law and reclaimed her children, though by then it was too late for her to become the mother she might have been. The fact is we were fortunate to have a grandmother who would do for us when we had a mother who could not and a father who would not.

Many mothers try to buy their families—with love or money. Sara's weapon was money, and it bought power for her for a while, but it did not buy what she wanted in the end. She thought she was manipulating her son, but he was only being a diplomat. He was kind to her, and she was kind to him. She gave to him, and he took from her. Maybe it was mercenary, but young men of his background in that day were used to taking. He took from her as long as it suited him, but he set his own course and neither his mother, nor her money, could make him change his mind.

I have to believe that if father had wanted to marry Frances Dana, he would have. After all, when he wanted to marry mother, he did, despite his mother's objections. So he let Sara take him on a Caribbean cruise first. And he had a good time. But when the cruise ended, his engagement had not. And if his mother wanted to build him a house with her own home connected to it, well, he would still have his new house.

Sara did not want him to enter politics, but he did. After his illness, she did not want him to return to politics, but he did. When she put her power to the ultimate test, she found she had none. She could buy *for* him, but he himself was not for sale. She went back to giving. He went back to taking. But by then they both understood the rules of the game. She understood that she must play it his way or drop out of the game. He was the winner. She did not want to lose every-

thing, she wanted her son, so she remained a member of the
family and instead resorted to buying control of his children.
But she was bound to be beaten here, too. We inherited his
independence. While we did not always wield it wisely, we
kept it. We all shamelessly took what we wanted from her. We
were as guilty as she was.

All in all, Sara Roosevelt was not the battle-ax she has been
pictured. True, she was a snob and a bit of a bigot. To Sara,
blacks were servants, and she knew few Jews except as businessmen. But she was a captive of her class and her time.
Time never moved for her. My parents were not so different
when they were young. Both of them were reared by WASPs
with a sense of superiority, and some of this rubbed off on
them. I recall a letter my mother wrote to my father on his
first day at Columbia, asking him if he found only "Jew Gentlemen" to work with. And later, my father did little to further the cause of civil rights for blacks in his presidency.

But my parents changed with the times. My father's record
indicated clearly that if civil rights had become an issue of his
day, he would have led the fight for black equality. Born to
the aristocracy, he nevertheless had a feeling for the common
man and always championed minorities. Nothing angered
him more than being attacked because he had so many Jews
on his staff. Accused of being Jewish himself, he once said he
wished he was. Mother, of course, developed an intense feeling for the oppressed, worked the latter part of her life on
their behalf and considered her crowning achievement in the
United Nations the Declaration of Human Rights which she
helped draft. They passed on to their children sympathy for
the underdog. Whatever else we may have been, we always
have been liberal in our relationships with people.

Sara Roosevelt was simply a woman out of her time and
place. She was the last of a kind, a woman who considered
herself a monarch. But she was a warm and loving mother and
grandmother. Like many of us, she wanted her way and was
guilty of getting it the wrong way. If she was guilty of anything else, it was of giving too much. She believed in decency

and we received many good things from her besides material things. All she has been given in return is the reputation of an ogre. It is unfair.

I remember granny's last years well. She became a sort of volunteer assistant president to her son, who tolerated her interferences with good humor. I recall one time when he was summoned to the phone to talk to her. Apparently, she did all the talking. Finally he said, "Well, Mama, let me put it this way. Even if I wanted to do that, I couldn't. It's against the law, and even the president obeys the law."

Even though he was the president, she was still trying to mother him. She had that family fear of drinking, for instance. She once said it was not good form to serve cocktails to the king and queen of England, who were visiting us. He retorted, "That's nonsense," and had cocktails served. They did not go to waste. I recall her often saying, "Franklin, don't you think you've had enough of your . . . cocktails for one evening?" Indignantly, he would retire to his private study, from which she was barred, to drink, though he did not drink a great deal.

To the very end she treated him as if he were a boy. Once when he was embarking on a presidential cruise, she advised him: "Keep yourself in order and your blood cool in going through strange climates." Another time she wrote, "Do be careful of your throat and don't speak until you have to." And another time, during a hot spell, "Do be careful about food and avoid fish and bad water. Do not drink with meals, but between meals."

In her last years before her death in 1941, Sara's love for her son was her reason for living. She wrote him: "Perhaps I have lived too long, but when I think of you and hear your voice I do not ever want to leave you." She lived to see him elected president three times, but her pride in him as president could not be compared to her feeling for him simply as her son. Father felt this, and he forgave Sara her excesses even if mother never could.

If my grandmother hurt anyone, it was my mother, but she

was to blame for being weak in her early years and not taking control of her own life as she did later. In her heart, I think mother knew this. Sara was not to blame for the problems that arose between my mother and father. In plunging into politics, father pulled his mother, his wife and their five children into a whirlpool of prominence in Albany and in Washington and in the world, a world in which that peaceful and idyllic country life of gentlemen and gentlewomen along the Hudson in Hyde Park and on Campobello Island was ours only once in a while.

III

Mother once confessed that she was completely naïve about sex and had not even kissed father until they were married. Sara supposedly counseled her to "do her duty." The evidence suggests she did this well. Married in the spring of 1905, she became pregnant in the late summer and had her first child within fourteen months. In fact she had six children in the ten years between 1906 and 1916. Anna arrived on May 3, 1906. Then I came, on December 23, 1907. The first Franklin, Jr., was born on May 18, 1909, and died on November 8 of that year. Elliott arrived on September 23, 1910. Then came the second Franklin, Jr., August 17, 1914, and finally, John, on March 13, 1916. We grew up during the rise of our parents to public prominence.

Uncle Teddy was president when Anna and I were born, but left office shortly thereafter, early in 1909. He remained an important political figure until his death early in 1919, when I was eleven. I clearly recall him commanding an audience in our home and blustering about being refused a regiment to lead into battle in World War I although he was only sixty or so.

The early Roosevelts were not politically active. They supported Democrats until the Civil War, when both branches rallied behind Lincoln. After the war, the Hyde Park Roosevelts reverted to the Democratic party, while the Oyster Bay branch remained Republican. Teddy Roosevelt was a Republican and the first member of the family to carve a career in politics. He was an inspiration to his nephew, Franklin, who would follow closely in his footsteps, though eventually they went their separate ways philosophically.

Teddy was tough. A military man, he advocated and fought in the Spanish-American War and found fame with his "Rough Riders." He supported a revolution in Panama so that our country could acquire the Canal Zone and build the Panama Canal. He was not always a humanitarian. He made an agreement with Japan that barred the emigration of laborers to the United States, in return for the assurance those already here would be treated fairly. He opposed independence for the Philippines until its people could be trained to govern themselves. He opposed civil rights for Negroes and their integration into this country's mainstream until they could be educated and trained on the level of the whites of that day. He and his brother Elliott both were sympathetic to white rule in the South. Their mother's family, the Bullochs, had property to protect there. He did enact some social reforms, but he was a snob. He believed it was the duty of the government to rule in the best interests of the citizens, and he considered it the calling of the upper class to do what was right for the lower class.

Teddy cut a powerful figure. A persuasive speaker, he had a deep impact on the public. Father cast his first presidential vote for him when Teddy was elected in 1904. He retired in 1908, but returned to challenge his successor, William Howard Taft, for their party's nomination in 1912. Losing, he formed his own "Bull Moose party," and ran anyway, but both he and Taft were trounced by Woodrow Wilson. By then my father was a Wilson man, and a Democrat.

Father passed his bar exams in the spring of 1907 and joined the established Manhattan law firm of Carter, Ledyard and Millburn. He admitted he was apprenticing for politics. Registered in Hyde Park, he became active in Dutchess County public life and let it be known that he was interested in seeking elected office. The party, seeing him as an electable young man with a good background and a well-known name, offered him the opportunity to run for the state legislature. The road, closed to many, was open to him, and he went up it, taking his family with him. He served in the New York State Senate in Albany from 1911 to 1913. In 1913 he was named assistant secretary of the navy and served until 1920. In 1916 he sought, but did not get, his party's nomination for the U.S. Senate from New York. In 1920 he was selected as the vice-presidential running mate of his party's presidential candidate, James Cox. Teddy was the front-runner for the Republican nomination until his death. Instead of facing Uncle Teddy, father's team opposed—and was trounced by—the Warren Harding–Calvin Coolidge ticket.

A year later, father was relegated to the sidelines by polio.

By that time, his family already had been drawn into the eventful and unsettled life of professional politics.

My sister and I were born about eighteen months apart and were closer than many brothers and sisters. We grew up on our Hyde Park estate, in houses in exclusive sections of Manhattan, Albany and Washington, and on Campobello Island. We did not have as many outside friends as most children, but Anna was a tomboy and I could play tennis and strenuous games with her, swim, sail and ride horses with her. The first Franklin, Jr., was born and died within one year. When Elliott arrived, Anna was four and I was almost three. Nearly four more years passed before the second Franklin, Jr., came on the scene and another year and a half before John was born. Franklin and John grew up together and were close, while Anna and I were well on our way by then. As the middle child, Elliott was more on his own.

For the most part, father left our rearing to mother. And she, for the most part, left it to our grandmother. There's no doubt that mother cared for her children. She read the right books on rearing children and sought out the best advice. She tried to do what was right for us, but had no confidence in her ability to do so. Sara had confidence in her own ability to do anything. As much as mother resented her mother-in-law's interference, mother let Sara guide the rearing of the children. Mother wrote Sara for advice when we misbehaved, and she seldom complained when Sara took charge. If mother even hinted her displeasure, Sara simply said, "Why, Eleanor, I didn't think you'd mind." Most of the time mother pretended she didn't. It was easier than pretending she could take charge.

Granny believed that fresh air, fresh food and castor oil were best for her "babies." When we were sick, we were practically drowned in castor oil. When we were away at school, we were sent at great expense fresh vegetables from the farm at Hyde Park. Once when she was responsible for one of us while father and mother were away, Sara wrote: "The baby is splendid, has his one big movement in the morning, and I do nothing but preach fresh air to nurse, who takes it in chastened spirit."

Granny was as hard on the nurses mother hired as she was on mother. She set up a watch and made pointed remarks about the hours our bedroom windows were seen to be closed. She talked mother into placing me and my sister in a chicken-wire cage hung outside our upper window for airing, which must have attracted attention above the sidewalks of New York. The cage was retired when one day Anna howled so loudly a neighbor threatened to report mother to the Society for the Prevention of Cruelty to Children. I am convinced I contracted pneumonia in that crazy contraption. After that, I was subject to constant colds and developed digestive disorders which led to ulcers. A heart murmur was also detected and I had to have rest periods daily. I hated my bad health.

Elliott also had his problems. He had weak legs which required him to wear braces in his early years. And he burned his legs falling into a beach fire. And, of course, the first Franklin's health failed fast. But the other children enjoyed good health. Anna was always robust, and the second Franklin was the hardiest of all. He was the most confident of all of us, too, and bigger, stronger and more outgoing than his "partner," John. The most thoughtful and businesslike of us, John envied Franklin his robust body and attitude.

When I was recovering from pneumonia, Sara approved my parents taking a summer cottage at Seabright, New Jersey. She felt the fresh air would hurry me back to good health. Actually, the place almost finished me. Anna accidentally pushed me off the porch in my carriage. I got even by stabbing her in the palm of her hand with a pencil. She carried the scar all her life.

None of us were angels. Anna and I used to drop paper bags filled with water on passersby beneath the sixth-floor window of our Manhattan home. Sometimes we threw stink bombs into gatherings of guests inside. We also had the usual sibling rivalries, squabbling a lot and fighting a little. Elliott was always the least disciplined of us. When he was three, mother wrote father: "Elliott bit James hard the other day. . . . I explained to him that boys did not bite. . . ." About that time, she reported that Elliott threw a kitchen knife at her friend, Jean Sherwood. He missed. And a few years later mother reported that he insulted Marion Dickerman, who was trying to tutor him. Mother's letters and journals are full of such episodes which suggest the rebellious role he was to play later in life.

Granny decided discipline would best be enforced by the importation of the proper English "nannies." I remember them as tough old biddies. The one we called "Old Battle-ax" was the worst. One time she pushed Sis to the floor, knelt on her chest and cuffed her about as an admonition to act like a lady. When Elliott knocked Franklin over in his highchair and then laughed, the old gal shoved Elliott in a closet and turned the key in the lock so hard it broke off. She just left him there. It was several hours before father came home and rescued him. Another time she locked Franklin in a closet so long that he claims he has claustrophobia to this day. I was fascinated by the way she smeared hot English mustard on meat. I was staring at it one day and she got so mad she made me eat the entire contents of the jar. It made me so sick I still cannot stand the taste of even the mildest of mustards on a ball-park hot dog. Once she didn't believe me when I told her I had brushed my teeth. She made me dress in my sister's clothing, hung a sign on my back which read, "I Am a Liar," and made me parade up and down East Sixty-fifth Street while other youngsters ridiculed me. I never forgot the humiliation. Nor did my mother, who wept when she found out about it. Mother and father frequently were furious at Old Battle-ax, but they did not give her the bounce until a drawerful of empty whiskey and gin bottles was discovered in her room. Even granny could not forgive her being a secret drinker.

As we began to grow up, we were given less strict supervision. Once we were freed from tyrannical nannies, granny spoiled us. So we put up with a lot of minor irritations from her. I hated, but tolerated, her calling me "Jamesie-boy." But in time some of Sara's Victorian teachings rubbed off on us. Looking back on it, I cannot believe some of the high-society snob language we used. I have some old letters I wrote home. One begins, "Dearest Mummy . . . I know I've been a wretch for not writing. It was simply grand to get your letter. . . ." It concludes, "Heaps and heaps of love." In another I wrote, "I've just been in a perfect bog. . . . This is my first epistle in ages. . . ." Well, that was the way I was raised.

I do not have total recall of those early days, and I remember little of my years in New York, except for the tall, narrow look and feel of the house my grandmother built for us. I think of it as a dark place, but then, it was illuminated only by gaslight. Apparently my parents graciously refused to let granny go to the added expense of wiring it for electricity, which was new at that time.

Nor do I remember much about our life in Albany. I do recall being taken by my father to visit a firehouse, and the thrill I felt when by chance an alarm sounded and I got to see the horse-drawn car rushing out. It was of no importance to me that my father was a state senator and a much-talked-of prospect on the political scene. I was only five years old when we left.

There were three children in the family when we went to Washington the first time. The last two were born during our first four years there. We spent about eight years in Washington, and before father's service as assistant secretary of the navy and his losing candidacy for vice-president were completed, I had become aware of his increasing importance and what our life was like. I remember our first house in Washington as one of many all-alike red brick buildings on our street. Again, it was gaslit and gloomy. Large trees in the front darkened the house, and a small garden in the back did little to open the world to us. Our second house was larger and brighter and had a large backyard. Daily life, dining and entertaining took place on the first floor. Our parents lived on the second floor. We children lived on the third. Servants took the top floor.

Yes, we had servants. In our way of life, we almost always had servants whether we could afford them or not. Father's prestigious position paid him only $5000 annually to add to the $12,500 in trust payments our parents had. Granny pitched in and we lived well. I went to St. Alban's School. I also went to dancing school at the British Embassy. This was mother's idea, not mine, and I hated it at the time, though I appreciated it later in life.

I only gradually became aware of the importance of father's position with the Navy Department. We sometimes went with him to his offices in the building that now is the executive office of the White House but at that time housed the State Department and all the military offices. I remember looking with awe at the marvelous models of every kind of ship, regretting that we were not permitted to take them from their glass cases to float them in the lake in the park. I recall accompanying father when he was part of a group that reviewed portions of the fleet. Once, after participating in an enormous banquet on board our ship, we ran into rough weather coming back across Chesapeake Bay and, to father's disgust, I lost my entire dinner. But then, mother often was sick at sea, too. However, we often went boating down the Potomac and picnicked on the Chesapeake Canal.

Those days are a lifetime removed from today, and I remember them with warmth. I remember Chief Justice White of the Supreme Court going around town in the most elegant carriage drawn by the most spirited set of horses I've ever seen. And I clearly recall driving through the streets of Washington with father in his Stutz touring car with the top down. He taught me to steer, but I couldn't drive the Stutz because it had such a stiff clutch that I couldn't press it down to shift.

Father liked to play golf, baseball and field hockey on Sundays. He wasn't a great athlete, but he was an enthusiastic one. He organized field-hockey games with recruits from the British Embassy who knew the sport. And he tried to teach baseball to a skilled cricket player, Ronald Lindsay. We kids told him he had to slide headfirst into the bases, and the first time he did so he skinned his face. Father was furious with us, but the young man, who later became Sir Lindsay and his country's ambassador to the United States, simply laughed it off.

When father was short of players, he would let Anna and me and our friends play. I sometimes caddied for him at Chevy Chase Country Club for twenty-five cents a round. I remember once when father's partner was Senator Warren Harding, who a few years later would head the ticket that defeated father's presidential team. He was an agreeable gent, and father really liked him. I don't remember who won, but father usually shot pretty well—in the eighties. Father tried to teach mother to play golf, but he gave up. She did become a competent horsewoman, rode regularly with Mrs. Henry Morgenthau and even won an award or two at shows. But she didn't stay with it. She really had little athletic skill and couldn't keep up with father. She was not a physical person, except that she had stamina, which she proved in later years.

When World War I began, Walter Camp, "the father of football," was brought to town to launch a physical-fitness program for the men in government. Father was one of his most devoted students. Sadly, I recall Camp writing, "Mr. Roosevelt is a beautifully built man with the leg muscles of the athlete."

Father and mother played a part in the social life of Washington during the 1920s and they often entertained important guests at our house. The servants did the work mother could not do. Sunday was servants' night out and mother usually fixed us an early supper of scrambled eggs, the only thing she could cook. One Sunday evening mother was in her dressing gown and father in his smoking jacket when the doorbell rang. Guests had begun to gather for a dinner party mother thought she had scheduled for the following night. She scrambled more eggs, father mixed drinks and the guests went home early. Mother did not enjoy entertaining, anyway, and was shy with strangers, while father loved an audience.

We met many of the most prominent people of the day in our home. The robust star of the *Tugboat Annie* movies, Marie Dressler, came to town to take part in a Liberty Bond rally. Father was assigned to introduce her. As she stood behind a high railing, the short, stout actress felt she could not be seen. Clumsily, she climbed onto the railing. "Hold my legs," she hollered to my flustered father. As he did so, gingerly, she fell backward onto him, almost crushing him. My father loved to repeat the story. Once, when he told it to Herbert Lehman at a dinner party, the then governor of New York laughed so hard he spilled his raspberry sherbet into his finger bowl.

Father had a feeling for history and always wanted us to make the most of our opportunities to mingle with the mighty. I remember he took me to meet President Wilson, who seemed a formal sort of person. I do not know where we met him, but it was not at the White House. I did not set foot in the White House until I accompanied my father in 1933 when he was inaugurated. I also recall meeting Josephus Daniels, who seemed a pompous but kindly old codger. As secretary of the navy, he was father's boss. Once, father and mother took Anna and me to Mount Vernon to meet visiting

King Albert, Queen Elizabeth and Prince Leopold of Belgium. A hot-rodder in his day, Leopold spotted a motorcycle and talked me into taking a ride on it that terrified me and my parents. Years later, when I visited Brussels and again met Leopold, who had become king, I reminded him of the incident. He just looked at me blankly and could not recall it.

In 1917 Anna, Elliott and I came down with whooping cough and were sent to Hyde Park, where we might contaminate our grandmother but not the rest of the family. That month, Marshal Joffre of France visited New York City. Granny was determined we meet him, whooping cough or not. She bundled us up and took us to the Frick Mansion on Fifth Avenue, where she'd been invited. I remember being kissed on both cheeks by this war hero with a walrus mustache. The hero of the Marne never knew how close he came to being infected, but he escaped unscathed.

For the most part, Sara did not now play as important a part in our lives, though she often visited us. I remember her playing the piano while we gathered around for a family sing in the evenings. Many evenings, father or mother read to us. We were closer in those days than we would be ever again.

I do not remember Lucy Mercer coming into our home every day to serve as mother's secretary. I certainly knew nothing of father's taking up with her while we and mother spent time without him at Campobello. I knew nothing until years later of mother's showdown with father over this affair and the agreement they reached which from then on made their relationship a formal one. Anna never was aware of it at that time, as far as I know, and the others could not have been. It is easy now for any of us to say we were, but it simply isn't the truth.

In those days, before father attained more important positions of power and mother moved out into the world, our parents had a fair amount of time to spend with us. Mother supervised our studies and daily activities. Father romped with us at night, tucked us in bed and kissed all of us goodnight. In spite of the lack of closeness later, we were always a family that embraced and kissed when we got together and when we parted. We sons kissed our father unashamedly, as is common in many countries. We touched without embarrassment.

With our entry into World War I, father's responsibilities increased and he became busier. By then I began to imagine his importance to be more than it was. I thought he was winning the war almost single-handedly. When in 1918 he sailed on the destroyer U.S.S. *Dyer* to tour the naval battlefronts overseas, all I asked of him was, "Please get me the kaiser's helmet, and, if you can, the kaiser, himself." Mother made more modest requests when he wrote from England to ask what gifts he should bring back. She wrote that Anna needed "6 new nightgowns & 6 prs. drawers," and Elliott and I needed "those knit stockings with turnover tops . . . you can get them cheaper in London than here."

Mother's vision was limited in those days, but she did what she could. She put on a Red Cross uniform and went to Union Station to serve coffee and donuts to the servicemen passing through daily. She set an empty place at our dinner table as a symbol of food being saved in support of Herbert Hoover's program to feed starving children abroad, which was his mission. Mother created controversy with an interview she gave a newspaper reporter. The story said that the food-saving program at the home of assistant secretary and Mrs. Roosevelt was regarded by the Food Administration as a model of its kind. It said that in addition to the seven of us in the family, there were ten servants, which there were not. Mother was quoted as saying, "Making the ten servants help me do my saving has been highly profitable."

Mother was at Campobello when the story broke, and it distressed her. It amused father, who wrote her: "All I can say is that your latest newspaper campaign is a corker and I am proud to be the husband of the Originator, Discoverer and Inventor of the New Household Economy for Millionaires. Please have a photo taken showing the family, the ten cooperating servants, the scraps saved from the table, and the handbook. I will have it published."

The world was reaching us, in any event.

Too much has been made of father seeking active duty
during the war. He had been discouraged by his mother when
he wanted an appointment to Annapolis as a lad, and now by
his wife when he sought to enlist in the navy in his thirties.
He was easily discouraged. He loved the sea, but he also was
proud of his position. Despite the patriotism of the times, he
was content to leave the physical fighting to others when his
superiors told him he could do more where he was.

Those were difficult times. I remember riots in the streets
of Washington. But what I really remember is not so much
my feeling for the protesting people as my fear that the violence would reach our doorstep.

It did. One night in June of 1919 while my parents were at
a party and the other children were at Hyde Park, I had
stayed home to study for an exam and was alone except for
the servants. I had gone to bed, but was awakened by the
sound of an explosion, breaking glass and screams. I ran over
broken glass to the bedroom window and saw smoke rising
from the house across the street. A bomb had burst at the
home of Attorney General Mitchell Palmer and had blown
out our window. My parents had just returned; they had
parked their car in a garage father rented several blocks away
and were walking home. Had they been a few minutes earlier,
they might have been blown to bits. They rushed to the house
to see if I was safe. Finding me standing by the window,
father embraced me so hard that, in my mind, I can still feel
the ardor of it. Mother merely asked, "Whatever are you
doing out of bed at this hour, James?" as if a bomb exploded
every hour. "Get yourself straight to bed," she ordered.
Which I did, while father hurried across the street to find the
attorney general also unharmed.

Examining the debris in the morning, I discovered an
unusual object, which I showed my father. He paled, placed
it in a napkin and took it to the police. It turned out to be a
piece of the assassin's collarbone. The anarchist had been
blown up by his own bomb. Mother wrote Sara: "James glo-
ries in every new bone found. . . ."

To a great extent, the end of the war marked the end of my youth. I was turning twelve and on my way to Groton and out into the world. The next few years altered our family life forever. In 1920 father failed in his vice-presidential effort and left the Navy Department. We returned to New York City, where he went to work for an insurance firm while planning his political future. But the following year he was stricken, and that future had to wait awhile.

IV

What I remember best about my youth was not our early life in Albany and Washington but our life in Hyde Park, which I will always think of as home, and on Campobello, which was our home away from home. I recall with warmth that time before my parents became less parents than people of the world, before the problems of their children became less important to them than their own and those of others in the world, before we were drawn into that world.

When I was growing up, Hyde Park seemed more my home to me than the many others I had. After father's death, most of the estate there went to the government. Mother willed her land to Elliott, who, needing money, sold it, and for this I can't quite forgive him. There are shops at Hyde Park now which should not be there, on the fringe of what is a national historical monument. It is hard to think of it as a monument, visited by thousands of tourists each year, preserved in a sort of unlived-in elegance.

When we lived there we loved it. Winters, we skated and played ice hockey on a frozen pond on the grounds of our adjoining neighbor, Colonel Archibald Rogers. We went sledding on a long hill leading to an area above the Hudson River. The run must have been a mile or more. Father was like a boy on those sledding expeditions. He would chase us back up the steep road so fast our lungs would ache from the cold air and heavy breathing. Summers he taught us to swim in the Rogers pond by throwing us in with rope attached to our waists. Mother barely learned to swim, though later she had a pool put in alongside her Val-Kill retreat, giving us our own place in which to swim. Father was a fair swimmer, which served him well later at Warm Springs when it became his only exercise.

As I recall it, we all had horses, including father and mother. We had twelve hundred acres in which to ride, between our property and the Rogers estate. We also rode on the Delano estate near Rhinebeck. Anna's horse, an agreeable animal, a Norwegian, was bred at the Delanos' and given to her. My horse was an Irish pony I named Truepenny, a hellion of a little fellow with a hard mouth, who used to run away from time to time.

Father always liked to drive around the Hyde Park area, visiting old friends. During Prohibition there were places he could go to get a brew or two while he chatted with people he'd known all his life. After his illness and the loss of the use of his legs, father received from the Fords a specially built car with hand controls that he could operate, and father drove it here and at Warm Springs for a few years. I recall when he took Sam Rosenman and Jim Farley for a drive one day to show off a new road he'd had built in the back woods. Like many of father's home engineering projects, it wasn't as good as he thought it was. And he wasn't as good with the hand controls as he thought he was. As they neared the bottom of a hill, he accidentally squeezed the accelerator instead of the brake. The car careened around a curve at terrific speed before he brought it to a screeching halt. Turning around, father found Farley almost in a faint and Rosenman crossing himself. Laughing, father asked his Jewish friend what in Lord's name was he doing. Sam said, "Driving with you, I'm taking no chances." Father roared. It became one of his favorite stories.

If father was not a good driver, mother was worse. She may

have been worse than anyone. She drove a car right into the back door of our Hyde Park house one time. Another time she knocked over one of the stone pillars flanking the driveway. Once she backed into a ditch. From time to time she gave up driving, but most of the time she kept trying. We boys, on the other hand, turned out to be spectacular drivers, suitable for speedways if not city streets and public roads, as our speeding tickets, especially in our youth, will attest.

Although it was father's home, Hyde Park remained his mother's domain until her death. He advised her on its operation, but she did not always heed his advice. For example, he wanted her to improve production on the farm or give it up entirely, but she kept it as her father had, as something for a gentleman farmer to have, with no thought of turning a profit on it. There were cows and chickens which produced milk and eggs, but only for our own use. The cream was so thick we could eat it with a spoon. During the war, granny did permit the fields to be planted for vegetables to ease the food shortage. Girls from nearby Vassar often pitched in, taking what they needed for themselves. We children were permitted to grow vegetables on our own little plots and we sold our produce to granny at outrageous prices.

Evenings in the main house we often had family "sings." We sang with enthusiasm, if not with ability. Father thought he was the best, but he may have been the worst. In Washington he sometimes went to the Methodist church simply because he enjoyed their hymn singing more than that of our own Episcopal church. "I love to sing with the Methodys," he'd say. He even took Winston Churchill to "sing with the Methodys" one Sunday.

At Hyde Park we went to Saint James Episcopal Church. Father's father had been a vestryman and his mother was active there. Father also became a vestryman, and, later, so did I. In time he became senior warden. After he became president and was responsible for the spending of billions of dollars, he was in his spare time responsible for the saving of a few hundred dollars at the church. In Washington we sometimes went to the Saint John's Church of Lafayette Square, across from the White House, which came to be called "The Church of Presidents." Here he was in the company of other officials of the government. At Hyde Park he was with old friends. Elsewhere, he hesitated at going to church because he resented being stared at by strangers during the privacy of his prayers.

Mother seldom missed Sunday services, but father was not above playing hooky on a beautiful day when livelier activities lured him outside. We were brought up to be churchgoers, but I can recall hiding under the bed and refusing to be coaxed out by mother one Sunday. Mother was furious, but father thought it funny.

Our parents believed in God and brought us up to believe, but I do not think father was really religious until later in life when he had become crippled and bore the burden of making decisions that would affect millions of lives. However, he always felt he would have made a marvelous minister. With his speaking ability, it's possible. When he was governor of New York, the minister at Saint James in Hyde Park was the Reverend Frank Wilson. When Reverend Wilson suffered an attack of appendicitis, Sara took it upon herself to telephone her son in Albany to suggest he might be of some assistance on Sunday. Swiftly father offered to conduct the service as a lay minister, but was disappointed when the rector advised him a substitute minister had been obtained. He got his chance later, though. When father was president and cruising the Bahamas on Vincent Astor's yacht on Easter Sunday, 1934, off Watlings Island where Columbus first landed in the New World, father invited the companies of American and British naval ships in the area to special services, had fancy programs printed and preached the sermon himself. He spoke of it proudly many times.

Reverend Wilson later became rector of Saint John's in Washington. Father invited him and Dr. Peabody from Groton to conduct special services on his inauguration anniversaries while he was at the White House. At the time of the 1943 anniversary services, Reverend Wilson was in training in chaplain's school in Norfolk. Father summoned him with special orders. After the minister arrived, father sent him to meet a VIP at the train station; it turned out to be Mrs. Wilson. At the time of the 1944 services, when Reverend Wilson was overseas, father had Mrs. Wilson brought in for the event.

Our warmest times at Hyde Park were at Christmas. On Christmas Eve we sat at father's feet while he read from *A Christmas Carol*, hamming it up magnificently. On Christmas morning we rushed to his bedroom to get to the stuffed stockings which hung from his fireplace. Smoking his first cigarette of the day, sipping coffee brought him by a servant, he watched us with affection. Mother would come from her room to join us. In our bathrobes and slippers we'd go to the library together to open presents spread beneath a decorated tree. After that excitement, we dressed and had breakfast. Through the day, family and friends would drop by. In late afternoon, dinner was served. Father carved the turkey and we had our feast. That night we might sing Christmas carols. Although it surely was not always so, it seems to me there was always snow on the ground and trees of the forest around us. It was as beautiful as a Currier and Ives print, traditionally lovely.

Even after we grew up, we gathered together at Hyde Park as much as possible at Christmastime to maintain this tradition. Our children took over roles we'd had as children. Our parents became their grandparents and adored their grandchildren. But as life and time tore us away, we could not always get back. Eventually, what had been was no more.

It was a grand house. After father and granny had built wings with bigger bedrooms, I inherited father's little second-floor room with the outsize bed Sara had gotten him to make sure his growth wasn't stunted. I used to keep my most precious possessions in that room—a stocking cap, a sweater, a baseball glove, ice skates, a book that had belonged to father —so I would feel at home whenever I returned from school.

As the years passed, however, I returned less and less often. And now that we have surrendered our rights to the estate, I go back only on ceremonial occasions. I do not know what happened to those possessions of my childhood, but they are gone as surely as is my youth.

A lot of my childhood—most of my summers, in fact—was spent on Campobello Island, part of the province of New Brunswick, Canada. It is just off the northernmost coastal point of Maine, joined to the tiny town of Lubec by what is now named the FDR Memorial Bridge. From Gooseberry Point to the East Quoddy Head Lighthouse, the island is only about twelve miles long. At its broadest point, from Snug Cove to Ragged Cove, it is a mere three miles wide. It is rugged, but beautiful. Except in midsummer, it is windswept, bitterly cold and battered by heavy waves. Its tides rise and fall more than thirty feet at the head of the Bay of Fundy. Even in midsummer its waters are too cold for all but the boldest of swimmers, but calm enough for pleasant sailing. I feel as though I can still taste the fresh salt air.

Some sixty years ago, it was not easy for us to get there. Usually we went by train from New York to Boston, which took six hours or so. In Boston we rested at an old-fashioned hotel Sara insisted we use because her father had stayed there. Sometimes we took a steamer from Boston to Eastport. Most of the time we took the late-night pullman train to Ayers Junction and switched to another train, heated by a coal stove, for the journey on to Eastport. Indians would board with baskets of handcrafts to sell. At Eastport we would transfer to a carriage, which took us to the dock. When the tide was right, a motorboat took us over to the island, and we went by rowboat to our own pier and climbed the hill to the house. Meanwhile our belongings, in forty or fifty trunks, valises, boxes and barrels, went separately by express to Eastport, by ferry to Welchpool and by horse-drawn dray to the hill. Men pushed our belongings in wheelbarrows up to the house. It took mother and the servants—usually the same ones, secured from the small, permanent population—almost a week to unpack. But once we were settled in, we stayed awhile.

Campobello was not *our* island. We had purchased houses there and were among the "summer regulars," grudgingly accepted by the fifteen hundred or so residents who lived in two villages, Welchpool and Wilson's Beach. Here, sardine fishermen and their families lived in houses with picket fences and flower gardens that looked as though they had been plucked intact from English coastal towns. Though it is a tourist attraction today—primarily because of father's fame —it remains much as it was yesterday, a simple place, unspoiled. Sara's house has been torn down, but ours remains, another monument.

Like most of the regular visitors, the family spent the summer while the man of the house came over for a few weeks when he got his vacation from work. Father loved life on the island more than any of us, but got to spend the least time there. Mother always liked it because she had her own home here, which she ran. As Sara got older, she seldom came. It was rugged, my father's kind of place more than my mother's, but we children never minded its inconveniences. Since we had no electricity, we lit the house with kerosene lamps and candles. Our food was cooked on coal stoves. We had a coal heater and a wood-burning fireplace. Mother read to us by firelight. Summer middays it might be hot, but the nights were usually cold. We dressed warmly and slept under mountains of blankets. We did have an indoor toilet, which was flushed by pulling a chain. The water came from a well and was heated in a boiler, but there was not a lot of pressure. We washed, but did not take daily baths. Of course, there were not a lot of conveniences in the cities in those days, either. Today Campobello does have electricity, running water and telephones. But in that yesterday there was no telephone, no radio. Mail came by boat across the bay, delayed a day. Newspapers came by mail, a week late. Of course, you could take a boat to Maine to get that day's newspaper or make a telephone call. After father assumed positions of importance, he made arrangements for urgent messages to be telephoned to

Eastport and brought to him immediately by boat, but I don't recall that there were any. The world seemed to turn more slowly in those days. Less seemed to happen. Perhaps we just didn't know what was going on until later, but it didn't seem to matter.

Today, with instant communication, the pace has picked up. Yesterday on Campobello, life was slow and there was a marvelous sense of isolation. We played in the woods, picked berries and walked the beaches. There was a kind of clay court where we could play tennis. We might take a dip in the icy ocean, but seldom really swam. Father tried to contribute a saltwater swimming pool to us and our neighbors, but it was a disaster. As usual, less the master builder than he believed himself to be, he had a hole dug, pipes installed and concrete poured. He devised a system whereby water would flow in from the ocean at high tide and out at low tide and be contained long enough to be heated. It never worked. The water became stagnant and stank. Over the harsh winters, the concrete cracked. The pool was not used; an eyesore, it eventually was filled in.

Father could, however, carve marvelous boats out of wood. He and Louis Howe spent hours at it, sailing and racing them. Father tried to teach me, but he lacked the patience to teach. He never attempted to teach us to fish, which on this island of fishermen was a waste. He did teach us to sail, maybe because this was the one activity he loved above all others and wanted us to love. He was a superb sailor. The straits and narrows around Campobello and the nearby islands are treacherous, the tides strong and tricky, but he knew them well. While he would not tolerate our fooling around on board a boat, he delighted in demonstrating his own ability with a near-reckless handling of his ship through rocky passages, so close to jagged reefs as to scare the wits out of us. He was one of the few civilians ever allowed to take the helm of massive naval ships, sometimes at full speed in foggy or other difficult conditions.

We had two boats during our days there—the *Half Moon,*

a sixty-foot two-masted schooner, and the *Vireo,* a twenty-foot single-masted sailboat. A local captain, Franklin Calder, was pressed into service to provide us our basic instructions in how to handle the sails and the tiller. Father took over to teach us the fine points. Actually, he expected us to learn by watching him. He'd sometimes explain how and why he did something, but seldom let us do it. Father never spoke about having been an only child, but he never worked up enthusiasm for a team effort with his children. Nevertheless, except for mother, and Elliott, who preferred horses, solid ground and the wild West, we became competent sailors. I love sailing and do not have my own boat today simply because I cannot afford it.

Father had his hobbies, but they were an escape for him, from us as well as from others. He never talked to us about his hobbies and never encouraged us to develop our own.

When father was not there, the most active thing we would do with mother was to have picnics. When he was there, the picnics became outings in the woods in which we threw a ball around, had races and played games. I remember father developed a sort of "hare and hounds" game in which our neighbors often joined. The "hares" would leave a trail of pieces of paper, while the "hounds" would try to catch them before they reached some predetermined destination. It wasn't easy, because the trail might be strung along the rocks by the beach at low tide and might be covered up by the time you reached it at high tide, or it might stretch along cliffs that were hard to climb. Father loved these rugged affairs. But these were not so much family affairs as community affairs. Father conceived of them as his contribution to island life, a way of getting involved with and seeing his neighbors. They would wind up as giant picnics with roaring fires illuminating the dark.

That splendid isolation of the island became a nightmare when father became sick with what turned out to be polio. We had trouble getting help and it took so long to figure out what was wrong with him. I was thirteen that summer of 1921 and seldom have been back since, but I think of the island fondly and often and cannot condemn it for what happened to father there.

We were reminded of it when Dore Schary wrote his play, *Sunrise at Campobello*, about that sad summer. When they made a movie of it, many scenes were shot in other homes on the island because they more closely fit the filmmakers' conception of what our home should have looked like. Our furniture was sturdy wicker, our belongings practical, the walls covered with floral papers. The filmmakers decorated more dynamically. Our dock was rotted, so they built a new one. With their magic, they made the sun rise at Campobello, though we faced west.

Life is not always as the movies would have it.

V

Heads of state have little time to be heads of families. Mother once said she was so busy being pregnant or having babies she had little time for anything else the first ten or twelve years of her marriage. But most of her children were reared more by their grandmother and by maids and nannies than by their mother. Meanwhile, father was too busy building his political career to play a regular role in our upbringing.

Anna was three and I was two when the first Franklin, Jr., was born in May of 1909. He was stricken with influenza, which apparently turned into pneumonia. Despite the desperate efforts of doctors, he never recovered. His heart finally failed a little more than seven months after his birth. My parents apparently took his death deeply to heart, but they kept their sorrow to themselves. They never could bring themselves to speak about it at any length and seldom mentioned the loss. They simply went on with their lives. Mother became pregnant within a month or two and gave birth to Elliott the following September, after which came the only long gap in their having children. It was almost four more years before the second Franklin, Jr., was born, followed by John less than two years later. Then they stopped.

While Anna and I had become one team, Franklin and John became another. Maybe because he came along after the death of the first Franklin, Jr., maybe because he was named for her father, possibly because he was the middle one and alone more than the rest of us, or because he seemed to need more care than we did, Elliott received the most attention from mother. You might say mother always liked Elliott best. As the women of the family, mother and Anna were close until Anna was in her teens, but mother was introverted, Anna extroverted; mother discouraged confidences, and Anna kept her own counsel and before long was going her own way. Meanwhile, mother remained close to Elliott. She used to sigh and say he seemed to have inherited many of her father's traits: He was unreliable and always in trouble; he just seemed to demand her attention.

I don't think father really had a favorite. Unless it was Anna. He was always a ladies' man, and she turned out to be his only little lady. And of course she was his first child. I was his first son and his eldest son and as such enjoyed a certain favor with him. But fate tore our parents further from us. When father was stricken with polio in 1921, Anna was fifteen, I was thirteen, Elliott ten, Franklin six and John four. While father and mother struggled through his ordeal, obviously we did not have a typical family life. To keep his name prominent while he was sidelined, mother got into the game, became active in public life and was away a lot. By then we had begun to go away to school and were seldom home. When father began his comeback, I was old enough to help him, but from then on neither father nor mother spent much time at home.

Mother felt guilty about spending so little time with Anna and me, so she did try to spend time with Elliott, Franklin and John when they were growing up. But father became governor while Franklin and John were in their early teens, and he had even less time for them than he'd had for the other children. I was able to work for him then, as Anna did later, and consequently we were closer to him than we had been in our youth. By then, mother was so busy she had little time for any of us.

While we were growing up we lived well, as far as material

things were concerned. We had handsome homes, and servants, and never went without anything of importance. We
attended the best schools, met many of the most important
people of our day and were on the inside watching as history
was being made. By contrast with the kind of lives most
young people lead, especially the poor, it's ridiculous for me
to complain. Yet on a personal level there was something
missing from our lives which even the most disadvantaged
youngster may have. We spent so little time alone with our
parents that those times are remembered and treasured, as
though gifts from gods. We never had the day-to-day discipline, supervision and attention most children get from their
parents. Ours was not an ordinary way of life.

One year, mother wrote a magazine article in which she
provided parents a seven-point code for the rearing of children. Among the points she made were, "furnish an example," "stop preaching," "stop shielding," "don't prevent self-
reliance and initiative," "allow your children to develop
along their own lines." Essentially, she suggested we allow
our young to grow up independently, watching their parents
rather than being guided by them. I suppose it was all she
dared to suggest. She concluded: "The next generation will
take care of itself."

In a day when the young were not so sophisticated and
independent as they are today, this was difficult for us to do.
I cannot recall any of us being counseled by our parents or
given any particular piece of advice. I cannot imagine going
to my parents with a problem. When we had problems, we
handled them ourselves or went to our grandmother. But you
did not discuss *personal* problems with granny. I never remember being in her bedroom. Nor, for that matter, in my
mother's very often. Certainly not when she was in bed. I
remember romping with father in his bed, but we never
romped with mother or granny. Mother once undertook to
read to Anna and me about the birds and the bees—literally,
the birds and bees. All I remember is the pollination of flowers. She never was tempted to try again. As we grew up, we

certainly never spoke of sex to our mother or grandmother. Nor did father do his duty. I learned from other children, I suppose. Or by experimentation. Later we were able to joke about sex with father, but only lightly.

Mother sometimes asked father to discipline us when we behaved badly, but he would not. Mother would leave one of us with him in his study and he'd take us on his lap and try to soothe our ruffled feelings and tell us to do right. He seldom laid even the lightest of hands on us, though he might tell mother later, laughing, that he had spanked us hard. Neither mother nor granny ever hit us, but, as I've already said, some of our nannies did.

Elliott has written of "the father we loved, the mother we respected." My first inclination was to differ with this. We grew to love and respect both of them. But on reflection I see there is some truth to what Elliott says. Father was able to give love more freely than mother and showed more warmth. Father could relax and, prior to polio, romp. Mother was always stiff, never relaxed enough to romp. She was a formal person who wore starched dresses to her neck. She found it easier to give than to get, to do for than to have done for her. Mother loved all mankind, but she did not know how to let her children love her.

The warmest moments I remember with mother were when as a boy I had to have my "quiet times," and in order to get me to stay put, mother used to lie alongside and read to me. It is sad she seldom had other occasions to unbend. I remember when Elliott as a boy in braces fell into a fire at Campobello and was badly burned while mother was on a shopping trip to St. Andrew's. Mother, perhaps feeling guilty about it, refused to make much of it. Writing father in Washington, she began by speaking of "the splendid cruise" she'd had to St. Andrew's and went on with other chitchat before even getting around to the accident: "When I got home I found that poor baby Elliott had fallen into the ashes of a fire the children had on the beach." We had been burning litter and the beach now looked quite nice, she noted. As for

Elliott, well, "The ashes got under the strops of his braces and burned . . . but he only cried a little. . . . Nurse says they are only skin burns."

I remember when I was seven or eight, my sister had expressed a desire for a watch for Christmas. I heard my parents privately say they thought she was too young, so I determined to get it for her. I took ten dollars from my mother's purse, bought the watch and presented it to a delighted Anna on Christmas morning. I saw my parents exchange meaningful glances. I suppose mother had missed the money from her purse, and she and father knew I did not have enough money to buy a watch. She could not bring herself to ask me about it, but sent me to speak to my father in his study. Father spoke quietly to me about the probabilities and I confessed. He praised me for wanting to please my sister, but said it was spoiled by stealing and hoped I would know better in the future. I was relieved by his gentle manner, learned from it and remember this sad moment warmly. I wish we'd had other such father-and-son moments.

Curiously, I connect one other traumatic moment from my childhood with a watch. A few years later, mother and father gave me my first wrist-watch for my birthday. The following summer I lost it in the sand at Campobello. I searched for it, but could not find it. I confessed my mishap to my parents, hoping they'd buy me another watch. But they would not, saying I had to learn to take care of my possessions. I was heartbroken. I am still saddened by the memory of it, but do think of it as one of the few times they tried to teach me an important lesson.

For father, the education of his sons meant Groton and Harvard. Except for Elliott, we followed in his footsteps. Elliott went to Groton, then rebelled and refused to go on to Harvard or any other college. We were not outstanding students. Anna got interested in farming at Hyde Park and went to Cornell to study agriculture, but left to get married before graduation.

When I first got to Groton I had led so sheltered a life and was so shy that I was afraid to ask where the bathroom was. Hard as it may be to believe, I did what had to be done in my pants or in the bushes. My soiled pants were stuffed in a box, which I buried in the bushes. I suppose I was surrounded by foul smells. Holding back as long as I could, I started to suffer stomach pains. Not knowing the cause, school officials suspected homesickness (well, I *was* homesick; at home I knew where the bathrooms were) and asked my parents to take me home for a few days to ease my adjustment. It was my grandmother, not my mother or father, who came for me.

After a short while I returned, resolved to manage better. I did well enough. I got fair grades in my studies, and, determined to make up for my sickly youth, I participated with fair ability on all the sports teams. I was always getting hurt, but father was proud of me anyway. He even came to see one of my football games, though I invited him to all of them. He was happy when I was elected prefect of Hundred House, which gave me the idea of being a leader. Father wrote me every month or so, but mother wrote weekly. It was one of the things she did so well, like always remembering the birthdays of everyone in the family. Neither wrote of personal things. Mother wrote me all the news, with warnings to take care of myself. Father wrote when he was disappointed in my grades, saying I should strive to meet the family's high standards. I didn't know until later that he hadn't done any better as a boy.

For the most part, father left my fate to Dr. Peabody. He was a tough old codger who kept his lads in line. Averell Harriman, a Groton graduate, once observed to his father that Dr. Peabody "would be an awful bully if he wasn't such a terrible Christian." The good doctor did keep after me, and I improved as I went along. However, one of my masters, James Regan, did more for me, reaching me as even my father did not. A marvelous man and an excellent teacher, Regan spoke to me not only of family standards but about my own potential, about becoming my own man. I don't suppose young men now lend themselves to such shaping by superiors as we did then, but I benefited enormously from his inspiration.

Groton did provide a new perspective on life in that I came to see that the sun did not shine exclusively on me. I remember how shocked I was when a student poll revealed overwhelming sentiment against the Cox-Roosevelt ticket in 1920 even though father had been, and I was, a student there. Insulted, I wrote father that clearly politics was a dirty game and perhaps he should give some thought to getting out of it and into something decent before it was too late. Fortunately, he failed to take my advice.

After I graduated from Groton, I was sent to spend the summer in the woods of eastern Canada in one of father's few attempts to do something he believed would be beneficial to me. He had a friend who owned a lumber mill, and he agreed to give me a job so I might learn what real work was like and be toughened by it. Reluctantly I went by train to Montreal, where I was given a ticket entitling me to ride in the caboose of a freight all day and all night until I reached the camp on the St. Lawrence River. I was welcomed without ceremony, given a bunk and sent out to sort logs. I did a variety of hard jobs for eighteen cents an hour for eight weeks. I wasn't used to such physical labor, but I was young and I got used to it. I never liked it, however, and I was lonely all the while. The men could not be convinced I was not a company spy, and they shied away from me. They were French-speaking and for a while I tried to teach them English, but the parish priest put a stop to this. The newspapers were in English, and the bosses did not want the men to find out about a world in which workers were better off.

I learned a lot about life there, but I never forgave father for forcing me into something that he himself had never been subjected to in his youth. The fact is that aside from my work for him, it was the only job he ever helped me get. His name may have done so, but he himself never opened a door for me, even when I needed it. Maybe it was just as well, but I would have liked to have had him offer to help me. He never sat down with me to discuss what I might want to do with my life and how he might help. The help he gave me was what he wanted to give me, not what I might have wanted.

I went to Harvard because he wanted me to go to Harvard, although I had my heart set on a smaller, less snobbish school, Williams College, where many of my friends were headed. I'm not sure why, but I never felt comfortable with the wealthy young men who were in the majority at Groton and Harvard, and never made the enduring friendships most students make in their school days. Instead, I joined and became president of the Phillips Brooks House, which, rather than being an exclusive social fraternity, was devoted to charitable activities. I worked with the poor in the settlement houses of Boston. I always supposed this made mother happy, though she never said so. Father preferred to speak of my membership in clubs to which he had belonged, and which I joined only to please him—the Fly Club and Hasty Pudding. I also joined the Circulo Italiano Club. He assumed it specialized in the study of Italian culture. The fact is, it specialized in the study of speakeasies, which I visited often, though I was afraid I'd hurt his reputation.

Father's supreme effort to give me guidance during my college days was to write a letter directed to the dean, but sent to me for comment before it was to be sent on. Among other things, he said, "He is clean, truthful, considerate of others, and has distinct ambitions. . . . He has at the same time, I think, too much of a love of social good times, like the rest of his crowd." He suggested I be encouraged in scholarship and discouraged in any social or sporting life, and wondered if I should not be found a part-time job. I did not send the letter on. Instead, I wrote father that I considered the letter unfair to me. It was never mentioned again.

I learned more in the streets of Boston than I did in my classes in Cambridge. I did well in those studies that interested me and less well in those that did not. A trick knee kept me out of contact sports, but I rowed on the crew. If father held my spending money to a minimum, it didn't matter because my grandmother more than made up for any amount I needed. Thanks to her generosity, I spent my summers traveling. I spent one summer in Europe, another in Scandinavia doing my thesis on government there, lucky to have doors opened to me. Once I got my passport mixed up with another person's, and it was three weeks before I had one that did not include a picture of a lady holding a poodle. A third summer I spent in Ireland with the Cushing family at a house they had borrowed from a fellow Bostonian. I was going with Betsey Cushing, and we had a happy holiday. I remember getting caught up in the excitement of bidding at an auction of yearlings and spending my passage money home on an attractive colt. Old Tom, who operated the estate, offered to tend the horse for me and ready him for racing. Excitedly I cabled the good news to my father, requesting more money. Calmly he cabled back that it was good to hear about the horse and I could swim home. But he told his mother about it and granny sent me the money to get home. The horse, which I sold at a loss, never won a race.

I was spoiled, of course. We all were. As, I suppose, the Kennedy, Johnson, Nixon, and Ford children were spoiled. Some may have the strength of character to overcome it, some may not. Some may be burned by the spotlight, some may slip into the shadows. I remember when we were children father used naval ships to travel to Campobello for a vacation and to take us off the island during a polio epidemic. Others in positions of power have done this sort of thing. Many still do. But today it would be difficult to defend.

When I was at Harvard, my father became governor. When he visited Harvard to speak at his old club at my request, it set me apart from my fellows. Years earlier Teddy Roosevelt had done the same for him at Groton. A few years after I left college, father became president and our lives were completely changed. From then on, we would enjoy a privileged, if pressured, position we had not earned or even asked for, but which we often used. I recall a time during the war when I was on leave and trying to get from Washington to Los Angeles as fast as possible. A snowstorm delayed my train to

Chicago and I was afraid I'd miss my connecting train to L.A.
I explained my situation to the conductor and he wired ahead
to have the train held in Chicago for the president's son. I
remember being escorted by railroad officials down the platform in Chicago while some of the waiting passengers booed
me. It didn't bother me. I accepted the power of my position.
It did not occur to me then that I had no real right to so
inconvenience others. There long ago came a time when I
became aware and ashamed of such unjustified and inconsid-
erate acts. Once I thought about it, I did not consider myself
better than anyone else.

I do not imagine Margaret Truman or John Eisenhower or
the Kennedy kids or the Nixon or Ford children hold themselves above others, but they are and always will be set apart,
their lives spotlighted. It was carried to an extreme with us
because our father was president longer than any other and
our mother carried on as a prominent public servant long
after his death. One or the other was a national figure for
thirty years. I rarely have been just Jim Roosevelt, for example, but almost always Franklin and Eleanor Roosevelt's son
James, though I have been a congressman, a United Nations
representative and a businessman. To this day it is so, even
though I am nearing seventy and my parents are long gone.
I often am introduced as the eldest son of the late president
and his wife.

My brother Franklin, in some ways the wildest of all of us,
got into a series of scrapes, several of them concerned with
careless driving, and resented the publicity a Roosevelt got
for acts that would not have been noticed if committed by a
Jones. Mother told him the advantages of his life outweighed
the disadvantages, but Franklin had the ability to accept the
advantages while refusing to accept the disadvantages. Once,
he was caught speeding on his way to Harvard and was taken
to court. When the judge found out who he was, he not only
dismissed the case but took Franklin home to dinner. When
father found out, he was angry, but Franklin accepted it as his
due.

At seventeen, John stayed out late celebrating on the day

father became president and moved into the White House. When John drove up in the wee hours he was refused admission because no one would believe the president's son would drive the disreputable jalopy he was driving. Guards at the gate refused to call the president, and John went to a hotel. A few nights after John moved in, he went to raid the refrigerator—only to find it padlocked. In the morning he complained to mother: "This is not going to be an easy place to live in. You not only can't get past the guards on the gate, you can't even get into the icebox." After he was arrested for reckless driving, a newspaper cartoon depicted father eyeing a car which had crashed into the White House, and a servant saying, "It's Master John, Mr. President."

John never played any part in father's political career. In fact, he turned Republican, though he kept quiet about it until father passed on.

Elliott and Franklin, meanwhile, fought a lot. Once they "borrowed" the family car, went joyriding and, arguing over who should drive, swapped punches while the car careened through the streets. Luckily no damage was done. Once, while playing football at Groton, Elliott went downfield under a punt and landed with both knees on the receiver, who suffered a kidney injury. The referee ejected Elliott from the game, and Dr. Peabody suspended him from school. Dr. Peabody wrote father that he had accepted Elliott's explanation it was an accident, but that he held him responsible because Elliott had a tendency to lose control: "I could see this when I coached him in rowing. . . . Criticised, he would seem to become angry. It made him an unpleasant person to coach. . . ."

I was at Harvard when this incident occurred, and father asked my opinion. I said that whatever Elliott's faults, father had been given no reason not to believe this incident an accident. Father wrote Dr. Peabody that if there was no reason not to believe it an accident, it should not be charged to any lack of self-control: "I am not making any excuses for a quick temper which at times he shows. . . . He is extremely sensitive to praise or blame. . . . But, apparently no one has given him an encouraging word. . . . You could try the experiment of encouraging him. . . . An inferiority complex at Elliott's age is . . . dangerous for later life."

If Elliott suffered an inferiority complex in later life, he concealed it cleverly. He wound up his checkered career at Groton by turning in a blank college-entrance examination paper so he could not be accepted at Harvard. Allowed to take a trip to the Southwest at nineteen, "Bunny," as he was called, simply dropped from sight, bumming around on his own. He was feared kidnaped until he wrote home for money, having not only spent what he had but run up considerable debts. Father, admiring his adventurous spirit, sent the money. Mother, relieved, did not reprimand father. A year or so after he married, he went back to the Southwest—without his wife, whom he never lived with again.

Of course, I had a temper, too. I didn't like Anna's fiancé, Curtis Dall, so I tripped him while we were ice skating. He carried a scab to the wedding ceremony.

After father's polio attack, Louis Howe moved into our house, moving Anna out of her room, and moving mother into the spotlight of public life. Anna accused him of stealing mother's attentions from her. He did. And he did not care. He felt mother was needed more in public than in her private life, that she had a higher destiny than merely being a mother. Anna was sacrificed to the cause, as we all were in a way. Anna argued bitterly with mother about this sacrifice, and when she got to college she refused to answer mother's letters. She quit college to marry and later admitted, "I did it because I wanted to get out of the life I was leading." It was a poor reason for marriage, but then the Roosevelt children did not have good reasons for many of the marriages they entered into.

I dated quite a lot during my college days. I found out I had inherited my father's feeling for the ladies. I still had most of my hair, I wasn't bad-looking and I had an important name, so it was easy for me to be a bit of a gay blade, though I wasn't wild. I took the daughters of prominent families to parties and dances. And when I met Betsey Cushing, I went overboard. After my senior year at Harvard, before my first year at Boston University Law School, we wed. We were not ready for marriage, but we thought we were. I had a lot of growing up to do. I have a letter I wrote my parents, another of those pompous notes I wrote in those days, and it is hard to believe I was already married. In part it said, "I hope Bets and I can mean as much to our children as you have me. . . . I've just been in a perfect tizzy. . . ."

I had no personal means to support a wife, but I was into independence. When Sara ordered a command appearance by us on a day we had a prior commitment, I sent my regrets. Sara didn't want regrets, she wanted us. She made it clear that if I did not honor her requests, I could not expect her to continue financing my college education. I got on my high horse, told her it was about time I started paying my own way and never again accepted any money from her.

My dean in law school helped me find a job in insurance to supplement the money my parents provided. But I did so well in my part-time work that I soon quit school. I had only gone to law school because father felt it might be helpful in politics or in any profession I pursued. And I had only chosen Boston University because I was a language credit short for graduation from Harvard and so ineligible there.

So ended my school days. And my youth.

One memory of my youth is more persistent than others. While I was at Harvard I came down with the flu. There are worse ailments, but none that make you feel worse. Mine was serious enough for the college doctors to decide I needed medical care and rest. I didn't want to go into the hospital in Boston, so I headed home, which was in Albany, since father was governor by then. It was a tough six-hour trip by train and I felt terrible by the time I got out of the taxi in front of the mansion. The butler didn't know me, but I asked him to call my mother to the door. When she came, she asked me what I was doing there. I said I was sick and wanted to go to bed in my own home. She said, "Well, then, for heaven's sake, let's get you to bed." She hustled me upstairs and helped me into bed, and that was the last I saw of her that night. I never saw my father that night at all. It seems I had come at an inconvenient time—my parents were having a dinner party for important people.

The next day a doctor was summoned and saw that I was treated. But I developed double pneumonia, was sick for three weeks and started to lose my hair. I can't help feeling my parents may have had their priorities mixed up. Maybe I'm wrong. Maybe I should have seen sooner that if you are born into a family like mine you must sacrifice your interests to some greater interest. I started to see it then, but I never have been able to accept it.

I do not blame my father and mother for any of our failures, no more than I give them credit for our successes. They were driven by their destinies, and we raced along behind them, at such speed that when we fell off we careened out of control. But no matter who or what parents may be, their children can create their own destinies. In our case, our parents being who and what they were, it was harder than it is for most. Our father and mother belonged to the world more than they belonged to us. What they could do for the world was far more important than anything they could do for us. Considering their circumstances, they certainly did what they could. Taking the grand view, it is insignificant that we did not have the kind of family life many others have, but I regret it personally. I feel they showed me in many ways that they loved me. I hope I showed that I loved them.

I remember when I was thirteen my father took me to Jersey City to see Jack Dempsey fight Georges Carpentier. It was a memorable day because Dempsey was a great hero, and because it was a great fight, and because I got lost in the crowd and was terrified until my father found me. But what made it most memorable was that it was one of the few times my father took me alone with him anyplace; he never again was able to take me or take care of me in that way. That was July of 1921, and father was only a few days away from the illness that would lead all of us down a different path.

VI

An epidemic of infantile paralysis spread across the eastern portion of the country in 1920. That year father lost his bid for the vice-presidency on the ticket with James Cox. Undaunted, father and his political adviser, Louis Howe, began to plan a campaign for the governorship of New York in 1922.

In August of 1921 father brought Louis to Campobello Island with him for his annual vacation. They traveled from New York on Van Lear Black's yacht, the *Sabalo*. Father's secretary, Missy LeHand, wrote mother that she thought father "looked tired when he left." The trip proved a rough one. The weather in the Bay of Fundy was cold and foggy, the sea choppy. Ever the confident skipper, the weary FDR manned the helm for hours on end.

On the island, father was so active that the Black party got tired and soon sailed back to New York. On August 10, father took us sailing on the *Vireo*. Spotting a forest fire on a nearby island, father, ever the conservationist, sailed his ship near the island, and anchored while we swam and waded ashore to fight the fire. We cut boughs and beat the fire out, but it was hard, dirty, smoky work. We were worn out and dirty by the time we got back to the boat and brought it into our dock. Father suggested a swim and led us more than a mile to the nearest swimming cove. We frolicked in the cold water awhile, then trotted home. The air was growing cold and we children felt chilled and went upstairs to change into fresh, warm clothing, but father stayed on the porch to go through his mail. After sitting there for a while in his wet bathing suit, he, too, began to feel chilled, so went upstairs to lie down for a bit and warm up. The chill persisted, however, and he skipped supper. By then he felt pains in his back and legs and was feverish to the touch, which worried mother and Louis Howe, but we'd all suffered from colds and the flu, from chills, aches and pains on the island, and we all naturally assumed father had come down with something like this. But when the problems persisted the next morning, the local doctor in Lubec, Eben Bennett, was summoned. We were relieved when he decided father merely had a "cold."

It is easy now to say we should have shown more concern and acted more efficiently, but we did not at that time have any reason to suspect the seriousness of the situation. Even after father began to have problems moving his legs, we didn't consider the possibility of polio, which was regarded as almost exclusively a children's disease. However, Dr. Bennett decided he needed another opinion. Louis Howe offered to go back to Lubec with Dr. Bennett to find a more expert diagnostician. After inquiries, the famed Philadelphia surgeon, Dr. William Keen, was discovered to be vacationing at a nearby resort. When he found out who father was, he was persuaded to come to the island to examine him.

Dr. Keen's diagnosis was that, possibly due to exertion, a blood clot had settled in father's spine, causing a "temporary" paralysis of the legs. Massage was recommended and carried out by mother and Louis. It turned out to be the worst of recommendations because in polio's early stages massage only increases the damage to the deteriorating muscles. This distinguished physician later sent us a bill for $600.

For about two weeks, father lay sick and helpless. Soon the tissue of his legs became so sensitive he could not even stand the pressure of the bed sheets that covered him, let alone endure massage. Mother, relieved periodically by Louis, slept on a couch in father's room and seldom left his side, doing what she could for him, growing more and more concerned daily. Writing his half brother, she worried, "I hope you will think I have done all I could." She asked him to meet Sara, who was returning from Europe, at the dock in New York. She had written Sara only that Franklin was not well.

Clearly he was not. Dr. Keen began to feel a personal empathy for his patient. In years to come he would praise father's "courage" and describe mother as one of his "heroines." He summoned Dr. Robert Lovett, an orthopedic specialist, from Newport, and it was he who made the diagnosis—infantile paralysis. We all were shocked. Mother's first reaction was panic. She wondered what would happen to them and their lives. Then she feared for the health of her children. However, Dr. Lovett decided that if we had not already shown symptoms of the disease and were kept in quarantine away from father, we probably would be all right. We were too young to understand the seriousness of the situation. Father was sick, that was all. Presumably, he would recover.

Dr. Lovett, to the best of my knowledge, never promised that father would recover. He did say that if father's determination to get well was sufficiently strong, he had a chance. Father perhaps read into it what he wanted to read into it. He wrote a friend that there was no question but that he would recover the use of his legs through several months of treatment, and that with the help of Louis Howe he would be able to keep up with his affairs. Carried from the house on a stretcher on September 14, he smiled and waved at us. "So long, my chicks, I'll see you again soon." Not wanting others to see his gubernatorial candidate on a stretcher, Louis Howe saw to it that father was transported in secrecy by boat to Eastport and by train to New York. There, Louis accompanied him to Presbyterian Hospital.

Much of this is all a matter of record by now, of course. What is not a matter of record is the ordeal that ensued, especially for father. It's easy to look back now and say that he contracted polio and learned to live with it; that with the encouragement of Louis Howe, Eleanor Roosevelt paved the path for Franklin Roosevelt's return to politics over the opposition of Sara Roosevelt; that he swiftly ascended to the governor's chair and finally to the presidency. But that isn't fair to father. It was more than three years before he hobbled briefly back into the spotlight, eight years before he became governor, and twelve years before he became president. The suffering and struggling of all those days, weeks, months and years are not to be taken lightly. I was thirteen when he was stricken and twenty-five when he became president. I grew up with his suffering and struggling.

You must remember that he always had been a physically active man who fancied himself something of an athlete and loved the outdoor life. He was not accustomed to being confined indoors to bed. He had rarely even been sick. Now he was crippled. It had to come as a dreadful blow to him. He lived a long time on hope, believing his paralysis to be temporary. It was seven or eight years before he faced the fact that his condition was permanent. That may explain why we never heard him complain about his condition or curse it; why he never raised his voice in horror at his helplessness. By the time he saw that he would not walk again and would spend the rest of his life in braces, on crutches or a cane or confined to a wheelchair, he was so accustomed to it he could accept it.

I was away at school when father was sent home from the hospital at the end of October. When I came home for the holidays that first Christmas, I dreaded the sight of him on his back with withering legs, but I went to his room determined to maintain my composure no matter what. He was propped up on pillows, exercising his upper body on trapezes and rings that hung over his head. Seeing me, he stopped, smiled broadly, thrust out his chin in that characteristic way of his, stretched out his arms to me and told me, "Come here, old man." I rushed to receive his embrace and was grateful to learn as he hugged me to him that whatever weakness had struck his legs, his arms were as strong as ever. I started to cry, but he just laughed and slapped me on the back and told me how "grand" I looked. Soon he had dropped to the floor and was roughhousing with me. Having easily beaten my younger brothers at arm wrestling, he challenged me. He beat me, too. He was astonishing, and I soon got used to his condition.

Still, he never admitted that this was the way it was going to be from then on. It was temporary, a test he could meet, a fight he was determined to win. He seemed to sense that his children wondered about the atrophying of his legs. He hauled back the covers and showed us his legs. They didn't look so bad. They would get and look worse and worse as time went on; but as we saw them often, the differences in them did not seem so great to us. He had learned, and he taught us, the anatomical terms for each muscle that led from his gluteus maximus, as if knowing them was one way of mastering them. How we loved to talk about father's gluteus maximus! He would work to wiggle one toe, straining and sweating. He never succeeded, but he believed he did. He reported to us the return of feeling and we cheered as though hearing of advances by our side in a football game. "By golly, I can really feel those muscles coming back," he would say. And we believed him because he believed it.

He wanted to believe swimming helped, so he swam. It was easy for him to swim, even without legs. It was something he could do; he did not feel crippled doing it. But when he hauled himself out of the water, he could not walk or stand, he was back where he had begun. He wanted to believe in Warm Springs, so he went there and swam in its warm waters and was sure it helped him. He invested in it and operated it and believed in it. It did him no good physically, but perhaps it did mentally. Maybe it was good doing, rather than not doing, trying rather than not trying, believing rather than not believing, but it did not do a thing for his legs during all those years.

He was almost forty when he was stricken. Maybe he was young by political standards, but not by the mortality of man.

He was a middle-aged man, entering the last half of his life, when he faced the fiercest fight of his life. It *was* a fight for life. Not to walk, as he first believed; that was beyond his reach. But just to live any kind of life at all, to be anything but a complete cripple, as his mother would have had him.

From the moment she received my mother's letter on landing in New York and hurried to his side, Sara wanted him to give up the life he had been living. She had never wanted him in the political wars anyway. Now she could not understand how he could consider returning to the battle. She wanted him to return to Hyde Park, to be as much of a gentleman farmer as he could be. It was Louis Howe, more than anyone else, who forced father to fight back. And mother, through the urging of Louis. And Missy LeHand, though she seldom is given enough credit in this regard.

A former newspaperman, Howe early recognized my father's political potential in Albany. He asked to join his camp and was given a job. It was Louis who took over father's reelection campaign for the state Senate in 1912 while father was flattened by typhoid. And Louis was father's key aide during his vice-presidential campaign in 1920.

Howe was a hard man to like. His clothes looked as though he had slept in them. They were constantly strewn with cigarette ashes. Yet he had an enormous ego. He thought he knew better than anyone else the public and its needs, politics and politicians. The fact is, he may have. Once you saw this, you could accept him and his ways. My father recognized what Louis had to offer and was flattered by Louis's admiration and encouragement. He didn't mind that Louis, seeing he could not sell himself, seized on father as a man who could be sold, as a vehicle who could be ridden to the top. Father saw Louis as a helper, not a rival, a first lieutenant who could never command. Father used Louis as much as Louis used father.

Like most well-bred people, mother disliked Louis at first. But she began to warm up to him during the vice-presidential campaign. She had gone along for the ride, but became a wallflower in the traveling party. She was neglected by father as he busily plotted strategy, worked on and delivered his speeches, played poker with the boys as the trains traveled across country. She was uncomfortable in the company of the newsmen and others who formed the group, and it was Louis who rode to her rescue, who befriended her, who brought her into the group, who asked her to dance, so to speak.

I believe Louis befriended my mother partly out of kindness—out of a feeling he knew all too well, what it was like to be a wallflower—and partly out of selfishness—out of a realization that a man's wife must inevitably play a part in his political life. Others credit him with sensing instinctively her hidden abilities, but I disagree, for there was no way he could have; they simply did not show through her reserve. In bringing her husband's speeches to her for review, in drawing her into conversations with newsmen, in engaging her in conversation himself, in penetrating that facade of hers, he apparently began to see that she was a sensible, sensitive, warm woman. It was then that she first started to emerge from her shell, that she first started to realize her hidden potential. She was grateful to him for it. She started to see Louis as more than a man who was ready to ride her husband to success. She began to befriend him and his family.

When father was stricken and later when it became clear that he had a long, hard road to any sort of recovery, I am convinced he would have dropped from public life completely had it not been for Louis Howe. Father was too busy with his fight for his life to think of his political future. It's easy now to look back and see that just up the road was the governorship and then the presidency. It was all but impossible then. He had a modest background, and unsuccessful vice-presidential candidates generally fade fast into obscurity. It was Louis who decided that the exposure of the campaign, even one they were bound to lose, would be beneficial. Louis predicted that father would be president one day. Father laughed it off. True, he was following in Teddy's footsteps, but he had no conviction that he could go all the way as Teddy had. Until his illness, all of us felt he had a future in politics. But the presidency? None of us saw that far into the future, though we could all dream. After his illness the dream died.

Louis Howe would not let his dream die. Maybe because it was too late to change horses. Perhaps he saw no one else who would offer him a ride. But he was not about to let fate cheat him of what he saw as his destiny. Stubbornly refusing to surrender his dream, he insisted father's illness was only a temporary setback and pleaded with father not to forget the future. At a time when his knees began to draw up and had to be placed in plaster casts into which wedges were driven to stretch the muscles straight, father grasped the hope Louis Howe held out to him and hung onto it as a man clings to life.

It was at this time that Howe turned to mother and enlisted her aid in this fight for father's life. He now was her friend too, the only one who offered her a place in her husband's political life, the only one who held out hope to her husband. He asked her to increase her public activities, to play a growing role in party politics, to keep her husband's name in the limelight.

She took convincing. It was so calculated it concerned her. She still lacked confidence in herself as a public personality. She had that high-pitched voice and plain appearance. But Howe worked with her on controlling her voice and helped her with her speeches. She may have made a hundred speeches with Louis her only audience, a critical but encouraging one. He urged father to encourage her, too. She became convinced that she should try.

Mother had already begun to try to right the wrongs of the world. Originally opposed to women's suffrage, she had with maturity begun to believe in it. She had worked for it as a member of the League of Women Voters, and when women got the vote in 1920 she took pride in the small part she had played. Then she wanted to work for women's place in political parties. She had become a Democrat only because her husband was one. She already knew the politicians of her husband's party. Sympathetic to the plight of working men and women at a time when unions were being formed to improve their working conditions, mother had become involved with the International Ladies' Garment Workers Union. An unsatisfied soul, she felt faint stirrings of need.

Sara was opposed to women in politics, especially her daughter-in-law. She had never even considered it a proper profession for her son. She did not like Louis Howe, and she did not like him pushing her son into politics. She was against it when he was given Anna's room in her son's Sixty-fifth Street house and allied herself with Anna against "that dirty little man." I was against him, too. My room was next to his, and we shared a bathroom. Everyone argued against him, but he did not hear the arguments because he did not want to hear them. He heard "higher voices." Mother wanted to do what Louis wanted. Torn, she sometimes broke down in tears. For her, it was what she later termed "the hardest winter" of her life.

As much as anything, it may have been Sara's opposition that steeled mother's decision to pursue the course laid out for her by Howe and encouraged by her husband. She had already begun to duck from under Sara's domination, standing up to her in matters that related to her husband and their children. "Sooner or later, I had to make a stand. I hated the arguments, but they had to happen," she once recalled. After she wrote father of one argument, he wrote her about a letter he had received from his mother: "It will amuse you as she says everything is going well between you."

Father sympathized with mother's struggle. He, too, had struggled. He loved his mother, but he recognized her faults. He loved his wife, too, and was pleased by her efforts to overcome her weaknesses. Ultimately he came to admire his wife more than he did his mother. He was amused by the battle between the two women, conducted as it was on a high level. Ever the diplomat, mother sometimes apologized to her mother-in-law for her stands. "I am so sorry I lost my temper and said such foolish things. I have no right to hurt you," she wrote her after one disagreement. But once the battle had been joined, mother would not back off and she continued to say what she felt should be said and to do what she thought should be done. What Sara thought became less and less important in our lives.

There had been that break between my mother and father, which I will discuss in the next chapter. It stemmed from my father's affair with Lucy Mercer. Mother neither forgot it nor forgave father for it. An understanding developed between them that, while the marriage would go on, their roles as husband and wife would be altered. However, she still cared for him, as he cared for her, a fact many biographers have forgotten. And when he was stricken, she took care of him with a selfless devotion which he never forgot. When she put aside her fears and agreed to try the role that had been created for her as her husband's ambassador to public life, she did so to prevent his mother from making him a complete invalid, to help him as she felt he should be helped, to take a part in his life and to assume a role in life for herself.

It is nonsense to assume either she or Louis Howe knew how far this role would take her. She remained reserved, plain, a nervous speaker, and in the beginning it was just something she could do that might benefit her husband and give him a reason to recover. But the more she did, the more she wanted to do. She felt herself filled with a passion for politics through which she saw the chance to right wrongs, to be of use. As she was accepted, she became less shy. As she succeeded, she became more aggressive.

At first mother was active in Dutchess County politics. She worked on behalf of the gubernatorial candidacy of Al Smith, the Democratic nominee to oppose the Republican incumbent, Nathan Miller, in 1922. She spoke to voters, drove them to the polls, did what she could. While Smith failed to carry her county, he gained ground there and did carry the state. He was grateful to her, and she wound up seconding his renomination at the state convention in 1924.

Encouraged by new friends Nancy Cook and Marion Dickerman, she increased her role in the League of Women Voters and in the fight for women's equality within political parties. She became an active and prominent member of the State Democratic Committee. She also worked on behalf of publisher Ed Bok's $100,000 public competition to come up with a plan with which the United States might work with other countries to preserve peace. The project and the winning plan, which proposed U.S. entry into the World Court and support of the League of Nations, were not received sympathetically by Congress, but attracted astonishing interest and aroused father's enthusiasm. He wrote her that he was proud of her. She wrote back, "You need not be proud of me. I'm only being active till you can be back again." But, by then, they both knew better. Mother had embarked on a voyage from which there would be no turning back. For some years, his public life and her private life had often kept them apart, communicating by mail. Now, for the rest of their years, they would be apart most of the time, linked largely by those letters.

For a while it was not clear whether father would return to public life. Louis Howe encouraged him, and so did Missy LeHand. She had gone to work for father as his secretary during his vice-presidential campaign. She was as attractive and animated as he was, and they were attracted to each other. They were relaxed and able to joke with one another. She continued as his secretary when he returned to law and business after the election, and she wrote to keep him informed of company activities during his vacation at Campobello.

After she was told of his illness, she was enlisted by Howe as a conspirator to silence. Until it became clear father would not recover for a long time and never completely, Howe chose to keep the seriousness of his illness secret. Missy wrote informal letters to father, gossiping about her activities to distract him from his own ordeal. He needed all the moral support he could get at this time.

Once the reality of being paralyzed, if only "temporarily," sank in, it was a difficult thing for him to handle. He once admitted to me that the hardest thing to endure was being deprived of performing the easiest tasks. Imagine the frustration of not being able to answer an insistently ringing telephone unless it is within reach; of not being able to go from room to room, or step outside; of not being able to retrieve something you've dropped. Eventually a device was designed for him which enabled him to reach down with a clawed stick to clasp an object at his feet.

With his increasing sense of helplessness, he developed a dread of fire. He used to lecture us on the carelessness which could cause fires, recalling how the original Delano homestead had been destroyed by flames. Very early in his illness he used to drop from the bed or his wheelchair to the floor to practice crawling so that he would be able to escape from a fire. He was embarrassed when we caught him practicing. He once confessed to me, "Fire is the one thing I fear. I have to feel I could escape on my own." We assured him he would never be alone, but he could not be sure, and furthermore found the idea depressing that he could not be left alone, as if he were an infant. He once reluctantly fired his valet, Irvin McDuffie, because McDuffie had drunk too much one night, fallen asleep in his room and failed to answer father's summons when it was time to be helped to bed. "I just couldn't take the chance it might happen again, at a bad time," father confessed sorrowfully.

Father was fitted for braces in Boston, but he never was able to walk any distance with them without support. It has been written that he eventually regained some use of his right leg and then had to wear a brace only on his left leg, but this is not true. He never regained the use of either leg, and he never was able to stand erect without both braces and support. The legs withered and got worse. It has also been written that I tried on the braces to see if I could walk in them, but this is not true either. I often wondered how they felt, but I never would have dared put them on. That would have been an insult to father.

I know the braces were heavy and hard to use. He admitted as much. He hated them. He hated putting them on in the morning and taking them off at night. In time, he did not do this every day—by that time he was not trying to walk and was willing to get about in his wheelchair or be carried. Technicians learned to make lighter braces as time went on, but they never were comfortable and he always took them off whenever he could. When I was traveling with him I would help him take them off when we had a few minutes' respite in the privacy of his train compartment.

In the beginning, he tried to master the braces. The first day he returned to his office for a brief visit, in the fall of 1922, his crutches slipped as he crossed the crowded sidewalk from his car to the door. He fell and found himself helpless. His call for help was answered by Basil O'Connor, a young attorney with offices in the building. Basil helped him up, into the building and into father's office. Basil visited with him and they became fast friends, later forming the law firm of Roosevelt and O'Connor. The partnership was dissolved before father's first inauguration but "Doc" O'Connor became father's personal lawyer.

The only other fall I recall father taking in public, contrary to stories of others, was at Franklin Field in Philadelphia in 1936, during the Democratic National Convention. I was helping him up the aisle on his way to make his acceptance speech after he had been renominated for the presidency. He was using my arm for support as he slowly made his way. Passing the poet Edwin Markham, who was seated on the aisle, father recognized him and reached out to shake the hand of this elderly, white-bearded gentleman. As he did so, his left leg brace became unlocked and he lurched, throwing me off balance. As he tumbled, his bodyguard, Gus Gennerich, and a Secret Service man, Mike Reilly, leaped in to help, and the three of us managed to catch him before he hit the floor. With remarkable poise, father instructed us to relock the brace, straighten his clothing and collect the scattered pages of his speech. Composing himself, he completed his handshake with the unnerved poet, then, reaching the podium, faced the crowd with a smile and delivered his speech smoothly. The people loved it.

It took awhile for father to accept his condition to the extent that he could deal easily with such situations without revealing any anger or embarrassment. It can't have been easy for a grown man to have to accept being carried about in the locked arms of aides, but father never complained. And the press protected his privacy to a degree that would not be repeated today. For instance, George Wallace, crippled by an assassin's bullet, is often photographed in his wheelchair. Father seldom was. He usually was photographed from the waist up, often shown seated when others were seated, often behind a desk.

A photographer named Sammy Schulman became a friend of father's, and I once asked Sammy why he and his fellows were willing to obey this unwritten rule. He said, "First of all, he treated us well, so we treated him well. There never was a public figure who was so accessible to the press, who was so responsive to them and easy with them, who treated them as equals and would joke with them. He was a decent human being, we genuinely liked him, and we didn't want to embarrass him. Then, you have to remember that he arrived during Depression days and remained into the war. These were hard times, and he was our hope. To have done anything to tear him down in the eyes of the public would have been unthinkable." When one photographer of an opposition newspaper did take such a picture and it was printed, he was ostracized by the others.

It amazes me how many people of that period were not even aware of father's handicap, although it was not really kept secret and he was pictured swimming in the waters of Warm Springs for recuperative purposes. Since he was not photographed in his wheelchair, or being carried, or being helped as he hobbled about, many people somehow assumed he had some limited use of his legs. Others simply never thought of him as a cripple. His opponents did not dare dwell on his handicap for fear of looking bad or of seeming to take unfair advantage of a foe.

Father, of course, was careful to refer frequently to his misfortune in ways that minimized its impact. In one speech

I recall, he detailed the man-killing schedule he had been keeping, smiled and said, "Too bad about this unfortunate sick man, isn't it?" This comment drew cheers from the crowd. In addition, he made appearances in the worst of weather, risking real illness up to the end, in an effort to convince the public he was as strong and tough and able to do what had to be done as the next man.

Politically, perhaps he was. Personally, he was not. I recall one incident that illustrates the sort of private life he led even after he had ascended to the highest office in the land.

Cruising at sea, he liked to sit on deck in the morning after breakfast. He had to be carried topside. When the time inevitably came when he had to relieve himself, he had to be carried below to the head, then carried back above. He was accustomed to this inconvenience, but he did not totally accept it.

One morning we found ourselves in fog so thick that the naval ships which always accompanied us to protect us could not be seen. Father and I were alone at the stern of the ship, and when it came time to help him below he suggested that, in light of the special circumstances of fog, a triangular extension on the stern could perhaps serve as a toilet seat; he could simply do what had to be done right there. Rather reluctantly, I agreed, settling him onto the "seat" and retreating to the flying bridge to permit him privacy.

No sooner had I reached the bridge than I realized the fog was lifting. And there, steaming up on us, were several ships of the convoy. As they closed in, father was bound to be visible. I shouted a warning. Startled, he looked around, realized the situation and hollered for help. I rushed to him, calling for assistance. "They can't see the president like this," father groaned. My brothers and I agreed. Without hesitation, we picked father up in that most unpresidential of positions and rushed him, pants down, below to the head. His dignity was saved, for the most part, and later he would laugh about the episode.

Father needed time to learn to accept his fate. Shrewdly,

Louis Howe gave him that time. At one point Louis had to admit to the press and public that father was paralyzed and that it was not clear how long it would take him to recover, but he never admitted that father would not recover fully. Eventually the realization sank in, but it was never voiced.

Louis kept busy maintaining political contacts for father. He encouraged father to write letters to various politicians on any number of topics to show a continuing concern with public affairs, and meanwhile had mother out in the world keeping the Roosevelt name out front. He reasoned correctly that when the time came that father understood he was crippled for life, he'd realize politics was the only life left to him. Here, his mind would matter, not his legs. He didn't have to dance to display his persuasive personality to the public. If anything, overcoming the obstacle of being crippled would endear him to the public. The world was full of losers, and they could identify with someone who had lost something. He would seem less privileged, less a product of the upper classes, less a representative of a rich and snobbish social set.

In a moment of weakness, years later, Howe admitted to me, "I worked out a schedule for your father becoming president, and we hit the timetable right on the button. He didn't know the details. No one did. I've never talked about it. But I worked out in my mind when the right times to make our moves would be, and we made them at those times and we were successful. I'll tell you, Jim, it would make a marvelous primer on politics, on how you can maneuver the right man to the top if you plan properly, and it would be something for historians to study in the future."

He was patting himself on the back, of course, but I believe he was telling the truth. I don't think he revealed his schedule to father, but father trusted his judgment and followed his advice. Howe never wrote that primer, but he should have. In all the years I've been in politics or observing politicians, I have never seen a more calculated campaign projected so successfully over a long-range basis, and I've seen a lot of maneuvering in my time.

Louis gave father time to begin believing in his ability again, and it did take time. In 1922 father accepted an invitation to visit Vincent Astor's home in Rhinebeck, New York. There, father swam in Astor's heated indoor pool. At one point he observed enthusiastically, "The water put me where I am, and the water has to bring me back." He became convinced that swimming was a therapy which would work for him, and the doctors did not discourage him. Any exercise was beneficial, though in father's case nothing was restorative. He built up the upper part of his body and used to point to his development with pride.

For a man who was crippled from the waist down, father enjoyed remarkably good health most of his life, until the last few years in fact. Gradually he began to develop kidney and other internal problems from years cramped in a sitting position. His heart became enlarged also, but since he died at sixty-three it is not unrealistic to assume he might have suffered severe physical problems by that time even if he'd never had polio. Father began spending his summers with Louis Howe in Massachusetts. Louis's family lived in Fall River, and the only time they saw him was on weekends, except when father joined him in Horseneck Beach. Father would sun himself on the sand and swim in the salt water, also taking treatment at nearby Marion, where he did exercises devised by the noted neurologist Dr. William McDonald. Father always loved the warm sunshine, sandy beach, salt water and clear air of the oceanside. He spent time on Vincent Astor's yacht, and in the winter of 1932 he went to Florida, rented a run-down houseboat—the *Weona II*—had it fixed up and cruised the Keys. He'd fish. And he'd find deserted beaches, strip to the skin and crawl through the sand to swim in the water, keeping an eye open for sharks.

Then he and a friend from Groton and Harvard, a Boston banker named John Lawrence, who also had lost the use of his legs, formed the Lawrence-Roosevelt Company. They bought a bigger, better houseboat for $3500, named it the *Larooco* after their "firm" and spent the next few winters cruising the backwaters with friends, fishing, swimming and, to be perfectly frank, partying. As far as I remember, mother was aboard the boat for only three brief visits in three years. I spent time there, as did the other children occasionally. Louis was usually there. So was Missy, who became the mistress of the boat and hostess to father's political cronies and friends. Louis had sent for Missy as soon as father bought the boat, wisely suspecting that father might benefit from feminine companionship. He urged her to encourage father to make as much of his life as possible.

It made me sad to see how difficult it was for father to get around, yet I marveled at how, outwardly, he did not let it affect his personality. He enjoyed life, and he had pleasant times on the *Larooco*. There were many happy gatherings of men and women who lived the good life.

Acting as his secretary, taking care of his correspondence and so forth, Missy was not, I'm convinced, father's mistress. The most important part she played was probably political. She trailed only Louis and mother in the matter of convincing father he was still capable of taking an important place in the world.

In 1924, at the suggestion of New York banker George Peabody, father visited a resort in Warm Springs, Georgia, where the natural heated pools were supposed to produce miracles of recuperation for patients with paralysis. He found he could "walk" in the warm water, and after only one day there wrote mother the place had done his legs more good than anything else had. Peabody wanted to sell the place, which was in poor shape, and in time father, against the advice of mother and more conservative associates, bought it for more than he could afford—almost $200,000.

The resort was run-down, but father set to work seeking contributions to help him repair and enlarge it. Edsel Ford, for example, contributed $25,000 for a glass cover so the swimming pool could be used year-round. Over the years, father persuaded many people to contribute funds. After he became president he sponsored annual "Birthday Balls" across the country with Warm Springs receiving the proceeds. He helped form the Georgia Warm Springs Foundation, and his purchase price was in the form of a loan to the foundation, which eventually was repaid by insurance on his death.

Father was seeking a miracle, as were the other patients there. While there were no miracles, I suppose most who went there benefited by the exercise and relaxation. Father felt close to the other patients. They shared a terrible affliction and common cause. He shared their resentment toward the able-bodied tourists who came to rest and who were reluctant to share the pool and other personal facilities with the "polios." His decision to "purchase" the resort stemmed as much from this resentment as from anything else.

Father persuaded a New York orthopedic surgeon, Dr. LeRoy Hubbard, to move in as medical supervisor and encouraged the construction of facilities for the physically handicapped to the exclusion of mere vacationers. I remember father telling me of a crippled youngster who spotted some "able-bodies" staring at him in his wheelchair. "Stick around!" he snapped at them. "They're going to feed us after awhile." Father was amused when a couple of the "push-boys"—the healthy youngsters who pushed the patients in wheelchairs—played a practical joke on a pair of visiting "able-bodies." One of the push-boys proclaimed that a dip in the waters had cured him of his "paralysis." His partner, who sat in a wheelchair, said he hoped it would work for him, too. "Well, why don't you start right now?" the first one said, suddenly throwing his friend into the water. In front of the shocked visitors, the "crippled" lad floundered about for a few moments, then leaped out and ran across the lawn hollering, "I'm cured! I'm cured!"

These youngsters were incorrigible. Sitting in wheelchairs and passing themselves off as "polios" too poor to afford to stay for the miracle treatments, they'd beg money from unsuspecting and sympathetic tourists.

If father was not cured by Warm Springs, he was helped

emotionally by his visits there. Afraid to stay in the firetrap of the old wooden main house, he rented cottages until his own cottage was built for him. This came to be called his "winter White House," and it remains a memorial to him, visited by thousands of tourists annually. Again, Missy presided over his home at Warm Springs. Mother seldom visited. We children often did and always enjoyed it, though we were almost ashamed of our good health compared with the people who were crippled.

Even after he became president, the residents of the community and the patients who stayed there considered father one of them and a "savior" of their resort, a friend rather than president. They called him "Dr. Roosevelt," as he counseled them on the care of their limbs and enjoyed an easy relationship with them. In short, he felt at home there.

Father found respite in the warm, sunny days and slow life of the deep South. It was here that he received his car, an old Model-T Ford rigged with ropes and pulleys father could operate without the use of his legs. He used to drive his "Tin Lizzie" around the countryside, often stopping to chat with the townspeople, especially at a secluded spot called "The Cove," where, though Prohibition was in effect, father would partake of some home brew.

Father was bemused by the southern attitude at a time when the rights of blacks were not yet recognized. To the best of my knowledge, prejudice on religious or racial grounds was distasteful to him. But it is only fair to admit that he grew up with blacks who were servants and secondary citizens, and it never occurred to him to take the lead in helping them.

I am going to tell you a true story that I have never told because I feared it would be misunderstood. Some time after father had become president, he was driving his friend and aide, Colonel Watson, a southerner, around the Georgia countryside. He teased Watson about bloodlines being mixed up in that part of the world because "you so-called southern gentlemen couldn't keep your hands off the black wenches." Father said half the children down there wound up with names like Thomas Jefferson Jones and Robert E. Lee Smith because of this. A bit further on, they saw a small black boy crying in the road. Watson brought the boy to the car. He was lost, and they offered to help him find his way home. First, however, feeling he probably would prove his point, father smiled at his friend and asked the boy his name. "Franklin D. Roosevelt Jones," the boy blubbered.

Father came to know the community so well that he enjoyed hearing the local gossip. In fact the postmistress used to bring the day's postcards with her when she stopped by so they could catch up on the "news" of their neighbors before the cards were distributed. He and his friends also engaged in poker games which floated from cottage to cottage. They gossiped for hours.

After father became president, he spent a lot of time simply eluding the Secret Service men assigned to watch over him. He knew the countryside better than they did and would make sudden turns while driving, speeding down back roads until he lost them, then driving back to the resort to await their worried return. Eventually there were three pools with connecting channels. When the Secret Service men weren't looking, father would dive deep, duck through a channel and surface in the seclusion of another pool, while his "guards" jumped fully clothed into the water to find him.

A bespectacled, earnest lady, Helen Lauer, used to give father therapy as he lay on a table at poolside. While he would try to raise his legs with as much strength as he had left in them, she would present muscle-building resistance by pressing down on them. Several times he relaxed his legs so suddenly that she was thrown off balance and plunged into the pool. Father laughed uproariously when she came to the surface spluttering, her hair streaming in wet strings alongside her face, her glasses hanging from one ear.

He learned how to laugh again in Warm Springs, in the company of others who suffered as he did. Here he never felt alone or left out. By 1926 he had sold the *Larooco* in order to invest in Warm Springs. He found one vessel or another to sail the rest of his life, and he never stopped visiting Warm Springs. He was, in fact, in residence there the day he was fatally stricken.

During this time, in 1924, father made one brief return to politics to keep his face and name before the public. He did it at the urging of Louis Howe. Ambitiously, Al Smith wanted to move up from the governor's chair in New York to the presidency. I do not like to use the word, but it is accurate to report that Smith was "conned" into allowing father to nominate him as the party's candidate at the national convention in New York's Madison Square Garden. With mother working as his intermediary in the Smith camp, Louis convinced Smith that having father nominate him would be dramatically effective. Smith bought this, assuming father was finished as far as full-time politics was concerned and could never become a rival. Smith also didn't know how completely crippled father was. He never realized the risk he ran of father not being able to make it to the platform or endure the ordeal of the speech. We knew it was a very real risk, but Louis Howe felt it was a risk worth taking.

Neither father nor mother was ever all that fond of Smith, nor did they regard him as a great man, but they supported him as the best man available to the party at that time. It had been only three years since father was stricken, however, and he was reluctant to return to the limelight merely to nominate another man for the presidency. Fearful he would fail and perhaps be badly embarrassed, he was not really ready to roll the dice. He took convincing. But he believed in Louis, and with the aid of totally separate pleas put forth by mother and by Missy, Louis was able to sell father on the effort.

I had accompanied him on previous public appearances. This time he asked, "Jimmy, would you care to come along and lend me your arm?" I accepted, of course, aware that I would have to lend him not only my arm but also whatever strength I had. I was only sixteen, but tall and strong. He secured a place for me in the official party as an alternate delegate, so I could sit with him and move about freely.

We arrived in New York early so that we could practice father's appearances. He didn't want to be seen in his wheelchair any more than necessary. He wanted to walk, with my help. At this time walking required such obvious effort that he determined we should arrive as early as possible each day so as to be seated before most of the others arrived. The process of seating him proved difficult. We practiced standing together by his chair while I took his crutches from him and supported him as he lowered himself into his seat. There was a woman delegate who was so enormous she'd had two seats set aside for her. I suggested father do the same, but he rejected the idea. He didn't want to call any extra attention to his situation. He asked only for an aisle seat, one with arms so he would have something to grip as he lowered himself. The audiences who gathered early in the galleries each day observed this ordeal and came to greet his gallant appearances with applause, which he respected but regretted.

He attended all the sessions, sitting on the crowded floor of the arena, joining in the discussions, casting his votes on the various proposals. Responsive to his every wish, I was his legs except for those occasional moments when I stole time with the pretty niece of the chairman, Senator Tom Walsh of Montana. I made sure I was at father's side during demonstrations, fearful he would be hurt in any boisterous activities. And at day's end, often late at night, actually, after most of the others had left, I helped him out of his seat, into his wheelchair and back to the hotel where we were staying. By the end of each day he was exhausted emotionally and physically, but he never complained. He'd say, "Well, we're doin' it, eh, James?"

The real test, however, was the nominating speech. He had decided he would walk with me to the platform, then walk alone to the podium. The day came and the test turned out to be as tough as we had feared. I was afraid, and I knew he was, too. As we walked—struggled, really—down the aisle to the rear of the platform, he leaned heavily on my arm, gripping me so hard it hurt. It was hot, but the heat in that building did not alone account for the perspiration which beaded on his brow. His hands were wet. His breathing was labored. Leaning on me with one arm, working a crutch with the other, his legs locked stiffly in their braces, he went on his awkward way.

In time I learned, and later Elliott would learn, to walk awkwardly also so as to some extent disguise his gait, but it was new to me then and I was aware of the silence of the delegates as we worked our way past them.

When we got to the rear of the platform, we waited. Father's grip on my arm did not lessen even as we stood there, though I doubt that he was aware how hard he gripped me. I never told him. His sweating increased. He was worried. He betrayed this by whispering to Joe Guffey, the Democratic national committeeman from Pennsylvania, to "go over and shake the rostrum." Guffey looked puzzled until father whispered the explanation that he wanted to be sure it was strong enough to support all his weight when he leaned on it. Guffey slipped forward and shook the rostrum. It seemed sturdy. Father nodded.

Then it was time for him to walk alone. I handed him his second crutch. I felt as though I could not breathe. He started forward, slowly, looking around to smile at the silent crowd. Step by step, his crutches carried him forward. He did not fall. He reached the rostrum. Leaning forward, he rested one crutch against it and raised one arm to wave at the crowd. He was still smiling. The crowd gave him an ovation.

I never in my life was as proud of father as I was at that moment. And he never again was as popular as he was in that instant. It heightened his image as nothing he had ever done. It has been dramatized, but no reenactment could capture the intensity of the drama that was played out that day. Rising to the occasion, father gave a magnificent speech, forever famous as the "Happy Warrior" speech. That was the phrase he used to describe his candidate. But it better described father than it did the nominee. That hour or so stolen from his sickness made more of father than it did of the man he nominated. I know Al Smith saw this and resented it, for he never again regarded father as sympathetically as he had.

I can still hear the echoes of the ovation father received at the conclusion of his speech. The cheering went on and on. It is in a sense still going on. The dramatic impact he made that day still lingers.

He did not walk back. He had proven his point, I suppose. Or maybe he was too worn out to walk anymore. He asked for his wheelchair. I saw that it was brought to him, and I pushed him away.

As I remember it, he said only one thing about it to me that day. When we got back to the hotel, he sat down wearily, looked up at me with a smile and said, "Well, James, we made it." It was he who made it, of course, not we, but it was his way of letting me share in that great triumph. He had done it. He had made it. And he took pride in it, as he deserved to. He never again spoke of it, but it was a symbol he could lean on in the following years as he gradually recovered some of his strength and mobility.

Al Smith was not nominated. Thus, in a sense, father failed. But while the speech failed in this respect, it succeeded in that it—and the dramatic effort that went with it—made father famous. In numerous newspaper editorials and columns from then on, it was said that father and not Al Smith or John Davis, the eventual nominee, should have been the nominee. And in the years that followed, father was accepted as the outstanding Democrat, though it would be a few years yet before Louis Howe would let father make his move. The gamble had paid off. Father remained in the spotlight even as he recovered in the shadows. Once again the future seemed to hold great promise for him.

There are those who say that having polio helped father in a strange sort of way. Possibly it did. It decreased his distractions. He could not get around and do as others could. It made him more human in the eyes of the public. On the other hand, if he had not been able to convince the public that he could handle his handicap, it would have curtailed his career. Possibly it increased his feelings for the troubled people of the world, but I believe that he was at heart a humanitarian who did not have to be crippled to care about others.

In short, I do not think, as has been suggested, that the ordeal of being crippled built father's character. I believe he had the basic strength of character to overcome his handicap. It was not easy, but many others have overcome their handicaps. Father, of course, was highly visible, and his example helped others. I suspect he was as much an inspiration as any man ever has been.

My father was a great man, but he was human and imperfect, as we all are. He had help, or he would not have battled back as he did. His great friend, Louis Howe, his wife, even Missy, who fit in somewhere between being a secretary and an intimate friend, gave him much of what he needed. He had his weaknesses, which he gave in to at times, but I do believe he deserves to be remembered best for his strengths.

VII

Father was, as I have said, human. He had a weakness for the ladies all his life, if you care to call that a weakness, and he had his romantic affairs, as do most men who have the opportunity. But his temptations were easier to respond to before he was stricken with polio. He was not able to give in to temptation afterward, contrary to what has been suggested elsewhere. Thus what might have been affairs of the flesh became affairs of the spirit. It is easy to make more of them than actually was the case, as I believe my brother Elliott did in his book.

From his youth until close to his fortieth birthday, father was tall, slender, graceful, athletic. He had fine features and a handsome face. He dressed like a dandy, and he had the gift of gab, a winning smile and an appealing personality. He was a charmer who loved to be the life of the party. Apparently a young man who was going places, he attracted the attention of many young women who wanted to go with him. Those who knew him in the early part of his life have written or spoken of his way with women, a winning way. Those of us who were with him a lot later in his life can tell you that even after he was confined to a wheelchair, he never lost his appeal. You might think of him as an older man, but he aged more gracefully than most; and after he aged, there were older women who were captivated by him.

As a physical personality, mother clearly was not in father's league. Men were seldom interested in her as a woman. Other things mattered to father when he made mother his choice. She had many wonderful qualities which people came to recognize in time. He, too, had marvelous virtues in addition to those that were obvious. I presume she saw the fine, hidden qualities in him, though I suspect that she was as flattered by his interest in her as anything else. She wanted very much to be a wife and mother, these were the roles she pictured for herself, and father made her an offer she could not resist.

Mother was a product of a Victorian background and I have no doubt she dreaded the sexual side of marriage, if only because she knew nothing about it. She had been brought up so formally she was not able to give herself freely to a man. She once told Anna, "Sex is an ordeal to be borne." However, mother shared a bedroom and a bed with father through our first stay in Washington and I do not believe there were any miracles of virgin birth connected with the arrival of any of us. It is possible, as has been suggested, that she knew no birth-control methods other than abstinence when she determined to have no more children.

While I am not a prude about sex or anything else, I must admit I find it difficult to speak about the sex lives of my parents. How many of you would care to detail the intimate affairs of your parents? It is an invasion of their privacy, which even their deaths do not justify. If I must, it is because their sex lives have become matters of intense interest and open discussion by others who are no more qualified, or are much less qualified, to discuss it than I. Another reason is a feeling of bitterness resulting from the suggestion that my father cared for many women, but not for my mother, and that my mother was not the sort of woman one would respond to physically. She has also been accused of being a cold woman. This is nonsense born out of the blindness of those who cannot see beneath the surface of a person.

Mother was formal, perhaps prudish. She was not given to

open displays of affection. If photographers were present, she did not kiss my father. I recall only one photo over the years showing them kissing. But I saw them kiss and embrace many times. Still, I cannot say that theirs was a warm, kissing, hugging, touching relationship. If he might have been given to that, she was not.

Without thinking about it, I accepted their relationship as a partnership, not a love match. I didn't think about it until I matured, married for the first time, began to see other marriages and became aware of how many ways there are for couples to live as husband and wife. Many are demonstrative, many are not. I do not believe demonstrations always show what people really feel for one another. I suspect that some who show more feel less. No one knows what goes on behind closed doors in the lives of others. I did come to know that my mother and father did not have the demonstrative relationship many married couples have, but I was always aware of a feeling of affection between them.

The demands of the lives they led kept them apart more and more over the years. They spent less time together than most married couples, even kings and queens, presidents and first ladies, because she was far more active than other women in her position ever have been. After he was crippled she became to a great extent his legs, his eyes and his ears, going places he could not easily go and reporting to him on experiences that would be of value to him. They had a marriage of the mails and wrote one another often. His letters were more affectionate than hers: "My Dearest Babs," he'd write. And he was thoughtful—he'd always bring her something from his trips. He spoke sentimentally of missing her. She, however, seldom responded to this sentiment.

After the Lucy Mercer affair, he held out his hand to mother many times, but she did not take it. I am sure the Lucy Mercer affair has led others to exaggerate the Missy LeHand affair, although I am disinclined to call, as others, including brother Elliott, have, father's relationship with Missy an "affair." But maybe I know some things others do not know.

I was a child when Lucy came into our home. As an adult I never met Lucy, nor did Elliott or any of my brothers. Only our sister, Anna, did, and then only late in father's life. I didn't even remember a Lucy Mercer existed until well into my life when I was having some sort of marital trouble and Cousin Polly said to me, "You know, your father was just as much a rascal as you." When I asked what she meant, she said, "Your father had an affair with your mother's former secretary, Lucy Mercer." She asked me if my father had ever spoken of it and I said he had not. (It was assumed, of course, that mother had not. Nor did she ever write on it in her several books.) Cousin Polly laughed and said, "Well, we better just forget it then. I'm sure your father regretted it, because he would never have wanted to make your mother suffer." Which I think is true. He did do some things he perhaps should not have done, but it is clear he tried to be discreet.

Although our parents never discussed it with us, more and more of the story slipped out over the years until father's old aide, Jonathan Daniels, published the details in a book he wrote in 1966 while he was editor of a Raleigh, North Carolina, newspaper. It has since been gone into at length, of course, although the whole story has never been revealed.

Actually, I think it was Cousin Polly who recommended Lucy to mother as a personal secretary in the winter of 1913 during our first stay in Washington, possibly with an ulterior motive. Polly rather fancied father herself, was not above flirting with him and enjoyed teasing mother about father's flirtations with others, which did not endear her to mother. Mother often spent time in Hyde Park or Campobello while father was in Washington, and mother did worry about him. She apparently tried to cover up by teasing him and laughing it off. She wrote Sara that father went back to the office often in the evening to review the females. And he did make the rounds of parties, dancing with attractive ladies, telling mother it was "a bore," but getting home late at times.

Lucy Mercer's mother had been one of the beauties of

Washington society, wealthy from her family's fortune in Virginia real estate. She married an Englishman, whom she divorced on a charge of adultery. She then married Carroll Mercer, a blue blood from Maryland but an undisciplined spendthrift who served under Teddy with the Rough Riders at San Juan Hill. The Mercers broke up and Lucy's mother had to go to work, first as an interior decorator in New York, then running an art gallery in Washington, to support her two daughters. Lucy had to work, too, when she came of age. She, her sister, her mother and her father all attended the same Washington parties as my parents and were known by them. She was not an outsider when she started to come to our house.

She was twenty-two, dark-haired, graceful and attractive, a lovely young lady by all accounts, when she came to work for mother. When mother was away, Lucy stayed to help with mother's business, and father, as is apparent from his letters at the time, began to make excuses for not joining mother when he was expected. Evidently mother began to be suspicious, and her fears were fed by the gossip of her relatives. As mischievous as ever, holding as little affection for mother as ever, Alice Roosevelt Longworth encouraged the affair by having father and Lucy to dinner when mother was out of town. Alice later said, "It was good for Franklin. He deserved a good time. He was married to Eleanor."

In June of 1917, father commissioned a naval yacht, the *Sylph*, for a short pleasure cruise, and included Lucy in the party. Arriving by small boat, mother later joined the cruise. Shortly after what must have been an awkward cruise, Lucy enlisted in the navy as a woman volunteer. However, father had her assigned to his office as a yeoman and she shortly joined him on another cruise, one that mother missed. Lucy's tour of service duty ended abruptly when she was discharged that fall by special order of the secretary of the navy as a "hardship case" because of the death of her father, although she was neither living with him nor responsible for him. In response to a pointed demand by mother, father had put in an appearance at Campobello that summer, and mother, playing up to Sara, apparently enlisted her help in seeking to put an end to father's affair with Lucy. But it was not that easily ended, it seems.

In the summer of 1918 father went to Europe for the Navy Department. On his return in September, he came down with pneumonia. Mother took care of him and in going through his papers discovered love letters from Lucy. Confronted with these, father could no longer deny the affair, as he apparently had up till then.

Elliott and others speak of this as the only hard evidence mother had, but in fact—and it has been a rather well-kept secret—there came to light during this time a register from a motel in Virginia Beach showing that father and Lucy had checked in as man and wife and spent the night.

In any event, mother's moralistic attitude toward marriage and life had been violated and she apparently asked for a divorce, offering father his freedom to marry Lucy. He, it seems, did not immediately refuse the offer, but Lucy, a Catholic, may have told him she could not marry a divorced man and the father of five children. As I understand it, Sara spoke sharply against any divorce, and Louis Howe said it would ruin father's political future.

Apparently, after everyone had their say, father and mother sat down and agreed to go on for the sake of appearances, the children and the future, but as business partners, not as husband and wife, provided he end his affair with Lucy at once, which he did. After that, father and mother had an armed truce that endured to the day he died, despite several occasions I was to observe in which he in one way or another held out his arms to mother and she refused flatly to enter his embrace. There was always an affection between them. After all, they had shared a lot and continued to share to the end. But she was brought up in an unbending way which worked against her ever forgiving him fully, and she could carry on better in this way than he. She was more reserved, while he was an outgoing man in these matters.

Mother swallowed her pride and permitted the marriage to endure, but it left a residue of bitterness that remained with her all her life. When the time came for mother to go out and make something of her own life, she did not feel it a betrayal of her home; he had broken these bonds already. After the affair she was less subservient to father and to his mother. She demanded respect from then on.

As an example, I recall that after father became president there was a time when mother insisted that the Young Communist League be permitted to visit the White House and that father meet with them when they gathered on the lawn. He gave in to this against his better judgment simply because consideration had to be given to her point of view. Mother was not a Communist, of course, but sympathetic to the rights of minorities to speak their piece, and this was at a time when it was not clear that communism was to be considered a curse. I figure father was an honorable fellow and was willing to go along with mother up to a point. But there were limits. He resisted doing some things mother wanted done, and refused others. It was not a situation where mother held a whip over father and he did what she wanted, or else. She did not blackmail him in any way. But she had a certain power to which he was willing to submit at times.

Claiming she had the memory of an elephant, mother said in later life she could forgive, but not forget, a wrong done her. Apparently father got something from Lucy Mercer he did not get from mother, but he forgave life for taking it from him.

However, much as mother might have wanted him to, father did not forget Lucy Mercer, even after she became Mrs. Wintie Rutherfurd in February 1920. They kept in touch over the years and father provided her a limousine so she might share, if from a distance, his moment of magic when he first was inaugurated president in 1933. On his trips to Warm Springs in following years, father occasionally took side trips to meet Lucy. These meetings were arranged by Bernard Baruch at his South Carolina estate near the Rutherfurd place at Aiken, North Carolina. After Lucy's husband died in 1944, father renewed his relationship with her. By this time he was in his sixties and she was in her fifties, and even if he had not been crippled, I doubt there would have been more than friendship between them. But it was a very real friendship and they shared the memory of a romance when both were young. He was a sentimental man and a good friend who was not about to forget Lucy even after life had drawn them apart. I am sure he needed a friend and felt she needed one. I suppose they could talk to one another as they could not talk to others.

In 1944 he spent a month recuperating from a severe cold at the Baruch plantation. Then and at other times he had meetings with Lucy. After Anna moved into the White House to assist father, she helped him arrange a number of meetings with Lucy and even presided over dinners at which Lucy was present. Lucy and Elizabeth Shoumatoff, the artist who was painting a portrait of the president, were guests at Warm Springs on the day he was fatally stricken. Jim Bishop presents no evidence for his sensational account of her weeping and wailing escape through the night from the death scene, and I suspect it was overly dramatized. A great man and a good friend had died, and to cry about it was to be human.

I doubt that father felt he was doing anything wrong in seeing Lucy, but I certainly can understand his keeping it a secret because he believed mother would take it badly and would be hurt. She *was* hurt when she found out about it. Yet, if father loved Lucy, as I suppose he did, I do not believe he loved mother any the less for it. I do not believe it logical to assume we can love only one person in a lifetime. I think of his long affair with Lucy as beautiful, not ugly. It is sad, certainly, if you love and are loved by someone with whom you get to share so little of life as did father and Lucy. Of course, mother did not see it that way. I suppose few spouses could. We think only of ourselves.

Mother was angry with Anna for participating in the

deception of the final years. But what was Anna to do? Should she have refused father what he wanted? She was not in a position to do so even had she wanted to. Accepting the confidence of father, should she have betrayed him by running to report to mother every move he made? A child caught between two parents can only pursue as honorable a course as possible. Anna could no more serve as mother's spy on father than she could as father's spy on mother. Anna suffered some private anguish, but she was as true as she could be to both our parents and she was blameless in this matter. Mother spent very little time with him during those last years. Anna did. So, too, at times, did Daisy and Polly. Lucy was there, too. And, until her fatal illness, Missy.

Now, the Missy situation seems to me something else as far as romance is concerned. If father had not been crippled, it could have been different, certainly, but he was. As his eldest son and the only one who served as his aide in the White House, I was closer to him than almost anyone else for a great part of his life. I traveled the world with him and slept in the same room with him at times. From my observation, it would have been difficult for him to function sexually after he became crippled from the waist down by polio. He had some use of his lower body and some sensation there, but it was extremely limited.

Of course, we should not use sex as the only yardstick by which to measure romance, but I believe that is what Elliott and others have done. I suppose father had a romance of sorts with Missy. After his forced break with Lucy in 1918, and after he became crippled in 1921, she filled a need and made him feel a man again, which mother did not do. Missy was a fairly pretty girl, as tall but more graceful and feminine than mother. She had a long face and a square jaw, but good features and beautiful blue eyes. She also had a sweet temper and nothing seemed to ruffle her. Missy pampered and flattered father. In fact, mother occasionally complained how Missy did whatever father wanted without question. If Missy considered father infallible, mother did not. Missy adored father, as he adored her. I suppose you could say they came to love one another, but it was not a physical love. A lot has been made of an incident when Missy was sitting on father's lap on the *Larooco*, but I recall that Anna and I often sat on his lap during the horseplay of parties aboard that boat. Father, I think, thought of Missy as another of his children. In fact, the record father and Louis Howe kept of happenings aboard the boat was entitled "The Log of the Houseboat Larooco, Being a More or Less Truthful Account of What Happened, Expurgated for the Very Young." Marguerite Missy LeHand was a wonderful lady. She went to work for Charles McCarthy when he was managing father's vice-presidential office during the campaign of 1920. McCarthy had been a secretary to assistant secretaries of the navy back to Uncle Teddy's time, but was supplanted by Louis Howe when father took over the post. Howe, in turn, brought McCarthy back to manage father's campaign headquarters. After the campaign, father talked Missy into taking a position in his law office as his secretary. She was as efficient as she was attractive, and all who knew her admired her.

After father became governor, Missy moved into her own room in our mansion in Albany. After he became president, she moved into a room in the living quarters of the White House. She lived with us for many years and we all accepted her as part of the family. It was not unusual for her to walk around the living quarters in her robe on occasion. There were times when father would ask her to take care of some item of business late at night, and at these times she'd be wearing a robe.

Elliott makes a lot of Missy being seen entering or leaving father's room in her nightclothes, but was she supposed to dress to the teeth every time she was summoned at midnight? This had become her home, too, and a certain informality was accepted accordingly. None of us thought anything of it at the time and to look back on it now and say, "Oh, well, I can see there must have been something to that," is utterly ridiculous. To smear her reputation, and his, on such flimsy evidence is absolutely unfair.

Born in upstate New York and reared near Boston, Missy

was half father's age when she went to work for him. Mother was seldom there, so Missy ran his home for father. With the aid of Grace Tully, she also ran the secretarial side of his presidential office. They shared that duty, and there was plenty for both to do. Because of her many years with father and her dedication to her work, Missy became one of father's most trusted confidants and aides. He didn't have to put on airs with her.

I was nearer Missy's age than father was and felt close to her. When I had to hire a secretary, I went to Missy and she found one for me. When the first one left, Missy found Kitty Gilligan, who stayed with me many years. After Kitty, there was Fayga Berkowitz, who was with me for a long time. A man can develop a close relationship with, even a dependence on, a personal secretary which has nothing to do with romance. Louis Howe had his own "Missy" in the person of Margaret "Rabbit" Terran (who later also worked for me for a while), and romance never entered into it.

I always felt I could talk to Missy. She did not force herself on the family and restricted her interest to father's concerns, but if we asked her for advice, she gave it. I remember discussing with Missy mother's resentment over the increasing role my first wife, Betsey, was playing in the White House and asking Missy if she thought I should talk to father about it. She said no, she thought I should leave it to my mother to make an objection if any was to be made, and that my father would bring it up to me if he felt there was anything to be brought up.

I also remember her coming to me once and suggesting that something father had said had led her to believe he'd like to talk to my insurance-business partner, John Sargent, about the social security program. So I brought father and John together and they did discuss the program at length, and father later said he got a lot out of it.

I could have gone in to see father at any time, but Missy was a wonderful go-between and I often relied on her judgment as to the best times to approach father on some delicate matter or other.

For the most part, though, Missy acted only at father's request and did not act on her own. Often, even when asked by father to get something done, she would get someone else to give the orders so that she could stay as faceless and as much in the background as possible. She refused to presume on her position even when it might have been in line with her role.

The only time I recall Missy using her powers of persuasion on father concerned her Catholicism. Like Lucy, Missy was a Catholic, and a really religious one. Knowing father had fallen out with Al Smith, also a Catholic, Missy suggested to father that he might benefit personally and politically from a meeting with Cardinal Spellman, whom she admired enormously. Father agreed. Missy came to me and she said she had father's permission to arrange a meeting and would appreciate it if I met the cardinal at the train station and took him to breakfast before bringing him to the White House. I was happy to do this because I admired the man, too. I was amused, however, because I could see Missy considered it her contribution to the church.

To the best of my knowledge, Missy had only one real romance in her life, and that was with William Bullitt, who later became U.S. ambassador to France. Father encouraged it, feeling, I think, that she had devoted a lot of her life to him and was entitled to a life of her own. She and Bill Bullitt went together for a while, and in fact became engaged. I don't know why the engagement ended—I believe Bill treated her badly —but from then on Missy devoted the rest of her life to father.

Much has been made of the money father left Missy in his will. I am the only one who knows the inside story, and if that is the last piece of evidence in support of a romance between father and Missy, I consider that case lost.

When Missy suffered a stroke in the summer of 1941 and was partially paralyzed, father felt an enormous sympathy for her distress. When she was released from the hospital, he sent her to his cottage at Warm Springs to recuperate. He visited her there, and he encouraged her in her time of need as she had encouraged him in his. Later, she tried to return to work for him, but she was physically incapable. She went home, but spent most of her last years in the hospital.

Missy had made little money in her service of father. He felt the children could care for themselves, but this faithful aide could not care for herself. Accordingly, father arranged with Doc O'Connor that his will be written so that the interest only on up to half his estate would be reserved strictly for such medical care as Missy might need. Mind you, it was not left to her personally, but to her medical costs.

Missy died in July of 1944, less than a year before father died. Elliott presumes that because he did not bother to change the will after her death to remove this clause, father must have wanted the world to know the importance of Missy in his life.

Father feared some would jump to this conclusion, but he denied it to me, personally, when he told me after his final inauguration in 1944 that he wanted me to be the executor of his will. He was sick by then. Contrary to what has been assumed, he did not believe he would soon be dead, but he was not well, and he was weary. He said, "I had the damnedest fight with Doc O'Connor over the details of my will, and I simply am not going to go through it again. I don't want to and I don't have the strength. Like all lawyers, Doc won't dot an 'i' without discussing it. If I go to him to rewrite it, I'll never last until the last 't' is crossed. I left half my estate to mother, and I left half my estate to Missy for her medical bills. Some may try to make something of that. They shouldn't, but they will. If it embarrasses mother, I'm sorry. It shouldn't, but it may. But the clause is written so that in the event of Missy's death, that half reverts to mother, too, so she gets it all. Missy didn't make it, her half already has reverted to mother, and so the clause is inoperative. I don't have to change it, so I won't." He sighed and added, "I owed her that much. She served me so well for so long and asked so little in return."

Father missed Missy enormously, which is why Anna was asked to fill in for her when Missy was stricken. He missed

Missy in a very practical way but even more than most men might miss their secretaries. Physically, he could not do for himself what most men could do, and she had seen to his needs.

Mother never disturbed Missy's domain, and to the best of my knowledge she never reproached father about any romance with Missy. I know she resented Missy's place in father's life, but she resented the place Betsey took for a while, too, and the one Anna, her own daughter, assumed at the end. What mother really resented, I think, was her own steel will, which would not permit her to assume her rightful role herself.

I have no doubt that one reason father liked to have Missy around was that she was attractive. He had few homely women working for him; that was not his style. But actually, though little has been made of it, more of a romantic relationship might have been built around Princess Martha of Norway.

The prince and princess and their children were in exile, living in Washington during the war, but the prince always seemed to be in Europe trying to look after the affairs of his conquered country, while the princess spent time at the White House or Hyde Park looking after father. At one time he tried to find a home for her near his in Hyde Park. The princess was an attractive and charming woman, and father obviously enjoyed her company enormously. He would kiss her hello when she arrived and good-bye when she left, and good-night if she stayed over.

For the most part, mother just did the dutiful things. She tried to get the family together for dinners on Thanksgiving and Christmas, for example, and she always arranged father's birthday parties. He had formed the Cuff Links Club, a collection of his cronies, and they always gathered together to toast his birthdays. Mother saw to it that the event came off. I don't recall him doing as much for her, frankly, though he always gave her presents at appropriate times. Mother preferred practical gifts. She didn't care for finery or jewelry. At any rate, celebrating occasions was a bit more than keeping up appearances; it was a sort of renewal of the ties that bound them. Shortly after each fete, however, she would be off on her own way.

It is sad in a sense that no one tries to suggest that mother had romances. It is sad because she was human, too, even if not a beauty. She was close to Louis Howe for many years (he was no beauty, either, of course; they used to compare newspaper photos to see whose was the homeliest), but I don't think there was ever anything physical between them. I do think they felt love for one another. I believe they sympathized with one another—these two who planned the parties, then sat on the sidelines and watched the beautiful people dance all the dances.

I think the best friend mother ever had, though, was Adlai Stevenson. I know they admired one another enormously and I could see they enjoyed being together. Had he been closer to her age they might have paired off. I know he was one of the few people she wanted to see in her last days. Even when she was on her deathbed and aware how bad she looked, she welcomed his visit. And he did go to her and was tender with her.

I believe there may have been one real romance in mother's life outside of marriage. Mother may have had an affair with Earl Miller. I write about it now because I believe it is important to realize that there are two sides to every coin; that as Victorian as mother may have been, she was a woman, too, who suffered from her self-imposed separation from father.

Miller was an extremely handsome and physical man, a former amateur boxing champion and outstanding horseman, a former police instructor and a state trooper. He was Al Smith's bodyguard during Smith's term as New York's governor, and he stayed on at the mansion after father became governor. Miller became mother's bodyguard, and though he eventually became director of personnel for the Department of Corrections, he remained with her for many years. His fellow officers originally teased him about being assigned to "that old crab," but she took an interest in him, her warmth won him over, and when others saw how he felt about her they stopped kidding him about his "awful assignment."

Mother was self-conscious about Miller's youth, but he did not seem bothered by the difference in years. He encouraged her to take pride in herself, to be herself, to be unafraid of facing the world. He did a lot of good for her. She seemed to draw strength from him when he was by her side, and she came to rely on him. When she had problems, she sought his help. He intervened on her behalf when Uncle Vallie went on a drunken spree at Tivoli, for example. He became part of the family, too, and gave her a great deal of what her husband and we, her sons, failed to give her. Above all, he made her feel that she was a woman.

If father noticed, he did not seem to mind. Curiously, he did promote a romance between Miller and Missy, but that did not last. Miller, who'd had an unhappy first marriage, later married a cousin of his first wife, and that ended the gossip about mother and him. But this was not a happy marriage either. He was divorced in 1934.

All the while, Miller had continued to see mother and frequently was a guest at Val-Kill. He saw other women, too, and she encouraged his romances. He married a third time in 1941, though he continued to see mother regularly. This marriage was a failure too, I believe. Maybe because of mother. Their relationship deepened after father's death and ended only with mother's death.

From my observations, I personally believe they were more than friends and that mother was more than, as she was described, "an aunt" to him. Joseph Lash in his excellent book, *Eleanor and Franklin,* glosses over the relationship as though to protect her reputation, but I believe this is a disservice to her, a suggestion that because of her hang-ups she was never able to be a complete woman.

I know Nancy Cook and Marion Dickerman did not like Miller. He could be crude, to be sure. Also, they may have been jealous of him, though not in the sense that some have hinted at. It has been suggested that there was some sort of unnatural relationship between mother, Marion and Nancy. I was close enough to them to say there is nothing whatsoever to this. It's true that they were close. In fact they shared Val-Kill. They shared it to the extent that the linen was embroidered with the initials EMN (Eleanor, Marion, Nancy). They also went into business together, forming Val-Kill Industries, which produced copies of antique furniture in a factory, and they bought, operated together and taught at Todhunter, a private girls' school in New York City.

All this started in the late Twenties, at a time when mother was emerging into the world and getting involved in her own crusades, and it lasted about ten years. I think the situation satisfied a need for companionship each of them had. They were among the first women's libbers, I suppose—at least they seemed determined to prove they didn't need men. I don't think Marion or Nancy ever married. They may have resented the fact that mother was married, but if so they were consoled because it was a flawed marriage. I do not believe there was ever anything sexual between them. From what I saw, friendship was all they felt they needed.

In this respect they may have asked more of mother than she was willing to give them. She enjoyed their friendship and got a lot from it, but as she began to see that there was more to life than the narrow limits they imposed, she began to break away from them. They bickered for a year or so before the break became final. Then the furniture factory, which was a losing proposition, was folded, and mother withdrew from Todhunter, turning over her share of the school to the other two, in 1938. After that she assumed total control over Val-Kill. Marion and Nancy were only guests who visited less often as the years went by. After father's death, and until mother's death, the three got together at times, but the friendship by then was diminished.

Father never interfered with mother's friendships. He felt she was entitled to hers as he was to his. It was part of their arrangement. Yet, for all that they were apart, both physically and spiritually, much of their married life, there remained between them a bond that others could not break.

Two moments stand out in my mind. One was when Sara died in September of 1941. Mother understood the depths of father's loss. She wrote a friend: "I looked at my mother-in-law's face after she was dead and understood so many things I'd never seen before. It is dreadful to have lived so close to someone for 36 years and feel no deep affection or sense of loss. It is hard on Franklin, however." She went on to write of Sara's loyalty to her family and especially to her son. She spoke of how much Sara had done for father.

Mother went to father and consoled him. She stayed with him and was by his side at the funeral and through the difficult days immediately afterward. She showed him more affection during those days than at any other time I can recall. She was the kind you could count on in a crisis, and father knew that.

When, later that same month, mother's brother, Hall, died and mother needed father, he did not fail her. She slept in her clothes in the hospital for ten days while her brother was dying, and I remember clearly the day she went to father and said simply, "Hall has died." Father struggled to her side and put his arm around her. "Sit down," he said, so tenderly I can still hear it. And he sank down beside her and hugged her and kissed her and held her head on his chest.

I do not think she cried. I think mother had forgotten how to cry. But there were times when she needed to be held, and this certainly was one. Hall had been a trial to her. His life had been a disappointment to her and to him, too. When it was over, I think it was the waste of it that hurt her. And she spent her hurt in father's embrace. It is too bad they were together like that so seldom.

VIII

As I said at the beginning, I want to take a personal look, rather than a political look, at my father and our family. I will leave it to the historians to judge his presidency, but I do want to consider him both as a political personality and as a pure politician—and he was both.

The family always thought of father as a politician. He was a super salesman, and even after polio impaired his appearance he remained impressive personally. That toothy smile of his was the stuff of which stars are made, and he knew how to use it. He'd jut out his jaw in his characteristic way, put his cigarette in a long holder that stuck out of his grin at an angle, and top it all off with a battered fedora—for the common touch. He struck his pose at appropriate times. He was an actor, putting on a performance. Although almost always seated, he nevertheless stood out from all others around him. He was "FDR," the first president identified by initials.

A superb speaker, father had as great a command of the "American" language as Churchill had of the "English" language. Father always sought from his speech writers the meaningful phrase that would endure after the rest was forgotten: "We have nothing to fear but fear itself," "The hand that held the dagger . . ." and so on. Like Lincoln's, we remember FDR's speeches because he bottled their magic in a few words we could remember.

John F. Kennedy captured this lightning too. But not Hoover. Or Landon. Or Willkie. Or Dewey. Or Truman. Or Eisenhower. Or Johnson. Or Nixon. Or Ford. What did any of them ever say that was memorable? Stevenson was a marvelous speaker, but what did he say? The lightning eluded him. He also lacked the common touch, which father had. Who ever spoke to the voters as father did in his "Fireside Chats"? From that first presidential address to the public when he began "My friends . . ." he had captured lightning in a bottle. No one has successfully imitated him. After that first one, every one of these "chats" started, "My friends . . ."

Of course, that was a different day, a time of trouble when the citizens of this country still trusted its leaders to lead them, hung on his every word and heeded his advice. He *was* their friend. Of course, all were not with him; he had powerful enemies who disliked and mistrusted him. But the vast majority of Americans were with him. They loved him and believed in him. It's true they did not see him through the intimacy of television, but I think this master of radio would have used television well, too. His was a personality that touched the public. He was the greatest actor of his time.

The Roosevelt name was a help from the first. Father had been active in Dutchess County politics to a limited extent, but had he not been a Roosevelt he would not have been considered a likely candidate for state office from that county. It was in 1910, when he was twenty-eight, that the Dutchess County district attorney, John Mack, sought father out to ask him if he was interested in running as a Democratic candidate for the state legislature. He was. He talked it over with his uncle, Teddy, who did not encourage him. Teddy regretted that his nephew did not share his political philosophies.

This happened when I was small, so I have only second-hand knowledge of what went on. I know Republicans had a tight hold on the office father sought, and he was an underdog, but he ran hard to reverse the race. He fell from a moving streetcar at one point, but pressed on, despite a sore elbow and leg. He toured the territory in an open Maxwell, a rented red touring car he had decorated with flags and banners.

It was an unorthodox campaign, but it worked, to the surprise of party veterans. He traveled two thousand miles to tell the people that he was owned by no one and that his only "boss" would be the people he represented. The bosses of his party did not approve of this approach, but they respected his victory. Although the Democrats did sweep the state in that election, father ran ahead in his county. He became only the second Democrat in fifty-five years to represent the county in the State Senate. And so we went to Albany.

His first term was somewhat spectacular, and, fortunately for father, it was successful. He made quite a show of wanting to kick out the bosses and clean up the government. This did not endear him to Tammany Hall in New York City and those who, though smeared by scandals, had continued to run the party in the state. In leading a fight to have U.S. senators elected by popular vote, instead of by appointment of the state legislature, in campaigning against senatorial candidate Bill Sheehan and for presidential candidate Woodrow Wilson, father opposed state bosses Charlie Murphy and Packy McCabe and made many enemies within the party.

He was young and heavy-handed at the time. Had not Sheehan lost and Wilson won, father's future in politics might have dimmed dramatically. But the world loves a winner, and Al Smith and the other party regulars accepted him into their inner ranks. Before his first term ended, he was being considered as a future gubernatorial possibility. And hard-bitten Louis Howe, who had left newspaper work to get into the fascinating business of politics, had asked for and been given a job on father's staff. After father was renominated for a second term, but stricken with scarlet fever, Louis, as I've already described, masterminded father's campaigns. Well known within the state by then, father won again in 1912 without having to wage the sort of campaign that had carried the first election.

That year he also served as a state delegate to the Democratic presidential convention in Baltimore, supported Wilson's successful bid for the nomination and won the respect of members of the Wilson camp, including Josephus Daniels, who would be Wilson's secretary of the navy. Father was invited to the inauguration in Washington. There Daniels, knowing Teddy had served as assistant secretary, invited father to take the post. It was what father wanted. He accepted on the spot. He resigned his senatorial seat and we went to Washington in 1913. Swiftly, he had shot into the spotlight.

Frankly, as far as I could ever see, father always felt he could handle any office better than the man in the job. Father apparently had barely settled in as assistant secretary of the navy before he was telling mother how much better he could do the job than the secretary. While Daniels dictated a modest growth for this nation's navy, father argued for the fast buildup of a powerful force that could swing swiftly into action if war broke out.

Secretary of State William Jennings Bryan and President Wilson sided with Daniels. But after German U-boats sank the *Lusitania*, with a loss of twelve hundred civilians, including one hundred and twenty Americans, Wilson came over to father's side. Bryan resigned, while Daniels remained to debate a big buildup with Wilson and father. The president could see, as father apparently had seen, that war with Germany was on its way. Wilson worked toward a "peace without victory" to the very end, but much of the world was already at war when, two days after the torpedoing of three more American ships, this country, in April of 1917, entered World War I.

Against the advice of Louis Howe, father ambitiously sought the New York State Democratic nomination for the U.S. Senate race in 1916, but was badly beaten in the primary by Jim Gerard, Tammany's nominee. Father never again, to my knowledge, disregarded Louis Howe's advice. On Howe's advice father turned down a bid to campaign for the New York State Democratic gubernatorial nomination in 1918. Another defeat might have finished father as a viable political candidate, and Howe reckoned the time was not right for father to make his move; he was not sufficiently known.

His early recognition of the forces in the world that were leading toward war served to increase father's prestige when he was proven right. He toured the fighting fronts at sea, gaining national recognition, and his efforts to increase the size and strength of the navy were regarded as having helped win the war. Father stamped himself a man of peace when he campaigned on behalf of Wilson's dream of a League of Nations.

Almost ten million soldiers had died and more than twenty million had been wounded in four years of war. Father and mother went to Europe to direct the dismantling of the naval forces located there. President Wilson and his wife also went to Europe, and by chance my parents and the Wilsons returned on the same ship, the *George Washington.* The president preached the League to my father.

From what father told me over the years, he admired Wilson enormously. He thought him "more a man of thought than of action, but a most thoughtful man." Although Wilson was sick, father supported the president's desire for an unprecedented third term. Later, of course, father became the first man to win a third term.

At the Democratic National Convention in 1920, father fought for Wilson. At one point he wrestled the New York State banner from a representative of Tammany to lead a demonstration march through the aisles as a portrait of Wilson was unveiled.

The doomed Wilson did not win. He had promised peace, but was blamed for delivering war. The war was over, and in its aftermath racial disorders were erupting in Washington, dissatisfied veterans were creating turmoil. The country wanted change. Ohio newspaper publisher and governor James Cox was selected as the Democratic candidate, though he had little hope of overcoming the Republican nominee, Warren Harding.

As I understand it, Cox wanted New York Governor Smith as his running mate, but Al, figuring the ticket was doomed to defeat, was not interested. He was looking ahead to 1924. When father was recommended as a replacement, Tammany boss Charlie Murphy expressed little enthusiasm, but if Cox wanted him, Cox could have him. It would take father out of any state race, anyway.

Louis Howe huddled with father. It was a long shot, they decided, but he should take it. Whatever the outcome, father would get national exposure. He could not be blamed when Cox went down to defeat. Teddy had been vice-president, so father, too, wanted the job. "I have a surprise for you lads," he told Elliott and me. A "spontaneous" demonstration erupted in his behalf.

Father, parted from Lucy, had made his deal with mother, and he was all work. Mother was notified of his nomination in a telegram from Daniels. She wrote Sara that he had little chance, then left to join him at his homecoming at Hyde Park. She returned to Campobello when he went on the campaign trail, and later she joined him on tour. We children were with him as much as we could be, which wasn't often in those school days. I remember I really thought he would win. After all, he was my father—he *had* to win. But the ticket never had a chance.

You wonder why men run when they have no chance. In many cases, it is better to be beaten than not to run at all. Father later said Cox felt that way, that Cox was seizing his one shot at the national spotlight. Besides, it was an honor. You may not remember that William Jennings Bryan was a secretary of state, but you remember he ran for president and lost three times as the nominee of the Democratic party. Stevenson and Willkie ran and lost, but are remembered. Nixon ran and lost, but bounced back to run again and win. It is not true that losers are always forgotten. Not even losing vice-presidential candidates.

Father campaigned hard for the ticket, crossing the country by train, becoming better known at every stop. He was not disgraced when Harding won with almost twice the popular vote and more than twice the electoral vote of the Cox team.

And, of course, father came back twelve years later to take the top spot.

In between there was that bout with polio, which father won, at least on points, though he wound up looking like a loser. He never spoke of the presidency—not when he was running for the vice-presidency, nor when he was temporarily out of the running—but I do remember him saying to me once, "I may not be able to walk, but I guess I could still run a good race."

I think he had his eyes only on the governor's chair at that time, though Howe had higher ambitions for him. He and Howe decided the way to stay close to the top was to talk Al Smith into bidding to regain the governership he had lost to Nathan Miller in 1920. This meant they would have to talk Smith into giving up a soft $50,000-a-year job as chairman of a trucking concern so he could seek to recapture his $10,000-a-year governor's seat. Mother helped persuade Al to run.

Smith was the one candidate who could keep publisher William Randolph Hearst from the party nomination. If you could have bought the job, Hearst would have become not only the nominee but the governor, and then the president. But it was beyond bidding. Smith's machinery ran the state party. If Smith wanted the nomination, it was his. And he wanted it. Mother seconded the nomination, and Al won to become governor again, beating, ironically, mother's cousin, Theodore Roosevelt, Jr., the Republican candidate.

In 1924 father made his dramatic return to the spotlight with his "Happy Warrior" speech nominating Smith for president. The fire roared for father, not Smith. Father also contributed the keynote address at the state convention where Smith was renominated for governor in 1926. Mother worked for Smith, and he won. Through Howe's manipulations, Smith was tied to the Roosevelts. It was a deal Howe made which brought Smith the support of mother and father in the race for the presidential nomination again in 1928, in exchange for Smith's support of father for the gubernatorial nomination.

Howe once told me, "The Republicans were winning by big margins. I believed they would win again in 1928. But I believed Herbert Hoover would be the nominee and he would be a disaster. I believed the time was right to put Franklin in a position to go for the presidency in 1932."

In Houston, father again nominated Smith. His was the first speech ever carried on nationwide radio, and though lacking one of his enduring phrases, it made a deep impression on all who heard it. The *New York World* reported the next day that father struck a posture that was proud despite years of suffering, that he obviously was a gentleman and a scholar. It concluded: "This is a civilized man. . . . For a moment we are lifted up."

Smith was nominated on the first ballot.

Father resisted the nomination for the governorship of his home state. Frankly, he was afraid of failure. He was not convinced the public would support a cripple running for an important office. He was not sure he could stand up to the strain of a campaign. Moreover, he thought he saw some signs of healing in his left side and he wondered whether, if he concentrated more on his rehabilitation, he might regain his mobility. He was not the typical reluctant candidate. His reluctance was real.

Howe was the one who convinced him: Father was not going to be allowed to live out his life sitting on the sidelines in a wheelchair, emerging only to support lesser men. Mother helped. By then, she was deep into politics, working for the women's wing of the party, making speeches, writing articles, printing a party paper.

It has been written repeatedly that mother opposed father's return to the wars. I take a differing view. I asked her once if she had in fact been opposed to his running. "Oh, no," she said. And then she was silent. Finally she said quietly, "No, I was not opposed. I thought it would be good for him. I thought it would help him to break away from Warm Springs before he became too deeply entrenched in running that resort. And I thought he might be able to help Al Smith win.

I had a lot of friends in the party by then. I had worked hard for the party. I believed in its principles. I was opposed to Tammany Hall, but I was not opposed to Al Smith. I wanted him to win, and I wanted the party to do well."

I do believe, however, that mother thought father would lose and that she was more concerned with Al Smith winning. From subsequent developments it became clear that she felt if father won, she would lose. She knew father had wanted her to become active in politics primarily to keep his cause in the public eye. She felt father would expect her to slip back into the shadows if he moved again into the limelight. On the other hand, she had become an important part of Al Smith's team. She felt that if he attained the presidency she would play an even more important part in public affairs. In this sense she was closer to Smith than to her own husband. Mother worked harder for Smith than for father. She appeared on Smith's behalf, and most of her other speeches were concerned more with Smith than with father.

But mother did encourage father to take a chance and make a race if it was what he really wanted. I told father he should run, and I believe my brothers did, too. I know Anna wired him, "Go ahead and take it." And father wired back, "You ought to be spanked." He was amused, but encouraged. I don't know how much we swayed him, but our belief in him had to help. Howe, of course, was behind him all the way, pushing him hard, and Jim Farley had jumped aboard to add a boost. And Smith, feeling father would help him carry his home state and New York's big bag of electoral votes, wanted "his man" in his old office.

Father was persuaded. He made up his mind to make the race. He once told me, "I just decided it was now or never." If they asked him, he would accept. He waited at Warm Springs to be asked while mother was at the convention in Rochester making halfhearted pretenses that father was unavailable right up to the time Smith and other leaders of the party told her that father was the one they wanted. She telephoned father and put the governor on the line. He talked father into taking a nomination he had already decided to take. Mother told father she knew he had to do what he felt was expected of him. She told others that she had not asked him to run; that it had been his decision. Which it was, of course.

At the time, my parents were budgeted to the dollar and were often short a hundred dollars here or there. After his losing vice-presidential race and prior to his being stricken with polio, father had joined Van Lear Black's Fidelity and Deposit Company of Maryland, a massive bonding house, and they continued to pay him $25,000 a year. He also entered a law partnership with Basil O'Connor, who guaranteed him $10,000 a year. In both cases he was paid less for what he could do than because his name brought in business. He himself was not a good businessman. Father and Howe lost money in all sorts of schemes to make a fast million in bonds, oil wells, shipping, lobsters, almost anything you can think of.

Now, with his announced intention to run for governor, Sara refused to lend financial support. Sara never gave a nickel to Warm Springs, either; she resented its hold on her son. When she warned him she would not finance his return to the political wars, he assured her he had no intention of asking her help. I suspect Sara was relieved. She assumed he'd be beaten. Her own income was something like $50,000 a year. It cost her half that to maintain Hyde Park. She liked to travel and lead the good life, and she really didn't want a drain on her resources so her son could pursue his foolishness. Consequently, he was left to his own resources. Although he would have to sever his financially rewarding private connections if he ascended to the statehouse, he did have his inheritance. And it helped when his half-brother, "Rosy," left him $100,000 in securities in 1927.

Unlike so many others, father sacrificed the good life financially to pursue politics and public service. He really believed he could do for others what other men could not do. While he hid his ego beneath a blanket of charm, it was enormous and it drove him to his destiny, all the while being dunned by this merchant or that bill collector. He was, in the end, one of the few men who did not prosper in the presidency, who did not leave office with more than he took into it. He was carried out of office, of course, but the will he left behind testified to the financial struggle he endured during his days in the White House. Oh, he lived well. We all did. But not only were we not wealthy, we were nowhere near as comfortable financially as has been believed.

Once he decided to return to the political wars, father, in his wheelchair, ran hard. He campaigned almost as hard for Smith as for himself, though I suspect Smith never believed this. Al was beaten before he began. He was not only an unattractive man with the big-city accents of the sidewalks of New York, but a Catholic at a time religious and racial prejudices were commonplace. In the bitter campaign that ensued, it was said by his enemies that he would be the pope's president, not the public's.

My parents' sense of fair play was outraged. They spoke against this sort of prejudice but were not heard. Perhaps they could have spoken louder. Father said in a speech, "I assure you that if Al Smith becomes president, our marriages will not be declared illegal and our children made illegitimate." In response to leaflets distributed in the South referring to "Al Smith the Negro Lover," mother wrote a southern newspaper that "Gov. Smith does not believe in intermarriage between white and colored people. He would not try to do violence to the feelings of southern people."

The Republicans were considered the "peace party," and the scholarly Hoover swamped Smith at the polls. Most significantly, Hoover beat Smith in New York State by one hundred thousand votes, while father beat Albert Ottinger by twenty-five thousand votes. This embarrassed Smith, whose feelings toward father cooled considerably.

Father trailed in the early returns, but simply refused to concede defeat. "I can't give up," he confided to us as we waited at home at Hyde Park for the radio reports of the returns. Around midnight, when Smith conceded and went to bed, he believed father had been defeated, too. But as the New York City votes were counted they carried father to the front and on to victory. His final margin out of four million votes was slim, to say the least: One vote out of every 160 turned the tide. He came that close to the premature end of what was to become the most remarkable career in the history of American politics.

His was not, as is assumed today, an easy career, in which a charmed constituency fell at his feet. No doubt there were many who admired him, but even among his admirers there were many who doubted his ability to perform effectively because of his physical condition. He won his narrow victory with the help of an energetic campaign and his good cheer. He told one audience, "Well, here he is—the helpless cripple my opponent speaks about. This is my sixteenth speech today." This attitude as much as anything else carried the day for him. He repeatedly stressed that he was an independent who did not owe anything to anyone except the people. And he repeatedly assured them that he was fully capable of withstanding the ordeals of the office.

Nevertheless, if he'd had a better-known and more interesting opponent, father would have lost. The Republicans underestimated him. They felt Hoover would defeat Al Smith so badly that the president would carry even an Al Ottinger into office. No one knew father's capabilities at that time, but he was a gallant figure and a persuasive speaker and he was able to beat Al Ottinger in what otherwise was another Republican year.

Father was a good governor. He had to be, or he would have been finished in politics. First came a show of strength; he had to assert himself as the governor of the state and the new leader of the state's Democrats; he no longer could allow Al Smith to take the lead. Crushed by his defeat on the national level, Smith was ready to reclaim his high position within his own state. If father now was the governor, Smith expected to stand behind him, showing himself to be the real power behind the throne. As far as he could see, father had no choice.

If it had not been for Smith, father would not have been governor. Father owed him a debt of gratitude and Smith expected to collect.

Smith made it clear he expected his cabinet to remain intact in the new administration. While father took his frequent rests in Warm Springs, the new lieutenant governor, Herbert Lehman, could run the state. Smith's aide, Robert Moses, could continue as secretary of state. And Smith's chief strategist, Belle Moskowitz, could stay on as his liaison with father, and as father's chief speech writer. Smith, of course, would approve all major speeches. It was a cold-blooded campaign to continue as a power in politics.

But father was a political animal, too. Finally in a position to assume authority and act independently, he went to work. He visited Warm Springs, but only to plot a power play with Louis Howe and Jim Farley. Robert Moses had said of father, "He'll make a good campaigner, but a lousy governor." Father remembered; Moses was out. Father admired Mrs. Moskowitz, but she had to go, too. Lieutenant Governor Lehman had to stay, of course, but Howe would head up father's cabinet as his chief aide. Farley would become the prime party man. Henry Morgenthau and others close to father would move into the new administration.

Smith ordered a conference with father on his return home to Hyde Park. It was the last such order father obeyed, and he did so to present the former governor with the new facts of life. Smith was upset. Where was Franklin's gratitude? Where was his loyalty? Father's only loyalty was to his new office. He assumed Smith had called on him because he believed in him, not because he wanted a hold on him. He did not see that he had debts to repay. "I will no longer be window dressing," father said. Later, in as diplomatic a manner as could be mustered, father told him, "I will lean on you for advice, Al, but I've got to be governor of New York and I have got to be it myself." He told Frances Perkins, "I'm awfully sorry if I hurt anybody, particularly Al."

Well, Al was hurt. He also was finished as a political force.

The public display of affection between my parents and Mr. and Mrs. Al Smith at the swearing-in ceremonies for the new governor at Albany the last day of January 1929 was strictly for show.

Father leaned on my arm as he took the oath of office on the family's old Dutch Bible in the same room where Teddy had been sworn in thirty years earlier. "This is some moment, isn't it, son?" he whispered to me. "It certainly is, sir," I said. And it was. I was twenty-one years old and awed. That was almost fifty years ago and I remember it as if it were yesterday. Herb Lehman's brother, Irving, a judge, swore father in. Father did become close with the liberal Lehman later, and he became as much father's man as he had been Smith's man.

On mother's advice and against Smith's, father made Frances Perkins commissioner of labor and elevated other women to positions of importance. If he slighted anyone, it may have been mother. He permitted her to resign her prime political posts without protest. He listened to her opinions and sometimes accepted her advice, but he did not make her a part of his team. I presume he felt it would have looked bad.

When asked by a reporter immediately after the election if she was excited by the outcome, mother had betrayed her inner turmoil by snapping, "No, I am not excited about my husband's election. What difference can it make to me? Since the rest of the ticket didn't get in, what does it matter?" So she dropped from public life, refusing to reemerge until after father became president and public pressure forced the First Lady to be seen.

Setting up their household at the governor's mansion in Albany, she gave her husband the big bedroom, assigned herself a back bedroom and gave Missy a larger bedroom near father. Mother retreated again into the shadows, seemingly satisfied to teach at Todhunter while her husband ran the state without her. He had plenty of help, but he was his own man and he ran his state as he saw fit. Howe didn't care, as long as father didn't harm his national image. They had their arguments, but father always loved an argument. He was a fighter. "I'm back into it with the boys in the state legislature," he laughed one time. "Well, there's nothing I like better than a good scrap."

Among other things, he fought for and won safety codes for factories, the right to be heard for labor, compensation payments for unemployed workers, pension laws for the aged. Prodded by Mrs. Perkins, he created welfare and work programs which were the basis of similar programs he was later to set in motion nationally. He pushed for the building of powerhouses along the St. Lawrence River to provide cheap electrical power for the farmers. He created conservation laws, and in fact was one of the early conservationists on the national battleground, though of course Teddy was there first. He was able to accomplish a lot in a limited time. He used the radio effectively, won popular support for his programs and was persuasive with the state legislature.

Possibly his most important move was against Jimmy Walker. Walker was father's Manhattan neighbor and the mayor of New York City. Father liked Jimmy. Almost everybody liked Jimmy. It was hard not to, no matter what he did. He may have been the most popular political personality in New York City's history. But Walker was a crook. He used his office to stuff his pockets. And when the newspapers revealed his misdeeds, sentiment to impeach him rose. People did not expect father to act against the pride of Tammany Hall; presumably, Tammany meant too much to the governor. But nothing meant that much to father. He appointed a special prosecutor, Samuel Seabury, to investigate the case and brought Jimmy to his knees.

Father always worked with Tammany, but he was not a Tammany man. He had aides at his side, but no cronies. There was none of the kind of cronyism that had crept into Al Smith's regime. Maybe father was just plain lucky. None of his staff betrayed him while he was governor, although he was subjected to betrayal later on as president. He committed no major blunders such as he stumbled into later in the presidency. He suffered no severe reversals as he did in the presidency. Of course, he was governor only four years and president more than three times that long, and the spotlight did not shine as brightly on him in the governor's chair as it did in the president's hot seat.

When father ran for reelection in 1930 against an unknown, Charles Tuttle, the Republicans had conceded him victory. Father felt he might win by 400,000 votes. Howe estimated the margin at 500,000. Farley went farther at 600,000. In their optimism, each tried to top the other. And yet each underestimated the magnitude of father's popularity in the state after two years as governor. He won by 725,000 votes, almost thirty times the margin of his first triumph and twice that of any previous plurality enjoyed by Al Smith or anyone else in New York. This victory made father the front-runner for his party's presidential nomination in 1932.

The stock market had crashed in October of 1929. Black Tuesday marked the beginning of a depression that was spreading across the country when father scored his stunning triumph in the election of November 1930. Louis Howe was right. Hoover was caught in a catastrophe. Unless Hoover righted the ship, the "peace party" would fall from the presidency, to be replaced by the "prosperity party" in 1932. All father had to do was keep his grip on the nomination.

As unemployment spread throughout his state, father created the Temporary Emergency Relief Administration, forerunner of the public works projects that would provide jobs for the jobless on the national level later. Father faced pressure to remove Walker from the mayor's office, but he delayed, maintaining a tight hold on Tammany as the Democratic National Convention opened in Chicago in the summer of 1932. Louis Howe's idea or father's? Both, I suppose. They were a team. But during father's four years as governor, Howe had nothing to do but plot tactics for the presidency. He was an expert whose specialty was winning elections for his client. Father did not fire Walker until after he had won the nomination, though before he won the election. I don't know how honorable it was, but father was no fool.

IX

Father was a great politician. He once said to me, "You can't be a great president without being a great politician. You can't do anything until you get in a position where you can do it. You make as few and as small compromises as you must make on your way to the top. You don't want to be compromised by your compromises." He also said, "Louis Howe and Jim Farley are great politicians."

Some of his greatness came from them. Howe, with the help of Farley, masterminded my father's rise to the presidency, and father was the first to give them credit. Father had an enormous ego, but he was wise enough to know he did not know everything. One of the secrets of his success was that he knew when to take advice. He was the boss—he made the final decisions—but often he acted on the advice of his senior aides. And they did not make many mistakes.

As I have said, father was the front-runner going into the 1932 Democratic National Convention in Chicago. Without confessing his candidacy, he had made it clear he coveted it, and Howe had spread the word, maneuvering Jim Farley into a high position in the party to press it. In addition he had father put ninety-second "pep talks" on records which were sent with autographed photos to the delegates. Father was not without opposition. Al Smith wanted the nomination again, which split father's home-state New York delegation. And John Nance Garner, the Speaker of the House, was being boosted by William Randolph Hearst. These foes were fiercely set against father.

Acknowledged candidates did not go to the conventions in those days. It was considered bad form, as if it would interfere with the presumed impartiality of the delegates. So father remained in the governor's mansion in Albany with mother. He did not tell her he had decided to make the run. Howe told her. Mother was annoyed with father because his sympathies for the League of Nations and the World Court had been silenced, and because he refused to commit himself on the subject of Prohibition, which he opposed, but which she favored. She was also annoyed because he refused to proceed against Walker and his Tammany mob. All to political purpose; he waited till after his nomination to go after Walker. But mother was not a political animal. She put ideals above elections, and father's ideals were not hers.

Meanwhile, I had gone into business in Boston and had been "adopted" by James Michael Curley. Curley thought I might be of use to him at some time. Father had appointed me his official representative to work with the Massachusetts delegation: "You'll learn a lot about backroom politics from Brother Curley," father predicted, with a grin. And I did, because the former mayor of Boston, congressman and future governor of Massachusetts was shrewd and sharp, one of the last of the big-city bosses. Like Jimmy Walker, Curley was a charming scoundrel, but father was perfectly willing to use him, and Curley was willing to be used as long as it was to his advantage. Curley wanted to be secretary of the navy. An Irish Catholic, he would also consider being named ambassador to Italy or Ireland.

We were swamped by Smith's strong forces in the Massachusetts primary, but later carried the state for father in the election. Father offered to make Curley ambassador to Poland. Curley was insulted, but father didn't care. He'd made no bargains with the man. He'd sought his help, but promised him no rewards. He didn't consider Curley fit for the positions the Bostonian sought, so he left Curley out in the cold. Later, father refused to intervene in a federal investigation of Curley. After father's death, Curley was convicted on charges of mail fraud and imprisoned.

I was at the convention in Chicago, working on behalf of father. Anna and Franklin were there, too. Louis Howe was in charge of father's headquarters in room 1702 of the Congress Hotel, where Howe had a "hot line" installed, connecting him by telephone to father's study in Albany.

Suffering from asthma, Howe had an attack shortly before departure and asked mother's friends Marion Dickerman and Nancy Cook to accompany him on the 20th Century Limited to Chicago. Later they said he lay in his berth most of the way, smoking cigarettes and gasping for breath. When he got to his hotel in Chicago, he lay on the floor, on the sofa, on the bed, even at one point on a dresser—because he supposed the air was better up high—still smoking cigarettes and gasping for breath. There was no air conditioning and it was hot. We were all soaked with sweat, but we were driven on by this man who seemed at death's door. At one point Farley lay on the floor alongside Howe to confer with him.

Howe and Farley decided father's best bet was to win early. At first they expected a first-ballot nomination, but by the time they got to Chicago the tide was turning against them. Smith had cut sharply into father's support and seemed to have him stalemated. There was talk around town that neither one could get the two-thirds majority—770 votes—needed, and that Garner would become a compromise choice.

Howe refused to permit father to commit himself on the major issues. Accordingly, columnist Walter Lippmann wrote of father as "an amiable man . . . who is not the dangerous enemy of anything." And broadcaster Elmer Davis termed him "the weakest of the candidates." But Howe knew this was not a popularity contest. It was a political contest. The delegates would decide it, not the public. Howe didn't care what the columnists wrote or the broadcasters said; he had his people dealing directly with the delegates.

Judge Mack, who had helped elect father to his first office back in New York, put father's name in nomination. The band burst into "Anchors Aweigh" as the inevitable demonstration erupted. They kept playing it as the demonstration continued, until finally Howe called down, "For God's sake, tell them to play something else, anything else!" The musicians switched to "Happy Days Are Here Again," and this became father's theme song.

The voting did not begin until 4:30 A.M. on the first day of July, a Friday. Farley brought Howe some ice cream, and they sat on the floor of the hotel room eating it and listening to the radio and hoping for the best. Farley later admitted Howe looked so bad there was doubt he would survive the ordeal. But Howe had worked so hard and waited so long, there was no way he was not going to play his part. And he was needed.

On the first ballot, father received 666 votes, Smith only 201. But father still was more than 100 votes short of the nomination. Back in Albany, as he admitted later, he was worried. Howe telephoned different delegations in a desperate attempt to gain votes, but by the second ballot had added only a few. When word filtered into the command post that some of the southern states were considering a switch to the Texan, Garner, Howe turned to the leaders in an effort to keep them in line.

On the third ballot, father pulled only 683 votes and remained 87 short. Smith had fallen to 191, Garner had only 102, but they had blocked father thus far. When the convention adjourned a little after nine in the morning, there was talk that a dark horse would be rushed into the deadlock to stampede the convention when balloting resumed that night.

Farley came from the floor to our room to tell Louis, "Texas is our only hope." Howe agreed. He telephoned father to talk him into compromising with this group that held enough votes to nominate him. The politician in father prevailed. He agreed.

Hearst, who no longer had political ambitions of his own, selected Garner as his front man in the "America First" movement that swept the country and threatened a serious break with our European allies. Hearst hated father, "an internationalist" and a man he could not control, and Garner agreed with his mentor. But Hearst was a practical politician; he realized he could not muster enough votes to capture the convention by allying Garner with Smith, only with Roosevelt.

When Howe telephoned Hearst to suggest an alliance, Hearst first asked that Garner be father's running mate, then he asked to talk to father personally to be assured father would not resume his support of the international groups. Howe agreed and telephoned father to tell him of the terms of their truce. Father telephoned Hearst to assure him he would not support the League of Nations or World Court in its crisis to come. Satisfied, Hearst consented to the merger.

When the deal developed, mother and others of similar persuasion were deeply disappointed. Father tried to reassure them this was strictly "practical politics," and to "have faith" in him "for the future," but when that future came, the opportunity to promote the League and the Court had slipped away.

The Hearst bloc consisted primarily of Texas and California. John Garner did not like the deal, but was convinced of the practical realities of the political situation at that time and agreed to take Texas with him into the Roosevelt camp. Hearst then dealt with Bill McAdoo, who convinced the California delegation to go along. Smith knew nothing of it. As the fourth ballot began that night, Al said, "Ah, tonight's the night." He had convinced himself the convention was going to turn from FDR to him.

When the balloting began and California was called on, McAdoo took the mike. "California did not come here to deadlock this convention, but to elect a president," he announced into a sudden hush. "When any man comes into a Democratic National Convention with the popular will behind him to the extent of almost seven hundred votes . . ." Bedlam broke out and few heard the rest of what he had to say. No one needed to hear the words to know what was happening. Smith's New York forces and Mayor Anton Cermak's Chicago group began to boo, but the cheers were louder. By the time Garner turned the Texas votes over, father's nomination as his party's presidential candidate was assured, although an angry Smith refused to release his delegates so it could be unanimous.

I telephoned home, where a celebration was in progress. As I have heard it, mother hugged Missy, and Elliott hugged John, while father watched happily. I felt tremendously thrilled.

At a time when air travel was not yet commonplace and in an era when candidates never invaded conventions, father had Howe announce that he was taking the unprecedented step of flying in to give his acceptance speech to the delegates in person. He asked me to meet the plane. Mother was with him, as was Missy and Grace Tully and Elliott and John. In fact, John was sick on the flight, and emerged looking it. Father had paid him no mind, working on the speech he and Sam Rosenman were preparing.

Farley and Howe went to the airport with me. Farley admired mother's work with women in politics and wanted her as part of father's team much more than father did. Alighting, mother went straight to Jim to say, "A fine job, Mr. Farley." Howe went right to father.

After I helped father into his car, Louis squeezed in alongside him, took the speech from father and read it quickly as we drove into town. There were things in it Louis did not like, and he argued about them with father. Finally, father snapped, "Dammit, Louis, *I'm* the nominee!" It was one of the few times I ever saw father lose his temper with Louis, and I believe it signaled that they had reached a turning point in their relationship. Howe had helped father this far, but now father took command, convinced he could go the rest of the way on his own if necessary.

Once, after they'd had an argument, father sent me to Louis to smooth things over.

"The old man thinks you're mad at him," I said. "He knows me better than that," Louis snapped. "He also knows I'm right and I'll be back tomorrow to argue with him some more. And, dammit, I'll win." Which is what Howe did the morning after father arrived in Chicago. He resumed his battle with father over parts of the speech, and he did win some points. "Only a fool never lost an argument," father once said. But Howe did not win his major point. He did not want to promise too much, but father planned a far more dramatic presidency than anyone envisioned and he felt he had a lot to offer. He concluded his speech: "I pledge you, I pledge myself to a new deal for the American people." Thus the "New Deal" was born. This phrase would forever remain symbolic of his administration.

The country was in need of a new deal. Of the 125 million citizens at that time, 17 million were unemployed. Men begged in the streets. Men too proud to beg sold apples for a nickel apiece, while others offered to work for a dollar a week. But there was no work to be had. In Chicago, Mayor Cermak permitted people who could not afford coal to dig wooden blocks from the sidewalks so that they could heat their homes. Many had no homes. In the Midwest and Southwest, drought brought dust storms, which in turn killed the crops and drove farmers west, their jalopies heaped high with their few possessions. Their dreams died in tents on the outskirts of California towns that had nothing to offer them. Throughout the nation, shantytowns sprang up to house those evicted from their homes. These were nicknamed "Hoovervilles."

Hoover had been elected on a promise of "two chickens in every pot." But he could not keep his promise. Certainly he alone did not cause the Depression, but he was unable to avert or reverse it. Even as the country was coming apart all around him, he pleaded, "Prosperity is just around the corner." No one believed him.

In June of 1932, some twenty thousand hungry veterans of

World War I marched on Washington to demand immediate payment of $500 bonuses voted them by Congress. They camped near the capital, but Hoover refused to see them. Instead he sent troops, led by General Douglas MacArthur and his aide, Major Dwight Eisenhower, to evict the veterans. The troops used bayonets and gas bombs. The shacks were burned to the ground and two of the marchers and two of their children died. Whatever hope Hoover had died with them.

Father took nothing for granted. When Hoover was Wilson's wartime food administrator ("Hooverizing" was the term for cutting down on the consumption of food), father had supported him. Hoover and his wife and my father and mother visited in each other's homes. In a letter to a friend, father once wrote of Hoover, "He is certainly a wonder, and I wish we could make him President of the United States. There could not be a better one." By 1932, however, father believed there could be a better one. Originally a liberal Republican who could work in the Wilson administration, Hoover had become a conservative on a different team.

A study of father's speeches reveals that he seldom made any direct references to Hoover himself. Father attacked the presidential policies and programs, or lack of them, but not the president. He really did respect Hoover. Later he lost respect for him. He felt that the Depression dictated drastic measures which were not being taken. Thus, although the heavy favorite, father conducted a hot campaign.

There were those who felt he was the least likely of candidates. Many of the voters were poor, and he was a man who never had known poverty. The workingman was in trouble, and he was not by ordinary definition a workingman. The presidency and the problems of the day demanded a strong man, and he was a cripple. A newspaper columnist wrote that father was no more than a pleasant man with no important qualifications for the job who would like very much to be president. But he was more and he proved it. He rolled up his sleeves and went to work.

I went with him on what was called a "whistle-stop tour," and we worked from six in the morning to midnight. Those were the days when the candidates covered the country by train, speaking from the rear platform to the assembled public and, hopefully, movie newsreel companies. Day after day father gave dozens of speeches. Since he was an excellent speaker and charming, too, he was cheered wherever he went, while poor Hoover, stiff and stuffy, was booed whenever he dared to venture forth. It was simply no contest.

Mother often went with us, as did other members of the family, including the glamour girls—Anna and my wife, Betsey. Father would introduce them, then turn to me, cocking his head to look up at me, and say, "And this is my little boy, Jimmy." He'd pause with the laughter, then add, "I have more hair than he has," and the laughter increased. I pretended to laugh too, but I didn't find it all that funny. I was indeed beginning to go bald, though I was only twenty-four.

Father had many a laugh at my expense. One of my jobs was to stay up all night, while father slept, to apologize for his absence to the slim crowds that showed up at the stops between two and six in the morning. At one such stop, a battle-ax of a lady ignored the handshake I offered her and announced, "Young man, I came here to see your father. Now you just go right in that train and fetch him." When I tried to explain how he needed his rest, she tried to hit me with an umbrella. I turned and ran, but she ran after me. Dad's bodyguard, Gus Gennerich, rescued me and he told father the story before I awakened the next day. Father found it the funniest incident of the tour.

Life was not funny at the time, of course. The Depression was the most severe of the many problems at home and abroad. Father later admitted to me he did not dare spell out the programs he planned because they were so drastic. In fact father spoke less of his own programs—even those he thought would succeed—than of Hoover's programs which had failed. Father spoke mainly in generalities, of federal aid to the poor, the farmer, the unemployed, of collecting money owed us from overseas loans, of balancing the budget, without saying how he planned to do this. As is so often the case in politics, it was safer to talk of what was wrong than of what one planned to do to correct the wrongs. Howe had him walking the middle ground. Father took a stand only when pressed.

The Walker case was one such instance; it commanded attention. With the nomination safely in his hands, father summoned the mayor to hearings in Albany. Acting as judge, the governor pressed the mayor to account for his unsatisfactory affairs, until Walker wilted and resigned under fire. Tammany tottered, afraid to fight the man who would be the next president.

Father influenced the selection of Farley as party chairman, and Farley influenced the election of father as president. Big Jim built a campaign team of six hundred supporters and set them to work building a basic unit of fourteen hundred more on the local level. He put mother in charge of the women's units, which were well organized. Everything was well organized. Since at the time it would have been considered unseemly to have mother campaign openly for father, she campaigned for Herbert Lehman as father's successor to the governorship of New York. With his success, they helped carry the state for father over Al Smith's unspoken opposition.

Father got little help from the egotistical Garner, who termed their team "like a mule—its strength is in its hindquarters." "Cactus Jack," as he was called, also said the office for which he campaigned, the vice-presidency, was "not worth a pitcher of warm piss." Father rather thought so, too —at least in Garner's hands. But father couldn't have cared less. He didn't need a lot of help from a vice-president.

I was with father while he followed the returns by radio, and I went with him to election headquarters in New York City when Hoover conceded defeat. Father flashed that famous smile as the congratulations rolled in during the early evening, but he seemed subdued. He had, of course, been confident of the outcome, as he had every reason to be. Father pulled in 22.8 million votes to 15.7 million for Hoover in the popular count. And father won 42 of the 48 states and 472 of the 531 electoral votes. It was one-sided.

It is interesting to note, however, that it was not much more one-sided than Hoover's victory over Smith just four years earlier. It became clear that although the incumbent has an enormous advantage over any challenger in such a political contest, one's performance in office could negate that advantage. I suppose father was sobered by this thought. Actually, attaining the office was sobering in itself. And father faced unusual problems in the office. It helped that his landslide carried with it Democratic advantages in the Senate and House. He would need the help of Congress if he was going to get his programs approved. And he had more programs to propose than anyone anticipated.

X

Father may have been guided into high office, but once he got there he went his own way. It is interesting to me that at the time he became governor of New York he rebuffed Al Smith's bid to be the power behind the throne, and at the time he became president of the United States he rebuffed Herbert Hoover's efforts to keep control of the course of this country. The feelings between father and his predecessors at both of these inaugurations were clearly cool, and the ceremonial roles he and mother had to play, first with the Smiths and later with the Hoovers, were made to appear cordial only by the acting abilities of all concerned.

Father was an immodest man, though his charm covered for him. He believed he was the man best suited to the task of leadership, and he proceeded accordingly. He used the power of veto more than almost any other president and seldom was overridden. If he had doubts about someone else's program, he would not support it. He believed he could find the best solutions to problems, and he pressed persuasively for their acceptance. He often assumed a dictatorial role, but I believe he was a benevolent dictator.

In all the years I knew him, there was only one time when my father worried about his ability. It was the night he was elected president. I think the enormity of the power he had inherited first struck him that night. It is one thing to run for it, another to get it. Suddenly father found himself in control of his country, to a great extent responsible for the lives of many millions. I think he was concerned about the fact that he was, after all, a cripple, though he would not admit this worried him. We went back to our Manhattan home that night and talked alone. After a while I helped him into bed and kissed him good-night. He looked up at me and said, "You know, Jimmy, all my life I have been afraid of only one thing —fire. Tonight, I think I'm afraid of something else."

"Afraid of what, father?" I asked.

"I'm just afraid that I may not have the strength to do the job."

I was surprised at the admission. It made me afraid, too, I think. I didn't say anything. Then he said, "After you leave me tonight, Jimmy, I am going to pray. I am going to pray that God will help me, that He will give me the strength and the guidance to do this job and do it right. I hope you will pray for me, too, Jimmy."

I looked at him and all I could do was nod. It was as though I was struck dumb by the moment. Whatever religion we had within us came to the surface with the enormity of the moment. I nodded and left him alone in his room, alone with the presidency, and I went to my room and did as he had asked me to do.

I think as he did the job he regained his confidence. If he called on God to guide him along the way, he did not confess it to anyone. But I know he was afraid of the job at first, as I suppose all presidents are, or should be. I know he thought a lot about fear in the following months and did not want to give in to it. As he said in his inaugural address on the Capitol steps, that cold, gray March day in 1933, in words partly borrowed from Thoreau, "This great nation will endure as it has endured, will revive and prosper. . . . So, first of all, let me assert my firm belief that the only thing we have to fear is fear itself. . . ."

Setting aside his fear, he went to work to try to bind the

wounds of this troubled nation and bring it back to health.

He went his way, not the way of Hoover or any other past president. In the weeks before the inauguration, Hoover wrote father frequently, asking his support for various stands, and father refused. As a lame-duck president, Hoover could do little, and father would do little until he took over. On the night before the inauguration, Hoover requested a meeting with father, and as a matter of formality father agreed. But instead of the traditional social visit, Hoover turned it into a final plea for joint action on banking and other situations. Father rebuffed him coldly, and there was no warmth between them from that day on. Hoover had wanted to emerge from the meeting with an announcement that they had agreed on courses of action, as if to say his regime had not been so bad after all, and his policies would be pursued even in the new regime. Father never gave him the opportunity.

Hoover departed in undeserved disgrace. The feeling remains that he did little to conquer the crisis in this country that developed during his presidency, but he did try many things. The Reconstruction Finance Corporation was born in his regime, for example, though father made it work and received the credit for it. Father's solutions stemmed the flow at least, until economic prosperity, which always accompanies wartime spending, turned the tide.

The cars in the motorcade that carried us to the inauguration were Pierce-Arrows. The company went out of business shortly thereafter; a lot of companies were going out of business at that time. I remember being in the reviewing stand—father, mother and I—for most of five hours watching the parade that was part of the ceremonies. No one enjoyed it more than father, despite needing to sit at times. But then he had to get to the office. The party was over and conditions were bad.

Five thousand banks had closed. The very night of his inauguration, Saturday night, the fourth of March, father closed the rest of the banks. I doubt that it was legal, but he did it, and in that troubled time no one tried to stop him. It hit the country hard, but he had to close the banks in order to re-structure them, after which he reopened them. The process took more than a week, and during that week, since people lacked money, a barter system emerged. People exchanged goods for goods. Father rushed an emergency banking bill to Congress and it passed on the night of March 9, permitting the Treasury Department to print paper money that was not backed by gold. Bundles of fresh money were rushed to the banks, which reopened on Monday, March 13.

The night before, father gave the first of his "Fireside Chats," addressing the nation through the medium of radio. The chats were conversational in tone; he did not speak *to* the people so much as he seemed to speak *with* them. Though they could not answer him, he made it seem as though he were answering questions. "You may wonder why . . ." he would say, or "You may ask . . ." He tried to answer the questions that would have been asked him had it been possible.

Father assembled his advisers and appointed his cabinet before he even took office. He would call in his speech writers and tell them the points he wished to make in his talks. They would go to the brain trust and get the facts straight and put them down in the simplest possible form. Sam Rosenman headed up his speech-writing team, although the great playwright Robert Sherwood and Tommy Corcoran contributed considerably to his speeches. They were masters of father's style—the informal flavor of his language, the easy tempo he wished to take. They'd supply a first draft. He'd go over it and ask for changes. They'd rough out a second draft and he'd go over that. And so forth. He'd write some of it out in long-hand. Or he'd dictate. He hated to write. But by the time he was set to go on the air, he had a speech in his hands that said what he wanted to say. "My friends . . ." he'd be-gin.

In that first speech he said in part:

I want to tell you what has been done in the last few days, why it was done, and what the next steps are going to be. The bank holiday, while resulting in some cases in great inconvenience, is affording us the opportunity to supply the currency necessary to meet the situation. I can assure you that it is safer for you to keep your money in a reopened bank than to keep it under the mattress. Confidence and courage are the essentials of success in carrying out our plan, and it is up to you to support it and make it work. It is your problem, my friends, no less than it is mine. Together we cannot fail. . . .

In a sense he was going over the heads of the politicians, directly to the public. War had been declared and "we" were ready to defeat the enemy. He was enlisting the support of the public in the Roosevelt Revolution, and though many of the political powers in this country did not agree with him, they dared not defy the public. The public needed help, and here was a man who was taking steps to help them, moving swiftly and surely.

Indeed, the customarily slow pace of the presidency disappeared with father's arrival. The first hundred days of his administration brought more major moves than the full four-year terms of many of his predecessors. Those hundred days became a yardstick against which all future presidents would be judged.

He told the people what he was doing for them. Life in this country came to a stop while he spoke. The people gathered around their radios to listen while their leader told them of the changes that were taking place in their lives. His personality projected powerfully over the airwaves. His speech was cultured, but soft and warm. I doubt that we ever again will pay such attention to a man and put such trust in a leader as this country did in my father. And he merited that trust.

I do not know if his solutions were always the best ones, but they were unselfish ones. They were designed not to improve his position but that of the people. He believed in his solutions and he was willing to carry each case to the people. He had more press conferences than any president except possibly John F. Kennedy. Father was able to talk to the press as well as he could talk to the people directly. They carried many of his messages to the people, and they treated him well, even in a Republican-owned industry. As I said, father was a salesman. He had some things to sell. And he sold them.

Journalists lost sleep trying to keep up with the furious pace of this crippled man, his aides and the Congress. As he had closed the banks, he opened the bars. He asked for and received broad powers to act independently and swiftly in economic matters. He pushed through the Federal Emergency Relief Act to provide funds for the states to distribute to the seventeen million unemployed. He got legislation to stop foreclosures on small home mortgages when such foreclosures were taking place at the rate of a thousand a day. He formed the Civilian Conservation Corps (CCC), which put two million young men to work in the forests and along the rivers of this country. He pushed through the Agricultural Adjustment Act (AAA), which guaranteed the incomes of the men and women who fed the country.

Farm-support policies remain controversial, but these kept the farmers from failing when they were in critical condition. Father also formed the Tennessee Valley Authority to provide power to the farmers and others in the Southeast. The TVA also remains controversial. It put the government in competition with private business. But it did what had to be done for survival at the time.

Finally, father forced through the National Industrial Recovery Act, which called for voluntary cooperation by industry to increase production and provide jobs, all the while shortening the work week and increasing wages. Public pressure made it as much mandatory as voluntary. If you didn't have an NRA sticker, your business was considered un-American.

Ten thousand telegrams of approval arrived at the White House each week. Hundreds of thousands of letters thanking the president for his help were delivered monthly. If some observers deemed FDR a dictator, if some said his "socialism" was evil, if some were concerned about the legality of some of his acts, it was difficult for them to defy the gratitude of the public. Millions remained out of work or in poverty, but FDR held out hope to them. Swiftly he helped some. The others supposed he would soon help them. He was a man of action at a time action was needed.

The first hundred days were only the beginning. Week after week, new deals emerged from the New Deal, peaking perhaps in January of 1935 when he created the Works Progress Administration. The WPA paid people to work. Writers received a minimum wage for writing, painters for painting. More important, jobs were created for the jobless, building bridges, roads, dams, airports, post offices. They changed the face of the countryside. Many WPA creations endure to this day.

Of course, father was not without enemies. There are those who feel he did damage to the nature of life in this country. If he did, he also did damage to the Depression. In any event, it's true that he effected more changes in this country than any man before or after him. To put it in its simplest terms, nothing came out of paychecks until father instituted the Social Security Act. To pay for his programs, taxes had to be increased, and eventually taxes were withheld from paychecks. During his three full terms in office, the population increased a little less than ten percent, but the number of workers in the federal government increased more than four hundred percent. Taxes alone could not pay for this, hence father not only did not balance the budget, he put it way out of balance.

Although they had been his social friends, father from the first declared war on big businessmen. In one of his first presidential speeches, he pointed out that the men who own but four percent of the securities in this country control the other ninety-six percent. "There, my friends," he said, "is the case of a ninety-six-inch dog being wagged by a four-inch

tail." Many of his acts depressed the profits of big businessmen, and many of his programs aided the workingman at a
time when the union movement was spreading, to the outrage
of big businessmen. A wave of strikes across the country
caused father to establish a National Labor Board under Senator Bob Wagner of New York, but big businessmen beat it
down. They were out to tame father.

On Monday, May 27, 1935—"Black Monday," as father's
faithful were to call it—the Supreme Court declared the NRA
unconstitutional. The vote was unanimous that father had
taken impermissible power upon himself, and that federal
interference in interstate commerce was illegal.

It was as though he'd been struck by lightning, but father
struck back. It was "a horse-and-buggy" decision, he declared.
Using all the persuasive powers at his command, he all but
commanded Congress to pass a new wave of bills. Originally
cool to the Wagner Labor Relations Act, he warmed up to it,
made it the hottest of his properties and sped its passage. It
may have been the most influential legislation he backed; it
put power into the hands of labor and its unions, power that
had belonged to the bosses before. The Social Security Act
was passed. The TVA legislation was strengthened. The
AAA legislation was modified. Before June was over, father
saw through to its passage a powerful share-the-wealth tax
bill that called for new or increased estate, inheritance and
gift taxes, and individual and corporation taxes aimed at the
high-income group. Under fire from the right, he swerved to
the left to the point where he was called not only a socialist
but even a communist.

Meanwhile, the courts of the country were issuing injunc-
tions restraining the federal government from conducting its
business. The Supreme Court declared the AAA unconstitutional. It went on to invalidate many minimum-wage laws. If
father had acted hastily in some instances, the Supreme Court
seemed determined to outdo him.

Father held his anger in check. It was not the time to make
waves. He was a politician and it was time to campaign again.

In 1936 there was another presidential election. Father's popularity was such that reelection was certain, but he was taking
no chances.

It would be his first campaign without Louis Howe. The
asthma with which this frail little man was afflicted had worsened during 1934, and by 1935 he was coughing so badly that
he was confined to an oxygen tent. From his hospital bed, the
dedicated campaigner dictated tactics. In April of 1936 he died.
Farley filled in for Howe as father took command of his own
campaign.

I walked him to the platform to accept renomination in
Philadelphia's Franklin Field. Before one hundred thousand
spectators, the president said, "We have conquered fear. . . .
We have new problems to solve. . . . This generation has a
rendezvous with destiny." It was one of his greatest speeches
and drew an ovation that lasted a long time. Cabinet member
Harold Ickes called it the greatest political speech he had ever
heard. It swept father on a wave of voter approval across the
country.

The opposition of such radicals as Huey Long, Father
Coughlin and Dr. Townsend probably increased father's popularity. The opposition of the du Ponts and other big-business
interests probably increased his popularity, too. I believe the
Republicans conceded defeat. In nominating Kansas governor Alf Landon, they sent into battle a modest midwesterner
who would not embarrass them, but could not win for them.
He had homespun virtues, but had no national name and had
not the charismatic personality to compete. He was a man
pulled out of the crowd to compete with a star. He never had
a chance.

When one national poll had Landon ahead, Farley laughed
it off: "The poll was taken by telephone. The Democrats who
are going to vote for Roosevelt by the millions don't even have
phones." While father predicted a decisive victory, Farley
went further, saying only Maine and Vermont would go for
Landon. He hit it on the head. Later he laughingly altered the
saying "As Maine goes, so goes the nation" to "As Maine goes,

so goes Vermont." In addition to winning 46 of the 48 states and 523 of the 531 electoral votes, father pulled 27.7 million popular votes to 16.6 for his foe.

In his final campaign speech, at Madison Square Garden, father assumed almost dictatorial tones. He said, "I should like to have it said of my first administration that in it the forces of selfishness and lust for power met their match. I should like to have it said of my second administration that in it these forces met their master."

At father's second inauguration, in the rain, Chief Justice Hughes of the Supreme Court read with a heavy tone that part of the oath that has to do with supporting the Constitution. The justice sat a few feet from me, his expression masked, as father stood in front of me and delivered an address that challenged the Court. In part he said, ". . . We must find practical controls over blind economic forces and blindly selfish men. . . . I see one-third of a nation ill-housed, ill-clad, ill-nourished. . . . I assume the solemn obligation of leading the American people forward along the road over which they have chosen to advance."

Less than a month later he dictated a message designed to alter the antiquated attitudes of a Supreme Court consisting of, as he put it, "nine old men." Indeed, their average age was seventy. The president proposed, in order to inject new blood into the Supreme Court, to ease congestion in the Court and increase efficiency, that for every justice who did not retire within six months of reaching seventy, the president could appoint a new justice, up to a total of six. The message was clear.

Father's foes called it "court packing"—and in this case he had more foes than he expected. Not only did members of the opposition party and the conservatives in his own party oppose it, but also many liberals he considered to be on his side. And Hughes was a shrewd foe. As the fight continued in Congress, the Court first upheld the Wagner Labor Bill, then the Social Security Act. Clearly, the Court seemed to be saying that it was not opposed to progress, only to that which was unconstitutional or illegal. Last-minute compromises collapsed. Father's plan died.

It was, I suppose, the biggest blunder of his presidency, the best-remembered of his embarrassments. I might point out here that he did not devise the plan. It was devised by Homer Cummings, his attorney general, at the suggestion of Ben Cohen and Tommy Corcoran. I suppose it doesn't matter who thought of the plan; father believed in what Harry Truman later termed, "The buck stops here." Father never tried to pin the blame for administration mistakes on aides, nor did he ever try to hide beneath the blanket of ignorance. It was and is the president's job to know what is going on. Father had help. He accepted advice. He also accepted the responsibility for the acts of his administration.

I remember father's staff was hard hit by the initial ruling striking out the NRA, and by the probability of other rulings killing other New Deal programs. I remember Ben and Tommy persuading father that they had to act before all they had built up was torn down. I recall that father agreed: "Well, let's figure out a course of action," he said. And they called in Cummings to devise an act which would alter the complexion of the Court. They tried to cloak it in respectability by tying it in with a pay boost for the justices, but that fooled no one.

I don't think father really expected the weight of opposition that he provoked. I remember asking him how he expected to get the votes for this, and he replied, "I don't think it will be that hard, Jimmy. Basically, the idea is sound. It should improve the Court. Everyone should see that." I said that it was apparent most people were against packing the Court with his appointees. He said, "That isn't the thing we're really trying to do." I told him, "Well that's what most people think you're trying to do, no matter what Ben and Tommy and Homer may tell you." Father laughed and said, "Well that may be, but it's not so bad for a president to have his kind of people in the courts. It's the same as having his kind of people in the Congress. Without it, it's hard for him to do his job."

Which is true, of course. Supreme Court appointments are for life, excepting impeachment or retirement, and it does pose a problem when a president must deal with men of entirely opposite persuasions, appointed by previous presidents. If the timing is right, appointments can create a Court that is predominantly conservative operating in a liberal era, or vice versa.

On the other hand, I must be honest and admit I personally believe the system is the best one yet devised. Presidential appointment is apt to be a lot less political in nature than congressional appointment or public vote, though it still must win the approval of Congress. Once a justice is appointed, he is perfectly free to rise above politics. The Court can serve as a check on a runaway president or Congress, bringing balance into play. And I am against forced retirement, though sometimes a sticky situation may develop, such as the recent one when Justice Douglas resisted retirement until long after it was evident he was physically incapable of contributing to the Court. Once a justice passes a certain age, the other justices perhaps should vote periodically on his remaining active or retiring.

As it happened, although he lost, father made his point. In fighting him, the "nine old men," only two of whom had been appointed by a Democrat, took a liberal turn. Father took defeat with a grace that surprised me. When I went to him after it was over and asked how he felt, he said, "I feel fine, Jimmy. No one bats a thousand. My batting average is high. I have no complaints. We lost the battle, but I believe we won the war." He said, "I think the agencies that have been or will be abolished have served their purposes, and it is time to take another tack, anyway. I believe the Court will conduct itself in a more considered manner now. It never was designed to operate politically in opposing a president. It should restrict itself to considering the constitutionality of the matters brought before it. But it must keep pace with the times, too. If my opponents want to consider this a defeat, let them have that pleasure. I've had my victories, too, you know."

Father had great respect for many members of the Court—Judge Brandeis, for example. Father was not against the Court, per se. Besides, over the next few years the Court voted in favor of several of his pet programs, and in time retirements permitted him to appoint several liberals.

Father was especially sensitive to southern opposition to his plan; perhaps because of Warm Springs he considered himself an adopted son of the South. I remember when I was invited to address the University of Georgia. Although I was asked to make a "nonpolitical" speech, I went to father and asked him if there were any points he wished me to make that would be helpful to him. He laughed and, in the words of Truman, told me to "give 'em hell." He suggested I might speak on behalf of his Supreme Court plan, which I did. I don't think they liked it, but they let me get away with it.

When it came time to make his appointment, father selected a southerner who had spoken in sympathy for his plan—Hugo Black. Father did so without investigating him sufficiently, and the Congress swiftly approved the appointment of this fellow member of their club. Only a little later was it revealed that Black had been a member of the Ku Klux Klan, as he himself admitted later under fire. In his own defense, he pointed to his congressional record as a liberal who supported civil-rights issues, saying he had long ago disassociated himself from the Klan. As the storm subsided, father let it pass, an embarrassment to him. Black later reaffirmed his liberal stance by his Court votes on civil-liberties legislation, and he became one of the great justices. Perhaps father saw that in him earlier.

Father's performance in the area of civil rights was spotty. He had grown up in a society in which blacks were servants. He was at home in a segregated South. Two of his personal aides were southerners—Steve Early and Marvin McIntyre. Father felt he should help improve the position of the Negro in this country, but he was far less passionate about it than mother.

At the urging of Farley, mother had become an active First

Lady. She went out and met the people, representing father. She spoke for him wherever she went and returned to tell him of the reception she received and what she had observed. She even became the first First Lady to hold her own press conferences, speaking candidly to the people through the media, primarily about women's problems in the world. In time she even took to writing her own newspaper column, "My Day," as well as magazine articles and books, commissions obtained for her by Louis Howe.

One of mother's trips took her to Appalachia, where she was so appalled by the poverty she found in the mining and strike-ridden areas of West Virginia and Pennsylvania that she approached father to enlist his help. He pushed through the Subsistence Homestead appropriation of $25 million to put 25,000 families on farms, but no one knew how to do it. He put mother to work at Allendale, the pilot project, but although she worked desperately on behalf of "her baby," it was an impractical plan doomed to defeat by one problem after another. It was another of father's few embarrassments.

Along the way, Negro leaders pleaded with mother to have their people included in the project. She sought this, but was voted down. Outraged, her interest in the plight of blacks increased, though she was rebuffed repeatedly. She was unable to talk father or Frances Perkins into appointing a black to a high post. With Walter White, she fought for but failed to get one antilynching law after another through Congress. She had only lukewarm help from a husband who was frankly worried about antagonizing conservative congressmen from the South whose support he courted.

With Mary McLeod Bethune and with the support of one sympathetic cabinet member, Harold Ickes, mother did advance the cause of the NAACP nationally. When the DAR refused to let Marian Anderson use their auditorium in Washington, mother invited her to sing at the White House. And mother resigned from the DAR, even as she had resigned from the Colony Club in New York after it refused Elinor Morgenthau's application because she was Jewish. Miss Anderson wound up with an outdoor concert attended by seven-ty-five thousand people near the Washington Monument, though mother considered it tactful not to attend herself. You must remember, this was a different day. Father fought for minorities. He took to his side Jews and Catholics. Because his name sounded Jewish, he himself was suspected of being Jewish and was attacked for it as if it were a crime. He reacted not by denying the bigoted rumors spread by such columnists as Westbrook Pegler, but by laughing at them and allying himself with Jews. And when he and mother were attacked along the campaign trail as "nigger-lovers," he reacted by becoming more sympathetic to mother's concern for Negroes.

With the coming of war, father worked on behalf of equality for Negroes in war and defense service. But he did not work as hard as he might have, and the cause thus did not have the success it might have had. Had the temper of the times made it more expedient politically, I am sure he would have; he was motivated by politics as much as by humanity. But I would be less than honest with you if I claimed he made many humanitarian moves to help his black brothers, even when pressured by mother. I also would be less than honest with you if I claimed I shared my mother's passion in this matter at that time. I was not, as mother was, ahead of the times. I have worked hard on behalf of blacks since then. I believe in absolute equality for blacks and believe we have a long way to go. But it was the blacks who brought me to this, forcefully opening my eyes. On my own I might have remained blind to the bigotry of my day, as father was in his day.

It was not that father was afraid of a fight. Frankly, he could fight dirty, too. Politics sometimes is a dirty business. During his years of feuding with the Supreme Court, he fought to remove his opponents from Congress. In Georgia, he stood on a platform in front of Democratic Senator Walter George and announced that if he had a vote he would cast it for the senator's primary opponent. He even launched a campaign against Doc O'Connor's brother John, chairman of the House

Rules Committee. This one worked, too. Asked about this abuse of friendship, father chuckled and commented, "Doc didn't like his brother either."

When a deadlock developed between Alben Barkley of Kentucky and Pat Harrison of Mississippi in a battle for the leadership of the Senate, father interfered in a way that the executive branch was not supposed to interfere with the legislative. It has been written and is believed that father favored Barkley. The fact is, he couldn't have cared less. Father favored the fellow who would favor *him*. The "Dear Alben" letter he wrote Barkley was not, as supposed, a promise of support for him, but a warning that if Barkley did not do battle in father's behalf, father would not do battle on Barkley's behalf.

It is not generally known that Barkley was so outraged he threatened to resign. Father backed down and promised not to butt in where he did not belong. But he did butt in. When Farley refused to help for fear of antagonizing Congress, father had Tommy Corcoran and Harry Hopkins take up the fight. Among those pressured was Bill Dietrich, a senator from Illinois. Father had Hopkins telephone an ally, Boss Kelly of Chicago, who convinced Dietrich to shift his support to Barkley, who wound up winning by one vote.

The president does not have the power to control Congress, but, if he knows how, he can pressure it to some extent. For one thing, he can work through a congressional leader such as Sam Rayburn or Lyndon Johnson, who knew how to use power. Father knew how to use his power, and how to court congressmen. For instance, he did not try to force his projects on them, but sought their support. He would get an influential congressman to introduce a bill on his behalf and let the congressman get the credit for it, though father had fought for it from behind the scenes.

For instance, father would call a senator to the White House and say that he knew the senator favored this or that bill, and would the senator work with the president's people in the writing of it, guide them on it and introduce it for

them? This form of flattery worked wonderfully well. I remember Sam Rayburn sponsored one of father's electrifica-
tion bills and helped it pass. And it was Rayburn's name that
was on the bill, not anyone else's. Rayburn was no patsy,
though. I remember him telling me he was well aware of what
was going on, but he favored my father's approach over that
of other presidents, and so went along with it.

Nevertheless, father was often at odds with Congress. He
had pushed them too far too fast. During his second term,
after the Supreme Court had demonstrated he had not always
been right, our representatives started to rebel and it became
difficult for father to do what he wanted to. The honeymoon
had ended. With the disappearance of the NRA, AAA and
others, the government by initials for which he would
forever be famous was altering.

Depression pressure had eased, but had not disappeared.
There still was considerable unemployment and poverty in
the country. Economically, the business community was suffering a recession. Like most politicians, father had promised
a balanced budget on his initial inauguration. Asking an adviser how to alibi this at his second inaugural, he was told to
forget it.

"I learned the lesson that a politician is not expected to live
up to his promises," father laughed. "If I tried harder than
others, I was popular for it. I did try."

Father entered into deficit spending with a flourish. This
was right up his alley. Before he came along, government did
little more for the citizens than police them and send them to
war, build roads for them and deliver the mail. With father,
we achieved the kind of government where money is spent
freely to improve the lot of the people. This money, of course,
comes from the people. Father was the first president to put
his hand in the pockets of the citizens. He'd take from one
pocket in order to put into the other. Of course, some cash got
misdirected in between. But since the rich were not going to
give to the poor, father had to act as a go-between.

XI

It was the war, of course, that put industry into full production, brought about almost total employment and finally healed the ailing economic condition of this country. I feel my father kept the economy alive at a time it was failing, however. I doubt that it would have failed, but I also doubt that it could have made as complete a recovery without his programs.

The threat of war, which worried the world during his second term, became the great crisis here, too. Of course, there was already war in much of the world. Japan was at war with China. Fascist Franco was winning Spain's civil war. Fascist Mussolini's Italy was overrunning Ethiopia. And Hitler, who came to power in Germany about the same time father became president in this country, was mounting a mighty war machine. First Austria, then Czechoslovakia fell. After the Nazis rolled into Poland, England and France declared war. By the middle of 1940, Italy enlisted on Germany's side. Both sides courted Russia.

While father sought to mobilize this nation and to extend aid to our allies who were being overrun, he kept telling the people he hated war and had no intention of sending our sons to die on foreign battlefields. He was walking a narrow line, which worried the America-firsters and other isolationists,

including such top politicians as Robert Taft, such dema-
gogues as Father Coughlin and such American heroes as
Charles Lindbergh. They spoke out against our taking sides
in European and Asiatic affairs and warned the president not
to interfere in the problems of other nations.

Father was likened to a Wilson, "who was elected on a
platform of peace and served on a wagon of war." The Republicans referred to themselves as the "peace party" and to the
Democrats as the "war party." You must remember that we
were less than twenty years from World War I; our wounds
were not entirely healed and we were far removed from
Europe and Asia because travel and communications were
not what they are now. Father did not dare tell the citizens
that war was inevitable. We know now that it was; we did not
want to think about it then. Father simply made us think
about it without committing us to our inevitable course.

Occasionally father let slip his true feelings. Once, when he
met heavyweight boxing champion Joe Louis, he felt the
champ's muscles and said, "These are the kind of muscles we
need to defeat Hitler and the Nazis." Joe looked puzzled.
Asked about it later, he said, "I didn't even know we were
going to war."

When England entered the war, father said, "This nation
will remain a neutral nation, but I cannot ask that every
American remain neutral in thought, as well. Even a neutral
has a right to take account of facts. Even a neutral cannot be
asked to close his mind or his conscience." And he added, "I
have said, not once, but many times, that I have seen war and
that I hate war. I say that again and again. . . . As long as it
remains within my power to prevent, there will be no blackout of peace in the United States."

Slowly, tactfully, he was modifying his stand against war,
suggesting that forces were at work in the world which might
make it necessary for this nation to fight. When Italy entered
the war, he spoke strongly: "The hand that held the dagger
has stuck it into the back of its neighbor." He was saying we
dare not turn our backs on our enemies, even while he did not

dare say we must support our friends. Winston Churchill had pleaded with him, "Give us the tools and we will finish the job," but for the time being father's hands were tied.

He had, however, a clear view of where we were heading. After his reelection in 1940, he sent me on a secret mission to the Middle East. I will discuss it in more detail shortly, but for now let me just point out that it was designed to encourage our friends to hold on until we could help. I was sent not because I was the best man for the job, but because I could be trusted not to call attention to the situation.

Just before the election, the war worsened overseas to such a degree that father's reelection was all but guaranteed. He had gotten us through one crisis, and it was presumed that now he could get us through another. As it became clear that war really might be inevitable, it became easier for him to get bills through Congress to arm this country, to help arm and supply our allies, to draft our young men into service "just in case. . . ."

During this time I had a conversation with father in which I discussed the dishonesty of his stand on war. I have never spoken of it, but this is a good time to do so because we are dealing with the realities of his life and of politics.

Father said, "Jimmy, I knew we were going to war. I was sure there was no way out of it. I had to delay until there was no way out of it. I knew we were woefully unprepared for war and I had to begin a buildup for what was coming. But I couldn't come out and say a war was coming, because the people would have panicked and turned from me. I had to educate the people to the inevitable, gradually, step by step, laying the groundwork for programs which would allow us to prepare for the war that was drawing us into it.

"If I don't say I hate war, then people are going to think I don't hate war. If I say we're going to get into this war, people will think I want us in it. If I don't say I won't send our sons to fight on foreign battlefields, then people will think I want to send them. I do hate war. I don't want to send our men to war. I tried to say these things in such a way as to say we won't go to war until we have to go to war. Sometimes you have to deny your political opposition the paint they need to present the public the picture of you they want to show. You can't feed your enemies ammunition."

I remember father saying, "Jimmy, I would have loved to have said that as president I was in a position to know what was happening in the world much more than was the public or even the members of Congress, and that I can see we are going to have to go to war sooner or later with the fascist forces and we'd better build up for it fast and perhaps even attack before we are attacked. But I couldn't say that because the public and congressmen didn't want to hear it and so wouldn't have believed it and would have turned on me.

"There were those who saw that this was true and helped me, but I couldn't take every congressman into my confidence because he'd have run off the hill hollering that FDR is a warmonger. I couldn't say we needed Russia on our side to win the war, because Russia is not our kind of country and I couldn't be pictured as a communist sympathizer. But the reality of life is that as Great Britain needs the U.S., so we need Russia to help defeat a formidable foe. So you play the game the way it has been played over the years, and you play to win."

So, in answer to the basic question of whether or not a politician can be completely honest with the electorate, I suppose the answer is he cannot be. If he is, he will not get elected and he will lose his opportunity to do what he believes has to be done. I think every president from Washington through Lincoln and Wilson to Kennedy has sometimes said what he felt the people wanted to hear, rather than what he really wanted to say. The buck stops with you, and once you decide you have to fight in Vietnam, you do what you feel is right. You know that a lot of people are going to think it's wrong, but you don't give the people a chance to say it before you do it.

I think father believed he really was needed in 1940 when a new election was at hand. After all, he knew what was happening in the world as no one else did. But I also think he loved the power of the presidency and enjoyed the privileges and prestige of the office enormously and really didn't want to walk away from it. He couldn't walk away from it, of course. He would roll away in his wheelchair to a life as a cripple without an active part to play, and he didn't want that.

No one had ever served a third term as president. Precedent was against it, if not law. Later, of course, the law was changed to prohibit a third term—after father had been elected to a fourth term. I don't consider this law a slap at father. It is a good law. The incumbent has so much greater a chance to win than any challenger that a popular president like father might be elected as long as he lived, and this democracy was not designed to be ruled by one man. And if he is not as good a president as father was, then the country is in a bad situation.

Although father was slow to commit himself to running again in 1940, I don't think he ever had a doubt about it being what he wanted. Mother didn't want it. I didn't want it. None of us wanted it. He was not an old man—he was not yet sixty —but he was not a well man. The demands of the office are awful, and he seemed tired to us. He'd lost a six-month fight for his Supreme Court scheme, and for the past couple of years he'd been walking a hard middle road down a country divided by its worries over war.

Thus we argued against his running, but he just laughed at us. Elliott argued the hardest. He even went to the convention as a delegate from Texas and opposed father's vice-presidential preference, Henry Wallace, by seconding the nomination of his friend, Jesse Jones. Father laughed it off. His own aides argued against it. Farley was dead set against his running. Of course, Farley wanted it for himself. Garner was against it. Garner wanted it for himself, too. Cordell Hull was against it. Mother wanted it for Hull. Father admired Hull, too. But the one he really thought worthy of it was Harry Hopkins, and Hopkins was too ill to go after it. Had Hopkins been well and electable, father might have stepped aside. Even Missy was against his running.

In the end father, as usual, piloted his own ship. "I think I'm needed," he said to me one day. "And maybe I need it," he smiled.

Shrewdly, father named two Republicans to his cabinet just before the Republican convention. He named old Henry Stimson, a cabinet member of the Taft and Hoover regimes, secretary of war, and Frank Knox, Landon's running mate in 1936, secretary of the navy. What father was saying to the public was that in this time of crises we needed to be led by the best men, regardless of their parties. The GOP hollered "foul," of course, but no one listened. As the war drew closer, the isolationist stands of Tom Dewey and Bob Taft loomed less appealing. American sentiment was stirred by Britain's stand against the Nazis.

Dewey and Taft led the early balloting for the Republican nomination, but a boom began for a dark horse, the chant "We Want Willkie" filled the stadium, and Wendell Willkie won a stunning upset on the sixth ballot.

While he liked and admired Willkie more than any man he ever opposed, father still wanted to win. In Chicago, the Democratic conventioneers seemed confused until father hit them where they lived through Alben Barkley. Alben told the conventioneers he brought them a message from FDR. The president, Barkley said in his speech, wanted to make it clear that he wanted the best man to be the party's candidate and they should feel free to nominate the best man. That shaft of lightning touched off a thunderous response: "Roosevelt ... Roosevelt... Roosevelt." He was a winner, so they wanted him. What the devil did they care about precedent? Like father, they wanted to win.

Willkie carried on a splendid campaign, pulling in twenty-two million votes, more than any loser, more than any Republican, ever, but he lost. Father got twenty-seven million votes, just five hundred thousand or so less than the previous election, but five million more than in his first election. Father picked off 449 of the 538 electoral votes, too. He said, "I'm happy I've won, but sorry Wendell lost."

Years before, father had sent me to meet with Wendell Willkie, to have breakfast with him at my house, to feel him out and report back. I carried back a favorable report. The rumpled Hoosier was a wise, strong man, more like father than many members of father's own party. Years later Willkie, with father's blessings, went on his "One World" tour. At one time father even approached Willkie with the thought of developing a third party, a truly liberal party composed of the liberal members of the other two parties. Wendell was interested. Had not death intervened, I'm sure Willkie would have become one of father's cabinet members and maybe his ally in the revolutionary third-party scheme.

Father had a lot less respect for Garner, and dumped him prior to the third campaign. For a while the old Speaker was helpful to him as a liaison with Congress, but after a time he didn't work at it. He was content to sit back and enjoy his position, and to criticize the president and wait for his time in the sun to come. When he started to suspect father was going to go for a third term, the crusty Texan became bitter and had such battles with the president that father stopped inviting him to cabinet meetings. I think father felt there wasn't a whole lot to Garner. He was a politician, pure and simple, without the redeeming virtue of wisdom.

Accordingly, father turned to Wallace, an intellectual liberal father admired as much for his mind as his liberalism. There was some opposition to Wallace, but not enough to outweigh the president's wishes. Wallace had not at that time moved so far to the left as to be called, as he came to be called later, a "Communist." When that time came, father was enough of a politician to give in to the party's demands that Wallace, too, be dumped, because Wallace's public image had been damaged and he might be a handicap to father.

Although today it makes a president look bad to as much as admit he picked the wrong man as his running mate, in father's day, and with father's popularity, it did not hurt him.

He fought the good fight for Wallace, he wanted him again for his fourth term, but he gave up the fight when he felt it was wise in order to insure himself the full support of his party.

When the party powerful named Truman, I don't think father cared who they named. I remember he approved Harry as one of the possibilities, but left the decision to the party head. As I recall, he said, "I wish to blazes they'd make up their minds. It really doesn't make that much difference." Father was an old-fashioned president who felt that the president didn't need a vice-president. We know now that father was dying by then, but I don't think he suspected. He was going to be president four more years and he didn't care who was going to be waiting in the wings.

Father didn't give Harry anything to do. He didn't tell him anything; he seldom even saw him. He let him do ceremonial chores and let it go at that. I am certain that father was sufficiently in love with this country, which had four times made him its president, that if he'd known he was soon to die he would have briefed Truman about all that was happening in the war and the way the peace was being planned by 1944.

I don't think father realized Truman was as powerful a personality as he turned out to be. Father felt Harry had done some good work in the Senate, but he still regarded him as a product of Boss Prendergast's Missouri machine, which he was, and a small-town midwesterner who in no way was big enough to become president. I don't think father thought about him that much.

I think Mr. Truman expanded under the pressure of the presidency. After father died, Truman had to take over cold. He didn't even know about the atomic bomb, and I don't believe he realized how much it would mean when he was first told about it. Father probably didn't realize how much it would mean, either, when he first was approached about it, but he became convinced to the extent that he gambled many millions of this country's money on the Manhattan Project. He had to tell leading members of Congress about it or he could not have gotten so much money appropriated for it. The project was disguised under other headings, but he picked his colleagues carefully and they made it the best-kept secret of such consequence of our time.

It was another case where he could not level with the public. In order to hasten the end of the war, and because they had to beat other countries to it, he could not tell the public they were bankrolling a superbomb that could kill hundreds of thousands of innocent people in a single explosion. If he had told them, he might have seemed a monster. To this day, some say he was. Some say all connected with that most lethal of weapons and most dangerous of devices were and are monsters. But at a time when hundreds of thousands of our soldiers were being killed in a war we did not start, the use of any powerful weapon which might turn the tide seemed wise.

On his third election, father said, "We must be the great arsenal of democracy. For us this is an emergency as serious as war itself." When war came with the Japanese attack on Pearl Harbor on December 7, 1941, he called it "a day that will live in infamy." He said, "With confidence in our armed forces, with the unbounded determination of our people, we will win the inevitable triumph, so help us God."

I feel, and I think most people feel, he led us to that triumph. He made mistakes. We made mistakes. They made mistakes. Wars sometimes seem to be won not by the men who do not make mistakes but by those who make the fewest. Father did not name men he liked to military leadership, but men whose work he admired. I think he thought of men like Eisenhower and MacArthur and Patton and Nimitz and Halsey and Arnold as military men who could lead.

I know he thought Admiral King the wisest of his staff of military men. I remember him being asked why he kept King in the White House instead of sending him up front to take command. He said, "The president has to have close to him the shrewdest of strategists. Most critical decisions must be made here. You don't send these men into the front lines where their lives may be endangered."

I also know father thought Marshall the wisest of his generals. But when I asked him why then did he make Eisenhower commander in chief, he said, "Eisenhower is the best politician among the military men. He is a natural leader who can convince men to follow him, and this is what we need in his position more than any other quality." Which, of course, was particularly astute in view of Ike's political successes later, though his administrations were not noted for remarkable wisdom.

I think father also thought of himself as a politician who could get men to follow him. I think he thought he could handle Stalin and Churchill as no one else in this country could. I think he thought that, left to their own devices, there would have been war between Britain and Russia. From things he said to me, I know he liked and respected Churchill, though they came from such different backgrounds and were such different personalities that at times Churchill frustrated him terribly. I don't think father liked or respected Stalin, but I think he trusted him for a while, maybe longer than he should have, and he never gave up the conviction he could convince old Joe to go our way.

In father's last days, near the end of the war, he was accused of giving Stalin too much in settling on peace terms. In light of later developments, maybe he did. He thought of Russia as an ally who was entitled to her share of the victory, which she certainly was. There was no way we could have fought side by side with Russia and then expect Stalin to ask nothing in return for his country's sacrifices, no matter the differences in our ideologies.

In 1944 there was no reason for father to feel he should not continue in the presidency. He was not well, but he had not been well for a long time. He felt he could continue to serve, no matter what Jim Bishop or others suggest in books blessed by hindsight. Father was weary, but we were at war, this was no time to change leaders. His slogan was "You don't change horses in midstream." By then we were winning, and he was the man we wanted to carry us to our ultimate triumph. I had been in the front lines far from the White House, and I thought less frequently of him as my father than I did as our leader. I trusted his leadership.

He may have been weary, but he still had his sense of humor. Accused of sending a ship to fetch Fala, his Scottie, he said, "These Republican leaders have not been content with attacks on me or on my wife or on my sons. Now they attack my little dog, Fala." And he laughed and the country laughed with him. He was a strong enough man to smile during a storm, and he had the sort of humor that helped our fighting men at the front endure. He was a fighter. He was symbolic of what was best in the fighting spirit of this country.

Father did not like Tom Dewey, who gave him a hard fight because so many really were worried about the wisdom of a fourth term. He considered Dewey a small man, so he fought him and defeated him. Father pulled in 25.6 million popular votes to 21.9 for Dewey and won 432 of the 531 electoral votes. At his inaugural he told me, "I am glad I won because I would not have wanted that man to win. I can lead the country as he could not. If they had put up a man I admired more, I might not have worked so hard. I am tired, Jimmy. But I have worked hard and I have won."

I think my father was the right man at the right time. If he was dictatorial, he came along at a time the nation needed that sort of leader. He was a wise man, if not an intellectual, and gave the country commonsense leadership at a time when someone had to make sense out of confusing situations. He had the sort of personality that appealed to people and led them to trust him, and at this time they desperately needed someone to trust. He was a practical politician who was able to get elected and get his programs passed and keep the machinery moving when it was most needed. He was a father figure and he gave his "children" of this country the sort of upbringing that enabled us to survive the most severe crises.

He was, as I have said, imperfect. I think when we look back we feel the internment of Japanese-Americans in the interior of this country, away from the West Coast, was a shameful episode in our history. He approved that. But looking at it from the point of view of that time we must remember that we had been victimized by a sneak attack by Japan even while Japan was talking to us about peace. We were right for fearing acts of sabotage by Japanese living here. Few protested the move. Maybe we would not do such a thing again.

It is easy now to say it was wrong to drop the atom bomb on two Japanese cities, Hiroshima and Nagasaki, and I think we all were completely dismayed by the suffering that ensued, but you must remember there was little objection to it at the time. If it beat Japan to her knees, then it was worthwhile. I believe that my father might have tried, as Truman did not try, to demonstrate the destructiveness of the bomb to Japanese leaders in some isolated spot before unleashing it on cities packed with innocents. But how would he have done this? Told them, so they could have shot down the bomber? And what if the bomb had not worked in its test run? We did not know it would. And had it not, the first time, no one would have known about it. But after it did work, I wonder why they had to hit that second city. I like to think my father would not have ordered the second bombing, but I do not know.

I do know that father planned to use the bomb, a fact which has been subject to question up until now. I learned about it when he brought me back from the South Pacific to play a part in his fourth inauguration, as I had in his first three. When I embraced him, I was overcome with the sentiment of the moment and tears came to my eyes. I must be honest; I was thinking of my possible death, not his, which I did not know was so close. When he asked kindly about my emotion, I said simply that although we were winning, we still had a lot of fighting to face and I could not know I would be coming back; that the invasion of Japan, for example, was bound to be bloody.

He said, softly, "James, there will be no invasion of Japan. We have something that will end our war with Japan before any invasion ever takes place." When I asked him what it was, he said, "I am sorry, even though you are my son, I cannot tell you. Only those who need to know, know about it. But it is there, it is something we can use and will use if we have to, something we certainly will use before you or any of our sons die in an invasion of Japan." He smiled and said, "So you come back to me, son."

I came back, but when I got there, he was gone.

XII

Because he was president longer than any other man and because so many men served with him so long, many of the men close to father became almost as famous as he was. The names of Louis Howe, Jim Farley, Cordell Hull, Harold Ickes, Harry Hopkins, Henry Wallace and several others remain better known today than those of others who played similar roles for other presidents in the years since. I served several years as father's secretary in the White House and, accordingly, got to know many of these personalities better than had I known them as only occasional guests at our home.

Smoking, coughing, sloppy, curt, Howe wanted desperately to be father's first presidential press secretary, but father felt him unfit for this public position, never offered it to him and to the best of my knowledge never had the heart to tell him why. Instead, father picked Steve Early as his press secretary and Marvin McIntyre as his appointments secretary. Missy LeHand, of course, was his personal secretary, assisted by Grace Tully.

Suffering failing health, Howe, who more than any other man was responsible for father reaching the presidency, drifted into the background of father's presidency, plotting reelection strategy, but dying before father's reelection. No one ever really took his place. Father had friends and advisers whose counsel he sought and sometimes followed, but no one came close to playing the role Louis had played for him. Father plotted his own strategy after Louis died.

Farley, who remained as party chairman and had been handed the plum of postmaster general after father's election, assumed a leading role in the president's private circle, but father never permitted him to play the sort of part Howe had. Howe, not father, had brought Farley onto the team. Both men admired Farley as a practical politician. Father liked Farley; he liked his warmth and frankness. He called Farley "a good guy."

But he seldom broke bread with him. He and mother were not friendly with the Farleys as they were with the Howes. Father knew Bess Farley didn't like him, and he resented it. He also resented the fact that she would not move from New York to Washington. Father never felt that Farley was unselfishly on his side as Howe had been. It was selfish of father, but he resented Farley's personal political ambitions.

When Farley told father he did not feel he should run for a third term in 1940 and could not support him because he wanted the nomination himself, father never forgave him. He replaced him as party chairman with Ed Flynn of the Bronx, an old friend. Mother was one of the main movers behind Flynn's selection. Farley, of course, fell apart politically.

Harry Hopkins came much closer to filling Louis Howe's shoes, but Harry was father's protégé, while father had been a protégé of Howe's. Harry was an earthy guy out of Sioux City, Iowa, and father delighted in polishing his rough edges, but Harry also had an exceptional intelligence. They met while Harry was working on welfare programs in New York, and father put him to work heading relief programs in Washington. It was Harry who worked out the work-for-relief concepts of the CCC and WPA. Later he served as secretary of commerce.

Father and Hop became pals—"Harry the Hop" as father called him. Father trusted him and respected his advice. He didn't even mind that Harry, too, wanted to be president. Father figured if he had to have a successor, he'd name Harry himself. But it wasn't to be, because father never stepped aside. Instead he sent Harry to England and Russia as his personal representative and had him by his side as his personal aide at Yalta and other conferences during the war.

Hopkins didn't get along with Harold Ickes—but then, no one ever got along with Ickes. Personally, I liked Ickes, but he was a hard man to like. He didn't like many people, including me. He was a very jealous man and he resented the hold I had on my father. He felt, rightly, that it came from blood, not sweat. He especially resented those times my father chose my ideas over his. But he sold my father on more things than I ever did. He headed up the PWA and resented conflicts which arose with Hopkins's WPA.

Hopkins, in turn, resented Ickes because he wasn't one of the "team." Ickes was one of the Republicans my father named to the cabinet. But he was a liberal Republican, and he was a real help to father because he had guts and didn't care what others thought of him. Several times I heard father ask Harold's opinion of some unusual scheme. Harold would usually say it was ridiculous. But father would say, "Well, I want you to present it to the public." And Harold would answer, "Well, explain it to me, then." And he'd present it. If it was accepted, fine. And if it wasn't, it was brushed off as another of Harold's brainstorms.

Ickes, father's secretary of the interior, was head of the PWA almost all of father's administration because he did a good job with it. Father admired him, and he was one of the few aides whose home father frequently visited. Ickes had a wife who was more attractive, much younger and much more liberal than he. She and father hit it off. Father could go there and play cards and let his hair down. Presidents don't visit in other people's homes a lot, but they do a little without publicizing it.

Jim Farley once told me he had sat next to Ickes at meetings for a year and a half and never said one word to him. Hopkins and Ickes, however, had a lot to say to each other, and both could be sarcastic and stubborn.

Father didn't mind conflict in his cabinet. He liked his

people to be independent and aggressive and he enjoyed the intramural skirmishes. He once said, "A good squabble keeps you on your toes. If a man won't speak his mind, I have no way of knowing if he has anything there."

Ickes spoke his mind. Originally an isolationist, he was one of the first to recognize the real threat of Hitler and to urge father to act. He was one of those who sided with father in his early efforts to mobilize this country.

Ironically, Ickes joined Farley and others of the party powerful in opposition, first, to father's third-term ambitions, and then to his selection of Wallace as his running mate. The fact is, while Farley wanted to be president, Ickes wanted to be vice-president—at least. Unlike Farley, however, Ickes did not depart the presidential party after the row.

Nor did Jesse Jones, though he might as well have. He also sought the vice-presidential nomination, and he not only opposed father's wishes on this, he opposed father. The Texas banker allied himself with the isolationists and fought father on issues of preparedness and aid to our allies. He was one of Elliott's Texas gang. After Garner folded at the convention, Elliott switched his support to Jones. When Jones folded, too, Elliott was out in left field. He had opposed father and lost. While they remained father and son, I don't think feelings were ever the same between them. Garner lost his hold on the Texas Democrats to Sam Rayburn. And Elliott's hopes for power in this part of the country caved in.

Originally, Jones headed up the RFC for father. In that position he became the most influential financial figure in the country. He fought with federal funds to break Wall Street's hold on the banks. Later he succeeded Harry Hopkins as secretary of commerce. He was a smart man who outsmarted himself. Father respected his ideas and listened to him and gave him a lot of authority until the 1940 convention. After that Jones lingered in the administration a few years, feuding fiercely with Wallace, until father finally fired him, replacing him with Wallace.

Jones was one of the few people father ever fired—or forced

to resign. For the most part he picked his aides shrewdly. He did not seek an all-star team of strangers; he preferred lesser fellows if they were good at what they did and he felt he could work with them. Father was more a man of action than of ideas, and accordingly he brought into his brain trust and cabinet mostly shrewd, tough men who were not afraid to fight. When they fought each other, he sometimes refereed, but more often he just sat on the sidelines and watched with impish amusement. His was not an intellectual group, as, say, was John Kennedy's. But father did have a few intellectuals in his group, such as Raymond Moley, Rexford Tugwell, Adolf Berle, Sam Rosenman and Bob Sherwood.

One of the first of father's brain trust to depart the team was Raymond Moley, the brilliant journalist who coined the term "New Deal" for father's first speech. A Columbia University professor, this cultured man was basically a conservative, but he thought he saw in father a man with whom he could create a partnership in power between big business and the government that could contribute to the country's stability. Father, however, preferred that government dominate big business. He admired Raymond's mind, but could not accept many of his ideas. He thought Raymond stuffy, and he would tease him. After an argument one night near the end of father's first term, Moley flew the coop to become a critic of the administration.

Others came and went—Bill Douglas, Robert Jackson, Isador Lubin. Most stayed. Rex Tugwell was an intellectual who remained. A noted economist who taught at leading universities and wrote books, he had advised Al Smith on agricultural problems and father brought him to Washington to serve in the Department of Agriculture. Tug was active in programs to improve the lot of farmers and farm laborers in those days, and he headed the Resettlement Administration, which sought to relocate farmers. He helped shape New Deal economic and industrial legislation. He was extremely active as an adviser to father during his first two terms and remained available to him in the 1940s after Rex became governor of

Puerto Rico. But father never felt close personally to Tug-well, who gave him ideas, but no warmth.

The same could be said for Adolf Berle, who was the youngest lawyer ever to graduate from Harvard and earned about every degree available there. A law professor at Columbia, he was recruited to father's team by Ray Moley. But though he served as special counsel to the RFC and later as an aide in Latin American affairs, he refused permanent posts.

By contrast, father considered Sam Rosenman a friend as well as an adviser and, accordingly, felt closer to him and made use of him and his ideas. Sam remained father's chief speech writer and trusted counsel throughout father's administration. When he died, I wrote his widow my regrets. Sadly, it turns out I was the only one from the family to write. Others forgot what he and others like him meant to father. He was a man of exceptional intelligence, but he did not have the mannerisms of an intellectual. He did not talk constantly of books he had read which father had not read. Father felt comfortable with him.

Bob Sherwood was added to polish speeches, and in the process he gave advice, too. What other president ever had an award-winning playwright as a speech writer? Sherwood admired father and wanted to work for him. He was not a full-time member of the team, but he was an important one. Rosenman wrote what father wanted to say and Sherwood was the technician who polished it to perfection. Together they contributed considerably to father's appeal to the public. By shaping what he said, they shaped what he was.

Father was friendly with Rosenman from their days together in Albany. He also was friendly with Tommy Corcoran, who jumped aboard early. The two were key figures in what was called "the kitchen cabinet," a brain trust that performed its function informally, as often over sandwiches in the living quarters as in some smoke-filled room in the working area of the White House. "The Cork" was a smiling Irishman with an attractive tenor voice and he told jokes and sang songs at family affairs. For this reason outsiders called him the "court jester." But he was much more. When it was time to get to work he was an important part of the team. He contributed wit and humanity to the discussions. He was a smart lawyer, young and aggressive, and he swiftly learned the ropes in Washington and wound up pulling a lot of strings for father.

Corcoran and Ben Cohen were called "The Gold Dust Twins" by political columnists. Ben lacked Corcoran's charisma, but he was brilliant and he plotted many of father's attacks on problems of the period. Father respected Ben's brilliance, and for a time Cohen and Corcoran were the two men closest to the president. But after a while Hopkins succeeded both of them. Allied with father, they also fought for father's favor, these varied aides of his. But "Pa" Watson was one who did not have to fight for favor. He was father's pal and his hunting and fishing companion. Originally his military aide—Colonel Edwin Watson—he became much more, a member of the inner circle. When wrangling erupted over the vice-presidential choice at the 1940 convention, father, listening to the radio with Watson at the White House, angrily wrote out his resignation and handed it to Watson. Watson took it to Rosenman and together they talked father out of doing something he really did not want to do. The resignation was crumpled up. Watson's strength was that he wanted only to serve father.

Bernie Baruch has been called an adviser, but he really was less. He got to father through mother. He flattered her and contributed to her causes. But I remember dining with him one night when he sparred with me in search of the least he could give her for some cause and still get gratitude in return. He had made a lot of money in Wall Street, but when he became an adviser to Wilson he found his true calling and wanted to advise everyone about everything, especially presidents. Hoover received him more warmly than father did. Later Truman gave Baruch a post at the United Nations.

It was Winchell who made an immortal of Bernie. He pictured him sitting on a bench in Lafayette Park, feeding the pigeons while waiting for the most powerful people in the world to come sit beside him and find out how they should run the world. Frankly, father considered that a grandstand play. "There's Bernie on the bench, the star on stage," he would say. Winchell billed Bernie as father's secret adviser, but father wouldn't take his advice. He considered Baruch smart, but he didn't trust him.

One of the funniest scenes I ever witnessed was a banquet Bernie attended with mother. Bernie kept falling asleep, and mother kept nudging him so he would awaken and applaud at the right time. After a while it was mother's turn, and she grabbed a few winks while Bernie nudged her at appropriate times. Obviously, they had worked out an agreement and it was successful.

Mother used to beg father to bring Bernie home for dinner and let him have his say and pay him some respect, but father would say, "Oh, let Jimmy do it," so I'd have to go and pay father's respects to Bernie. Bernie didn't like it, but it was better than nothing and he couldn't be sure I wouldn't carry back his words of wisdom to the president. It was always a difficult chore for me. Bernie was supposed to be hard-of-hearing. He'd manipulate his hearing aid so you'd think he hadn't heard something you said. But after a while I learned he heard what he wanted to hear.

Working both sides of the fence, Bernie did betray mother later by arranging meetings between his South Carolina neighbor, Lucy Mercer Rutherfurd, and father. Despite his advanced age, Bernie always liked the ladies. He was close to mother, father's mother and father's former lady friend, which was quite a parlay.

Mother was part of father's "kitchen cabinet" and did play a part in his decision-making, even if he didn't always sympathize with her causes. It is not generally known, but on the day of the nominating speeches at the presidential convention in 1932, she wrote Marion Dickerman that she couldn't bear to think of herself as a president's wife out in that bright spotlight and didn't want to live in the White House. Nancy

Cook, Marion's friend, showed the letter to Louis Howe, who ripped it up and made her swear to keep the contents from father. He never found out.

After his election, mother also confided to her friend Lorena Hickok that she never wanted to be a president's wife. And yet she may have been the best. She was the first First Lady to hold press conferences. In fact she held her first press conference two days before father held his first as president. She did so to ease the demand on her for individual interviews, but she avoided discussion of directly political topics. However, from the time beer was made legal again—the first of the thrusts that would lead to the repeal of Prohibition— and she announced at her regular press conference that she would serve it in the White House, hard news with a political angle began to emerge from these sessions.

Later she began to do magazine articles, magazine and newspaper columns ("My Day") and even books. While these were not purely political, they had a political impact. Father was aware of this. He edited her book *This Is My Story* rather ruthlessly and would have edited, or had written for her, the columns and articles in his favor if she had given him the opportunity. But she was becoming independent. When there were complaints about her receiving $1000 an article, she ignored them because she did not consider the complaints justified. I doubt that today a president's wife would be permitted to receive pay for articles unless she donated the cash to charity, but mother treasured her private income. She did give much of it away, but only as she wished.

Mother maintained an incredible pace as she traveled representing her husband. She seemed to pop up everywhere. A *New Yorker* cartoon of the period depicted a coal miner deep in a shaft looking up in surprise to see her. "Why, it's Mrs. Roosevelt," he said. Meant as a joke, it became reality when she went into the mines in West Virginia to see for herself the harsh working and living conditions the Appalachian people were subjected to.

She always seemed to be leaving on or returning from some

trip, but she always picked up information to pass on to father and he listened to her reports, having grown to respect her wisdom. He appreciated the fact that she made him look a lot more liberal than he really was.

As I said earlier, it was largely through mother's influence that Frances Perkins became the first woman member of a presidential cabinet. A social worker and reformer, she had been a member of New York State industrial commissions under Al Smith and had impressed mother. Although mother always said, "Now, I don't want to butt in, Franklin . . ." mother made suggestions which he sometimes approved. At her suggestion he appointed "Ma" Perkins state industrial commissioner when he was elected governor, and U.S. secretary of labor when he became president.

Frances was a bit of a busybody—she had something to say about everything—and she had no sense of humor. Father liked to tease people who had no sense of humor in an effort to get a rise from them. More than once he teased "Ma" until she rose in righteous indignation. She was a stuffy sort and we used to laugh about the little hats she wore. But she was a good person.

Much like a benevolent boss, father was for the working-man, but not for labor unions, really, so the workingmen liked him and the labor leaders didn't. Frances soothed a lot of troubled waters for him. She authored a great deal of labor legislation for him. And she helped draft the Social Security Act. She served throughout his administration and was one of its most effective members.

Father did not make all of his cabinet appointments on merit, no more than does any president. All were not permitted to play important parts in his administration. All were not noteworthy. He regretted some he made. He repaid Bill McAdoo's support by making McAdoo's man, Dan Roper, secretary of commerce, and later called him "as comical as a crutch." Father made deals to get what he wanted. When "Cotton Ed" Smith of South Carolina was blocking Rex Tugwell's nomination in the Senate as undersecretary of agriculture, father got him passed with a bit of patronage, naming one of Smith's men a U.S. marshal. Unfortunately, the fellow had been charged with homicide at one time. Meeting Tugwell, father announced cheerily, "Today I got you in trade for a murderer."

Father named Bill Woodin secretary of the treasury as much to repay a campaign contribution as anything else. Father liked him, though, and he liked father. An accomplished musician, Woodin used to take his violin to work at the White House because playing it during breaks relaxed him. I remember during some of those all-night sessions in the first hundred days father would say, "Will, why don't you get out that violin of yours and play it for us?" And Will would get it out and play it while everyone relaxed.

As secretary of the treasury, Woodin didn't do much. Father's fellow Grotonian, Dean Acheson, then a young and ambitious man, filled in for him frequently as undersecretary. But Acheson ran afoul of father by refusing to sign an order devaluating the dollar in 1933. He told father it was someone else's job, not his. Father told Woodin that if Acheson didn't resign, he'd be fired. Woodin told Acheson, suggesting a straight letter of resignation without a carbon copy.

Acheson wrote the resignation, but he included his reasons for quitting and he kept a carbon. When Woodin, himself ailing, resigned later and Acheson attended the ceremonial swearing-in of Woodin's successor, Henry Morgenthau, father admitted to me he was "flabbergasted" at Acheson showing up but admired the man's aplomb. It tickled his fancy. He grinned at Acheson and later shook his hand and complimented him on his "good sportsmanship."

Morgenthau was one of the men closest to father during his lifetime. Born to wealth, he was a gentleman farmer and a neighbor of father's in the Hudson Valley. Father and Henry's father had a bad experience when they invested in coin-operated machines at one time—another of father's frequent bad investments—and father came to think of the old man as smart, but shady. He thought the younger Morgenthau was completely honest, but less smart. However, mother was fond of Henry's wife. They worked together in women's politics and the two families became close. Father made Henry business manager of his first gubernatorial campaign, then an agricultural administrator, first as governor, then as president. Henry played a part in trade deals with Russia and supported father's radical policies regarding gold. He soon was moved into the Treasury, becoming secretary in 1934.

I think father wanted to be his own secretary of the treasury so he picked someone who would do his bidding. Frankly, I think father thought of Henry as a loyal dog who would do as he was told. Henry *was* loyal; he'd do anything for father and did little for himself. Henry was also stuffy, so father teased him a lot, and since his feelings were easily hurt, he was constantly resigning. Father never accepted the resignations, so Henry never left.

Traditionally, father's "Cuff Links Club" played poker the night Congress closed shop. They played until the Speaker of the House called to say that unless the president had any pressing business, Congress would adjourn.

One such night Henry was far ahead but couldn't cash in his chips until the traditional adjournment. Father whispered to me to telephone a message to the Speaker, then Congressman Bankhead of Alabama. I did so.

The Speaker's call came at nine. Since I had warned him, he was not surprised when father said loudly, "Why, Mr. Speaker, you mean you have to stay in session at least another hour? Well, all right, I'll be right here." Turning back to the table, he said, "Deal the cards."

A disappointed Morgenthau dealt. And started to lose. When he had lost everything, I slipped away and telephoned father on the pretext I was the Speaker announcing adjournment at last. It was after ten and Henry was busted when the game broke up.

The next morning when he read in the newspaper that Congress had adjourned at nine on schedule, he flew into a rage and resigned again. Again, it was not accepted.

In time father did come to feel that Morgenthau was a pretty smart fellow after all, and he'd sound him out about different matters and respect his commonsense approach. Henry was one of those few who recognized the threat of war from Nazi Germany and other fascists as early as father did, and Henry actually authored the Lend Lease Act, which finally provided real help to those countries that would be our allies.

Henry was not easy to live with, however, because he was possessive about father. He courted father's approval at every turn and resented my place alongside father. We never got along because of this. He also resented Harry Hopkins's place alongside father, knowing he could never replace Harry. And he resented Harold Ickes's efforts to replace Hopkins. Old Henry and the abrasive Ickes had many shouting matches, battling bitterly over the years, yet Henry, like Harold, remained for the duration. (The amount of loyalty father pulled from opposing personalities really is astonishing.) Henry did change over the years though. In fact, after his wife died he married a younger, more beautiful lady and became quite the social butterfly.

I suppose it is of no importance, but I am struck by the similarities in the names of many of father's associates— Henry Morgenthau, Henry Wallace, Harold Ickes, Harry Hopkins, Harry Truman. I don't suppose you can include Louis Howe and Cordell Hull in there, can you?

Hull had been a judge and a congressman and chairman of the Democratic National Committee in the 1920s. A member of the House of Representatives, he was elected to the Senate in 1932 but did not serve, resigning to serve as father's secretary of state instead. He served twelve years. Father really respected the small-town Tennesseean and he wanted to repay the power Hull had wielded on father's behalf in Congress.

However, to contradict what Elliott said in his second book, father never really respected Hull's knowledge of foreign affairs. He felt Hull came from the sort of background that did not prepare him to be an internationalist. For this reason father made Ray Moley undersecretary of state and had him handle many international matters. In fact he sent Ray, not Cordell, to an important international monetary conference in London early in his administration. And when Ray returned, father had him report directly to the charter boat on which we were taking a vacation cruise along the coast of Maine.

Hull was hopping mad that father had sent Moley and raised hell, threatening to quit. But he didn't. When father didn't want people to quit, they didn't.

When, to father's disappointment, he saw that he and Moley just weren't in agreement and Moley left, Hull did take command—as much as father would let him. Our foreign policy really was father's. He did not even include Hull in some of his wartime Big Three conferences. Father wanted Hull as his running mate in 1940 because Hull was willing to stay in the background. Father never considered Cordell presidential stuff, though mother and some others did.

Father never gave a hoot about the chain of command which so many politicians live by. If he wanted to see someone, he saw him; he didn't make a request through channels.

At one point, long before the war, father had Colonel Evans Carlson assigned to China, instructing the marine to look into the communist setup there and the ways we might wage a war in the Pacific. Father even set up a mailing system so Carlson could report to him directly.

The brass knew nothing of it, and when they found out about it they were furious. They made life in the marines so difficult for Evans that he actually left the service for a while, though he returned when war came. I wound up serving under him as his exec in Carlson's Raiders.

I believe Carlson's reports made father distrust Chiang Kai-shek at a time when others thought father should be supporting him. At any rate, father felt the assignment was worthwhile and he didn't care whether the generals resented his bypassing the chain of command.

Father appointed an old Harvard classmate, Sumner Welles, as undersecretary of state. Welles had worked in government for many years in ambassadorial roles and later helped set up our Good Neighbor policy with South American countries. A formal person, he seemed to father suited to an international role, and he took on many assignments that normally would have been Hull's. Accordingly, Welles and Hull quarreled regularly. This didn't disturb father, who considered Hull and Welles an ideal team—one a man of the people, the other a man of the world.

Later, Averell Harriman went on many missions for father that normally would fall to members of the State Department. Heir to a railroad fortune, Averell added to the fortune in railroading, ship construction and banking. Harry Hopkins brought him into the Roosevelt administration as administrator of the NRA, and Averell served in other offices after that. Building on a business relationship he had developed with Russia he was the ideal man to be ambassador to the Soviet Union. He represented father in difficult dealings with Stalin and Churchill.

George Marshall was more than a military man, of course; he was a brilliant man. I think the Marshall Plan was one of the most effective political plans conceived on an international level. And Averell Harriman administered it marvelously well, though it is interesting he did not administer the FDR Memorial Commission especially well later on.

A brilliant man, Averell filled ambassadorial roles later for presidents Truman, Kennedy and Johnson. In between he served as governor of New York before being beaten by Rockefeller, who also served father as an administrator for Latin-American affairs in the 1940s. Harriman was a low-key kind of fellow. If he'd been more aggressive he might have attained greater heights. At one time he made a slight bid for the presidency, and he might have been a good president. He would have been a good secretary of state for father, but maybe father didn't want one that good.

Bill Bullitt, a charming chap who found favor with the

family, served father as ambassador to, first, Russia, then France. Bill wanted to be secretary of state, but father felt that he lacked stature.

According to Elliott, in his second book, Bill set up Sumner Welles for public disgrace. Welles was married but rumored to be bisexual. On a trip to the Midwest he was taken from a train by police on the charges of a porter that Welles had made homosexual advances to him. Welles believed Bullitt had bribed the porter, and father may have believed Welles. In any event father took no action. And no charges ever were pressed.

To my knowledge, father never spoke of it. He did not mention it to me, and Elliott does not say father spoke of it to him. It may be that father didn't want to know about it. He was not the sort to proceed on rumors. He would not have wanted a man's career to be ruined because of rumors. As far as father was concerned, a man's private life was his own business. As long as he did father's business well, that was all father wanted from him.

When Welles resigned before the year was out, father felt he had lost an important aide. At seventy-four, in ill health, Hull resigned the next year. Ed Stettinius stepped up, but never swung weight.

Lesser members of the team, the secretaries—Missy Le-Hand, Grace Tully, Bill Hassett, Marvin McIntyre and Steve Early—swung weight by the ton. Missy saw father more than any other single person; he respected her and she had his ear. While for the most part she devoted herself simply to doing his bidding, of necessity she had to take on a lot on her own. With Grace's help, Missy screened some of father's visitors and contributed to some of his correspondence.

Marv McIntyre did most of the screening of visitors. He learned who father wanted to see and who he did not want to see. He also knew who father had to see, whether he wanted to or not, and often made persistent and pointed suggestions along these lines. If he felt father had hurt someone's feelings, someone he didn't want to offend, Marv might suggest that father invite the fellow in for a visit. Father often followed Marv's suggestions.

Bill Hassett had a curious job. Originally he was a sort of chief clerk: It was his job to keep track of important papers; he was responsible for getting papers to the people who were supposed to sign them, getting them signed and back where they belonged. He ran between the White House and the Hill, got to know everyone and became increasingly important. Eventually he became a secretary, somewhere between Missy LeHand and Steve Early, but actually he was a historian; he kept track of the records. Father had a feeling for history and his place in it, and he wanted to leave behind something like the Franklin Delano Roosevelt Memorial Library which stands today in Hyde Park.

(As an aside, it is interesting to note that there is material in Hyde Park which has never been opened and, by father's will, is not due to be opened for years. It is difficult to defend Richard Nixon, but I might point out here that he was not the only president who did not want all that took place in his office made public. Father was another one who felt he was entitled to privacy even in the presidency. It is easy to say the presidency belongs to the public, but it is hard to approve putting a spotlight on any man's every word and gesture. We all say things to one man we would not say to another. We sometimes use words we should not use. We go one way, change our minds and decide to go another way. It seems to me a president, as much as any other person, should be judged on what he does, not on how and why he does it.)

Steve Early's job was one of the most difficult in Washington, but it was not as difficult for Steve as it was for his successors. The press secretary is on the firing line; he is the link between the president and the press, and the press and the public. He is subjected to questions he may not be able to answer or may not want to answer. He sometimes is an apologist, covering up problems that the press is determined to uncover. The resulting friction between the presidential press secretary and the press often causes sparks and touches off fires on both sides.

However, Early did not have to do father's job for him. Father was his own press secretary to a great extent. Father held almost a thousand press conferences when he was in the White House. As for frequency, possibly only John Kennedy later came close to it.

By contrast, Richard Nixon went many months between press conferences, losing touch with the press and the people. He was afraid to talk to the media and the public in any situation in which they could talk back. He did not hold himself accountable for his actions, apparently.

Father loved the give and take. He spoke openly with the men and women of the media, was on first-name terms with them, joked with them. A couple of times he called them to an "important conference" at Warm Springs and, when they assembled, trotted out some livestock so he could lecture the reporters on the importance of having good mules and sound stud bulls on a farm.

Another time father followed the famed H. L. Mencken to the speaker's stand at the 1934 gathering of the famous Gridiron Club of Washington correspondents at which Mencken had ripped into Roosevelt's New Deal. Father proceeded to rip into the press. He spoke of its "stupidity" and "cowardice" in a way that was most unlike him. Everyone, especially Mencken, was stunned, and started to seethe with indignation—until someone realized father was quoting directly from a book of essays by Mencken himself. As this word was whispered around, the other journalists began to eye Mencken with amusement. Father finished it all off by stopping in front of Mencken on the way out and shaking the startled critic's hand.

There were other critics who were not easy to laugh off. One was Westbrook Pegler, who had a way with words but wound up a hatchet man, trying to chop everyone down to his own level.

At first Pegler wrote approvingly of father and especially

of mother and of the New Deal. Then—and this is not generally known—Pegler wrote father suggesting he wouldn't
mind being offered some position of importance on the team.
When the offer was not forthcoming, Pegler turned against
my father's programs and against both my parents personally.
He began to write about them with increasing nastiness that
went beyond the bounds of decency and occasionally sank
into bigotry. In his eyes, mother went from "the greatest
American woman" to "a disgrace to the presidency" in short
order. Day after day he damned father in awful ways.

Pegler was entitled to be critical, but not tasteless.

We were still young, and after one particularly vitriolic
piece Elliott suggested we do something about it. We went to
father and I proposed that we defend the family honor by
waylaying the columnist and giving him a sound whipping.
Father was amused at the thought of it, but warned us off on
the grounds it would do him far more harm than good. "Not
that it isn't a grand idea," he added with a grin.

Privately and impishly, father sometimes worried his aides
by threatening to speak profanely of his press adversaries. He
did needle his critics caustically at times. After a dressing
down by Missy and Felix Frankfurter, later an appointee to
the Supreme Court, father scribbled a memo in pencil in June
1935: "I, Franklin D. Roosevelt, do hereby solemnly agree to
submit, in ample time for full discussion, to Marguerite Le-
Hand and Felix Frankfurter any and all proposed attacks,
direct or indirect, upon the press or parts thereof, under any
form or pretext, so help me good [sic]." It is signed "Nerts—
Franklin D. Roosevelt," and witnessed by Grace Tully.

At times father did become bitter and vengeful. Pegler
appeared primarily in Hearst newspapers. Hearst no doubt,
and perhaps deservedly, expected more from father than he
received for supporting father's presidential nomination. Father never bowed to Hearst, so fell out of favor with the press
lord. Hearst, his editors and his columnists criticized father
and his policies, continuously editorialized against him and
supported his opponents.

At one time father apparently ordered the income tax records of Pegler and Hearst studied in search of irregularities, but to no avail. A similar study, however, eventually led to the imprisonment of Moe Annenberg, publisher of the *Philadelphia Bulletin*. Thus I cannot in good conscience say that father never used his power in an effort to punish opponents. When angry he could be vengeful. But these occasions occurred less frequently perhaps than with many presidents. Most of the time he had the grace and good humor to laugh off or shrug off foes and their criticism.

No one, not even a president, should be above criticism. No one, not even my father, is or was always right. Although it is not for me to say, he no doubt made many mistakes and deserved criticism many times. I myself did not agree with everything he did. But there is a partisan sort of criticism, strictly along party lines, that pounds away at a president beyond the limits of good sense, and there are always a few critics who go beyond decency in making comments that are in the worst possible taste. I admire father for not acting in anger more often than he did, for holding his temper, maintaining his composure and conducting himself with good-humored dignity most of the time.

Eventually, Pegler fell into disrepute. In time, people came to see him for what he was. His exceptional way with words was overshadowed by his outpouring of venom, and in his last years he had a hard time selling his column to a single newspaper. Today people dismiss his impact on father. But this is hindsight. During father's presidency, Pegler was a popular and influential columnist who did damage to many undeserving people. He stands out among critics of father because he was by far the most unfair. His attacks on mother, in particular, partly as a way of getting at father, are a low mark in journalism.

The Hearst newspapers had a history of what can only be called "yellow journalism," and they, too, tumbled badly in public esteem after a while. However, we should not forget the role they played in shaping life in this country, a role that went far beyond merely opposing father.

For the most part, I think the media does a difficult job well. I have been involved in what might be called scandals at one time or another in my life and hurt by public reports, some of which were neither accurate nor fair, but I still think the majority of people in the media conduct themselves well.

Hearst was clever. He took Elliott and then Anna and her husband John Boettiger to work for him. He even allowed them the leeway of cooling the heat that other members of his group gave the president. He did not demand that they join in attacks on father. It's clear he considered them his pipeline to the president. But if he figured it would give him a grip on father, it didn't work, because father was not about to take the advice of his sons and daughter or anyone else if he did not agree. He didn't try to stop Anna and Elliott from working for Hearst. He always felt we should be free to do as we wished, even if it reflected unfavorably on him.

I recall one day during the war when my wife and I were driving north to San Francisco, we happened on the entrance to the Hearst estate at San Simeon. I'd heard a lot about the unusual mansion he had erected there, but this was long before there were public tours of the place. In fact there were signs all over the front gate reading, "Private Property . . . No Admission . . . Proceed At Your Own Risk" and so forth.

This challenged me. I was spoiled, the president's son, used to going where I wanted to go. So, against the advice of my wife, I just drove in, and up the hill. After a while I saw a sign that said, "Go No Further Unless You Have an Appointment." Then another one which read, "Beware of Wild Animals." This was followed by others which hinted death was imminent if you proceeded. I drove on, expecting to be attacked by dogs or blasted by bombs or bullets at any moment.

Apparently Hearst considered the warnings sufficient, because we reached the front door unscathed. Mr. Hearst's secretary came to the door. He was a bit stuffy until I introduced myself and my wife. He pointed out that I didn't have an appointment. I admitted I'd come on impulse, and he said that as long as I was there, he'd see if Mr. Hearst could see me. I replied that would be awfully nice.

After a while he came back and said that Miss Davies and Mr. Hearst were not up yet (although it was eleven in the morning), but that they would like to have us stay to lunch. I accepted the invitation, and he said that in the meantime he'd have us shown around the estate.

We got a three-hour tour and it was really impressive. Most of San Simeon was long since finished and in use, but a tower and one wing were still being reconstructed stone by stone with the most exquisite stuff from Europe. I'll admit I was awed.

At about two o'clock Hearst brought Marion Davies down, unblushingly, and we went to dine in the baronial hall, sitting opposite each other at a long table that seated forty-nine, I was told. At this time visits to the "Hearst Castle" by film stars and other prominent people already had become legend. I could see his guests were treated well. There was a butler behind each of us and a swarm of servants to serve luncheon for four. It was wonderfully well organized. And the food was fabulous.

Even though I was a president's son, I was impressed. I felt their way of life removed them from reality. Yet, I found I liked him, and I especially liked Marion Davies. He was an impressive person and a cunning conversationalist; she was beautiful and charming. We talked of the war, which by then was going well, and we discussed politics. He made it clear he didn't approve of many of my father's policies, but he said it in such a way that I felt I could defend them without being rude. We talked of Anna and Elliott working for him. He said they were doing well.

It was apparent to me that he enjoyed having power and being close to others who had power. Let's face it, I had done little with my life up to then and I would have meant little to him if I had not been a Roosevelt. I'm sure it was the only reason Anna and Elliott were part of his team, no matter how capable they might have been.

We left about 4:30. Expecting perhaps thirty minutes with the great man, at most, we had been there more than five hours.

Father tolerated such attempts to use his children as a means of getting to him, and father himself was not above using members of the press to get what he wanted if he could. He used Winchell, Drew Pearson and H. V. Kaltenborn, for example, feeding them inside information and allowing them to use his name freely in exchange for favorable comment for himself and his programs. Like Pegler, Winchell eventually came to seem less than admirable and fell into public disfavor. For a time, however, he was a highly influential columnist and broadcaster and his support helped father's image immensely.

Father liked Drew Pearson and his wife, and they were really rather friendly. Their friendship didn't prevent Pearson from putting father down at times, however, nor father from striking back. At one press conference after Pearson had criticized him in a way father considered unfair, father made some remarks about those who write inaccurately and said he'd devised a decoration for them. He pulled a dunce cap out of his desk and said that the guy who got to wear it that week should stand in the corner awhile to reconsider what he had written. And he called Pearson up and placed it on his head. A good sport, Pearson went and stood in the corner and laughed along with everyone else.

One day a friend of Marion Dickerman's, a Wall Street broker, presented her with a copy of a book entitled *Frankie in Wonderland*. It was written by Latham Reed and was a takeoff on the Lewis Carroll classic. The friend read her some of the ridicule of Roosevelt, expecting her to be upset. To his surprise, she asked for a copy she could present to the president. He said, "You wouldn't do that!" She assured him she would. "He'll love it," she said. Shaking his head, the man handed her his copy.

Marion gave the book to father at a dinner that night, and, as she expected, he found it funny. In fact a few days later, at a picnic for the press at Hyde Park, he pulled it out and read some of it to the guests gathered around a roaring fire. He read them the story of how Little Frankie, "tired of having only one state to play with" and anxious to "get rid of that rowdy little Smith boy who always wanted to play with his toys," was inspired by the sight of the "White Rabbit," and thought if he could perform such tricks as pulling a rabbit from a hat he might become popular enough to "be given 48 states to play with."

Everyone laughed. "What can you do with a man like that?" wondered a writer for the opposition press.

If the owners of newspapers and radio stations were generally opposed to father, their reporters were not. Father won over the working press. He felt he needed all the help he could get, even if he could go to the people directly through his "Fireside Chats." As I said earlier, the sympathy he stirred among photographers and other working people of the press was responsible for his seldom being pictured as a helpless cripple. The story behind the Sumner Welles incident was also not widely reported. When there were stories that father did not feel should be made public, he could trust the press to keep secrets.

During the war, publisher Frank Knox happened on a story that would have been big but might have jeopardized national security. Knox called it to father's attention and agreed, when asked, not to publish it. This impressed father. When he needed a new secretary of the navy, he selected Knox, who, though a Republican and part of the opposition press, was otherwise qualified. He did a good job, too.

There were times Steve Early had to deal directly with the press. And there were times when he lost his temper with the press, especially when they'd been drinking together. Occasionally they lost their temper with him, too. But for the most part, he managed marvelously with the press. He was a former newspaperman who had worked on father's vice-presidential campaign of 1920. He was brought back in 1928 because father believed he was the best man available.

In a way, he and father were pals; he was a member of the Cuff Links Club, part of inner-circle, high-level discussions. He worked well with Louis Howe and other key aides who followed Louis. Early's was not a casual, passing appointment. He was meant to stay and he stayed.

Early respected the press and was respected by them. Steve could say, "Look, you're trying to put me on a spot, but I can't help you out in this case. There is something here and it's going to develop, and when it does I'll tell you all about it, but I simply can't talk about it now, and that's that." He was not evasive unless it was absolutely necessary. He leveled with the guys and he kept his promises to them. If he did a better job than others who have held that post, it may have been because father leveled with *him*.

Because he was able to keep everything that happened in perspective and brought such a keen sense of humor to the problems that arose, life with father was fun in the best of times and endurable in the worst of times, whether you were a member of his inner circle or just outside it.

XIII

Following his first election to the presidency, but prior to his inauguration, an assassination attempt was made on my father's life.

In February of 1933, father had gone to Florida to fish and rest aboard Vincent Astor's yacht and had gone ashore to address an American Legion group at an outdoor park in Miami. Many members of the elite rode in the caravan that carried the president-elect to the park.

After father finished his short speech, a crowd gathered around his car, and one man—an out-of-work bricklayer named Guiseppe Zangara—pressed forward and pulled out a gun. Shouting angrily at "everyone who is rich," complaining "too many people are out of work," Zangara fired five shots.

A woman standing near Zangara hit his arm, causing each shot to hit a different person near father, but father himself was not hit. Anton Cermak, the mayor of Chicago, was shot, and was pulled into father's car while Secret Service agents and police rushed into the crowd and grabbed the gunman.

Astor and his companions also pulled one of the wounded into their car and were about to take him to a hospital when agents jumped onto the large trunk rack and onto the running board of their limousine, began beating on the windshield with their revolvers and ordered the Astor chauffeur to "drive to the jail." Astor refused, arguing that he had a wounded man inside and intended to follow the Roosevelt car to the nearest hospital, which he did.

It was only after they got there that they discovered the officers had Zangara handcuffed to the trunk rack and were leaning over him to hide him from spectators. At the hospital they hustled him into another car and took him to jail.

Father had held Cermak, bleeding, in his arms all the way to the hospital. There the mayor was rushed into the emergency room. Soon Astor and others arrived with some more of the wounded. When he found father, Astor asked, "Don't you think you had better telephone Eleanor and let her know you're all right?" Father smiled and said, "Your mind, Vincent, works rather slowly. I did that five minutes ago."

Later, Ray Moley marveled at how calm father was. There was, he said, "not so much as the twitching of a muscle, the mopping of a brow, or even the hint of a false gaiety" to show he was unnerved by the threat to his life.

Father later told me, "I think they really were after Anton." And indeed the newspaper reports suggested it had to do with a Chicago gang war. But the fact is, Zangara, when interviewed later, said he wanted to get the president—not father, in particular but anyone who happened to hold that position of power at the time.

After poor Cermak died—he was the only one seriously injured—Zangara was convicted and executed in March of 1933.

Clearly it was nothing to take lightly, but father was a fatalist. Although, in his crippled condition, he would have been a lot less able to get away from an assassin than most men, he accepted the risks and refused to worry about them. Maybe because he knew he couldn't get away it was easier for him. Actually it is clear by now that any suicidal assassin has a good chance of getting to anyone, no matter how nimble, no matter how many Secret Service men surround him.

At that time we were not as preoccupied with assassins. It's true there had been assassinations around the world—the president of France and the prime minister of Japan had been assassinated only a year earlier, and the premier of Japan had been assassinated a few years before that. But no American president had been murdered since William McKinley was shot in 1901, when father was a young man.

"Since you can't control these things, you don't think about them," father said at the time. And although he could not walk among the people, he appeared in public in open cars and on the back platforms of trains and at public gatherings regularly without being concerned with danger.

Although it was not publicized, he got threats on his life through the mail and (indirectly) over the telephone fairly often. But I don't think anyone was ever apprehended or prosecuted other than Zangara.

Security was not always what it should have been. I recall, for example, one evening when we were watching a movie with some guests in the White House living quarters. When the lights went on for intermission we saw a young man standing by father, whose seat was always on the aisle. No one knew the man, but only a few people moved between him and father.

As it happened, he was a cousin or nephew of Henry Morgenthau's and had simply introduced himself at the front gate, without credentials or an invitation, and been permitted to proceed unescorted into the building. It turned out he wanted an autograph from the president. He got his autograph from father, who laughed it off, but there was a bit of head-knocking in the security detail after that.

Another incident that points up the difference between today's tight security and yesterday's more casual approach involved mother's friend Marion Dickerman.

On a visit to the White House one day, Marion was treated to a description of the history of father's desk. Made up of timbers from the salvaged HMS *Resolute*, which was abandoned during a quest for the Northwest Passage in the 1800s, the desk was presented by the royal family of Great Britain to the president of the United States. My father read Marion the plaque that described the gift.

At Todhunter School in New York the next day, Marion related the story to her students. One asked for a copy of the message on the *Resolute* desk plaque, and Marion promised to copy it when she returned to the White House.

On her next visit she remembered her promise as she was about to leave to catch a train. Alone, despite increased security precautions against espionage in those prewar days, she hurried down an empty corridor to the president's study. Finding the door open, she entered and went to the desk. In the gloom, she found some matches in father's desk drawer and lit one after another while she copied the inscription. Then she left.

The next morning Secret Service men were called to the Oval Office when the president's chair was found pushed aside, his drawer full of secret documents open, the papers on his desk scattered, burnt matches in the wastebasket. Fingerprints were taken, but none matched those of the staff. An intense investigation was under way when Marion's secretary telephoned mother's secretary to check a few of the words Marion had scribbled in the dark, and the secret visit was revealed.

Marion apologized to father, but he ordered her to report to the FBI to be fingerprinted and given an identification card she would have to carry if she wished to visit the White House again. Over her objections, he insisted she do as he asked. I'm not sure she found it funny, but he sure did.

"He never let me forget it," she said later.

I remember when I accompanied father on a South American "Good Neighbor" tour. The president of Uruguay, Gabriel Terra, came aboard our cruiser and, in discussing a ceremonial parade in Montevideo in which we were to participate, seemed concerned. Asked why he was nervous, he confessed that this was to be his first public appearance since he had been shot and wounded in another parade a few months earlier. Father laughed and said, "Welcome to the club. I've been shot at, too. We can't worry about these things. Don't worry, we'll have a great time. We'll be surrounded by security men."

When we got to the car, father further reassured him by suggesting, "I'll let my little boy Jimmy ride in the jump seat directly in front of you so you'll be shielded." He thought that a splendid idea, though I did not. I wasn't a little boy by any means, but I didn't protest. I just did it, and I was scared. Fortunately there was no gunfire.

Father and I often teased each other about the incident later. "Better the president's son than the president," father laughed. He just simply never was willing to dwell on and worry about the possibilities.

Having survived polio, he may have considered himself indestructible. "I'll last a long time, I'll outlast my enemies," he would laugh, obviously undeterred by his crippled condition.

The extent to which father had come to accept his condition is illustrated by a remark he made when Arthur Godfrey wanted to become a navy pilot in World War II but was rejected due to a severe limp resulting from an automobile accident.

Godfrey appealed to mother, a fan of his from the old days in Washington, and she in turn appealed to father. He called in a navy doctor and asked why Godfrey had been refused a commission.

"Because he has bad legs," the doctor said.

"Can he walk?" father asked.

"Well, yes," the doctor admitted, "he can walk."

"Well then, give it to him," father said. "I can't walk and I'm the commander in chief."

Years later, in assembling an historical collection of recordings, Fred Friendly ran across a recording of Godfrey's moving description of father's funeral procession. When he played it for Godfrey, Friendly not only got permission to use it, but free radio and television plugs that made the record a surprise smash hit.

Once he accepted the situation, father was a lot less embarrassed about being lifted, carried and helped about than those who had to help him. In fact it was he who eased our embarrassment and helped us laugh about it. I remember one time Gus Gennerich and I locked arms so we could carry him, and as we walked Gus started to swing him, singing, "London Bridge is falling down." Father laughed so hard I thought he was going to fall.

If he ever was embarrassed about his circumstances, he never said a word about it. He simply wasn't going to let it spoil his life.

He loved life, and for all the burdens he bore, he got a lot of fun out of life.

He loved losing his Secret Service protectors, regardless of the risk, and he constantly played practical jokes on everyone around him. A couple of times he had his bodyguard, Gus Gennerich, climb up on the roof at Warm Springs or Hyde Park on some pretext, then had a hired hand remove the ladder, stranding poor Gus.

"Pa" Watson was also a target of my father's practical jokes. We were on a cruise south of Key West once when Watson mentioned to father that they were nearing a famous military establishment on one of the islands and perhaps they should pay a courtesy call. Realizing that Watson did not know the fort had been closed down long before and left in the hands of an aging Negro caretaker, father instructed Watson to arrange a presidential visit for the following day. Watson wired the War Department to do so, and I presume father contacted the department, because they did not reply to Watson's wire.

The next morning as we approached the island, Watson stood on the bridge with binoculars and grew increasingly concerned since he could see no flags, no signs of life. He was not only worried that they were not prepared for a presidential visit, but that something dreadful might have happened to the men. He went to father and said, "Mr. President, I'm terribly upset. Something's wrong at the fort." And my father smiled and said, "Oh, I'm sure everything's all right. You see, it's been closed for a long time, but there is a colored caretaker there who I'm sure will be happy to see us."

Watson was furious when he realized that he had been tricked. The last thing he wanted to do was to go ashore to pay the president's respects to the caretaker of a deserted fort, but he had to do his duty. Later, of course, he laughed about it. Father loved people who could laugh at themselves.

When father was at sea with favored companions, news bulletins were delivered daily. Father frequently inserted his own "news" into the batch, which often caused consternation among his companions. Once he inserted a dispatch that the New York State Supreme Court had reversed all decisions handed down by Justice Freddie Kernochan, one of the passengers, and was "demanding a probe of this discredited justice." Another dispatch reported that the U.S. Supreme Court had invalidated all "quickie" divorces obtained in the western states, which hit home with a number of the passengers.

Father often operated "pools" on baseball games and football games. I found, in his handwriting, an account of a pool he had on the St. Louis–Detroit World Series in 1934. Serving as bookie, he had recorded: "H. the Hop [Hopkins] $37 (won); Pa [Watson] $4.50 (won); Steve the Earl [Early] $25.50 (lost); J. the Rose [me] $6 (lost)," and so on, adding up to a profit for father of $51.

The "pool" I remember best was one we had during our South American voyage. It concerned King Edward and the outcome of his affair with the American Wallis Warfield Simpson, big news at the time. There were a number of possibilities and we put up stakes and wrote down our predictions, which passed into the protective custody of Pa Watson. I remember father laughing as he wrote his prediction.

When King Edward went on the air to announce his abdication—becoming the duke of Windsor—to marry the woman he loved, Watson brought out the slips and read our predictions. Father's was missing. When he found out, he was upset. He told Watson, "You've got to find that slip and destroy it. If what I have written ever gets out, it may mean war." He was kidding, I am certain. Clearly, he was concerned.

The missing slip never was found, even though we searched the ship, and father never told me what he'd written. I think it must have been risqué.

During the war, father frequently had to deal with Joseph Stalin. After he returned from Yalta, someone asked father about Stalin. Father did not want to discuss the Soviet chief with the person who asked the question, so he said Stalin was the sort of person he didn't want to discuss, adding ominously that he'd heard Stalin had poisoned his wife.

The fellow went away without knowing whether to take father seriously or not. Presidents are not supposed to make up stories that might be taken seriously, but father was the sort of person who did.

Father and Churchill always referred to Stalin as "Uncle Joe," as if he were some black sheep of the family. At first they probably didn't believe he'd be so tough to deal with, but as time passed and we got well into the war, they found him more difficult than they had expected. I remember father saying, "Uncle Joe is smarter and stronger than I thought he was."

Stalin was sensitive to his position as a junior partner who needed help, but Churchill, too, needed help. I think Stalin knew that his country would carry a heavier burden of the war than had been expected, and would in a short time develop power equal to or beyond that of its partners. He was stubborn in his demands and difficult to negotiate with.

Father may have thought he could humor Joe out of his stubborness and succeed in negotiations with him where others would fail, but I believe he was fooled. I think father felt he was responsible for Russia's regime receiving worldwide recognition in 1933 and expected more credit than he received from Stalin.

I also think father was sorry about having let the League of Nations dissolve, and was determined to carry on the Wilsonian concept with the United Nations. He was insistent in his last negotiations with Joe that everything be done to make this a reality. This was one of father's final successes, though later Stalin and his successors simply disregarded many of the agreements made with their allies in the final stages of the war.

For that matter, Churchill was not easy to deal with, either. He felt the United States did not ally itself with Great Britain early enough in the war, nor provide enough help soon enough, and I think father agreed. Politically, father just had to stall. As late as November 24, 1941, while still negotiating with Japan, he told Churchill, "We must all be prepared for trouble, possibly soon." Two weeks later it came, and we went to war.

Father and Winston seldom agreed on how to wage the war. They worked it out, but father always favored a well-ordered battle plan, while Winston favored all-out assaults. It was a basic difference in their personalities: Father took a little time reacting to situations and deciding what to do, while Winston reacted quickly and preferred fast moves.

Father always felt he was the one who held the Big Three together. Perhaps he was, but I think their meetings were difficult for him. He was not well, while they were iron men. He sipped a drink now and then, but Winnie and Joe hit the bottle hard and Winnie always smoked cigars. Father liked to get to bed early and get up early, but they went in for all-night sessions and then slept late.

I was away at war and not with father at many of the Big Three conferences, but I did accompany him once when he saw Winnie early in the war, and I know how hard Churchill's habits were on him. Another time I remember father saying, perhaps prophetically, "These all-night deals will be the death of me yet." He was smiling when he said it, yet was somewhat serious at the same time. These "poker games" were intense and the stakes were high.

Later on, I had an experience with Winston which was rather poignant. It happened after father's death, when Winnie was nearing his. I was in England and was invited by Lady Churchill to visit her husband. "He'd like that," she said, "and maybe it'd perk him up a bit. He's been a bit down." So I paid a visit to him.

I was saddened by how feeble he was. But when he saw me his face lit up and he held my hand and asked me to sit and talk to him. From time to time he'd ask me if I remembered someone I'd never met, and he spoke about a message he'd sent me, when he'd never sent me a message in his life. At first I was puzzled. Then I realized he thought I was my father. It was awkward and sad as he started to reminisce about private experiences he'd had with father.

Lady Churchill, fortunately, caught on quickly and leaned over and whispered to him, "Winnie, this is not your friend Franklin; this is his son, Jimmy." At first he was confused, then embarrassed. He was terribly disappointed and his expression and posture seemed to sag. Shortly Lady Churchill, with admirable poise, suggested her husband needed his rest and thanked me for my visit. He returned to his bedroom and I departed. I thought, so this is the way the world ends for us! Perhaps, then, it was better for father to be stricken while still in command, and taken mercifully fast.

Charles De Gaulle, leader of the Free French forces in England, did not, as captain of a conquered country, command a berth in the Big Three. While Churchill favored De Gaulle, father favored Henri Giraud. Father approved of the return of France to French rule but reluctantly approved the return of such colonies as Indochina. This turned out to be the first step toward a war in Vietnam, which eventually would claim two million lives, including almost fifty thousand Americans. I don't think either father or Churchill saw how important De Gaulle was to France. I know they both considered him a pompous ass, almost impossible to deal with. De Gaulle never forgave father for saying that De Gaulle fancied himself "the modern Joan of Arc."

Years later when I was with Investors Overseas Services, we planned to move our office out of Switzerland across the border into France. It was a small community, Ferney Voltaire, and we expected to set up an international school to take care of our children as well as those who lived there. The mayor told us we needed government approval and asked us what we planned to call the school, so that he could submit a name to Paris. Bernie Cornfeld suggested we call it the Eleanor Roosevelt School. The mayor said that was fine; he didn't expect any problems and we could expect approval in short order.

Weeks went by without a word. Eventually the embarrassed mayor called on me to report that the name was not acceptable to Premier De Gaulle, who had suggested we name it the Joan of Arc School. I had to laugh because it showed me old Charlie not only had a long memory, he had a surprising sense of humor, too.

Long before this, in the long hot summer of 1942, Churchill visited the United States to confer with father and was our guest at Hyde Park. He agreed to a swim in the Val-Kill pool before lunch, but we had to find a pair of bathing trunks wide enough at the waist to fit him. A pair was found among a number of suits accumulated over the years. He also asked for some cotton.

He was a remarkable sight when he emerged in his suit with cotton in his ears, a wide-brimmed sun hat on his head and a long cigar in his mouth. Setting the hat and cigar aside for a few moments, he jumped into the pool and bounced about like a rubber ball for a few moments. Then he emerged to dry himself, don his hat, take up his cigar and sit in the shade, waiting for a full bottle of brandy. He could do justice to a bottle of brandy.

Once he asked for a butterfly net, but we had none. Presumably he wished to chase a few butterflies. I'm sorry we missed that sight.

A few years before the war, King George and Queen Elizabeth visited father and were entertained at mother's Val-Kill cottage at Hyde Park. I had been in London and was asked by father to arrange the visit.

Ambassador Joseph Kennedy arranged for me to stay at Windsor Castle. I was coached in the courtesies, but flunked the tests. I forgot to bow, and instead presented my hand when introduced to the king and queen. Smiling, each shook my hand. Later, at dinner, I was so busy telling tall tales to the queen that I neglected to finish my soup. It was terrible soup, but because of rationing you had to finish one course before another was served. The others were eating their fish when I realized I had a cold bowl of bad soup to finish. I started shoveling in spoonfuls, but the queen saw my plight and motioned to a servant to relieve me of the bowl.

At Hyde Park, to granny's horror, father served hot dogs to the king and queen. Father didn't stand on protocol and they seemed to enjoy this bit of Americana. Afterward he offered to take them for a swim, one sport in which father could participate.

They had brought modest one-piece suits. Nevertheless, when we got to the pool father asked me to tell an assemblage of press photographers that in this case pictures could not be permitted. Reluctantly I did so, to wails of anguish. The press departed and we swam.

Later granny served a formal dinner for the royal couple. To her horror, father had drinks brought in before dinner. She had been horrified a bit too often to suit father. He said to the king, "My mother thinks you should have a cup of tea. She doesn't approve of cocktails." The king, who had little to say, thought this over for a few moments, then observed, "Neither does my mother." Whereupon they grabbed their glasses, raised them to one another in unspoken toast and downed their martinis.

Dinner was a disaster. The food was fine, but first a serving table loaded with fine china collapsed, then a butler tumbled down the stairs, spilling a trayful of decanters, glasses and ice at the feet of the king and queen. I suppose you could say we just didn't know how to carry off these formal, royal affairs as well as the British. When the china crashed in pieces, Uncle Rosy's widow, Mrs. James Roosevelt Roosevelt, a guest, spoke sharply to granny: "I hope, Sally, that none of *my* dishes were broken." We'd had to borrow plates to have enough.

Despite all of this, when war came, we were allowed to fight on England's side.

One of the best examples of father's playfulness came when
Joe Kennedy was named ambassador to England. The father
of future political leaders, he always had a hankering for
politics. He became chairman of the Maritime Commission
and was first chairman of the FCC, but he wanted something
bigger and better. He was often critical of father's New Deal
policies regarding big business, but he was, in a way, an old
family friend, and when the chips were down he supported
father.

After the 1936 campaign, he made it clear he felt he deserved
a reward—which he did—and he hinted broadly that the reward he had in mind was the post of secretary of the treasury
—which was out of the question. Father was not going to
remove Henry Morgenthau from the office. Father did not
tell Joe in so many words, but in time it became clear to him.

One day father said to me, "We've got to do something for
old Joe, but I don't know what. He wants what he can't have,
but there must be something we can give him he'll be happy
with. Why don't you go see him and feel him out and see what
you can come up with?"

This conversation took place several times, and each time
I went to see Kennedy. I saw him so often, in fact, that we
became friendly. He had a lovely place in Maryland and we'd
sit around in the evening talking.

One evening Joe said that if he couldn't be secretary of the
treasury, there was one other job he'd consider: "I'd like to be
ambassador to England." I was surprised. I really liked Joe,
but he was a crusty old cuss and I couldn't picture him as an
ambassador, especially to England.

I said, "Oh, c'mon, Joe, you don't want that." And he said,
"Oh, yes I do. I've been thinking about it and I'm intrigued
by the thought of being the first Irishman to be ambassador
from the United States to the Court of Saint James's." I
laughed and admitted it would be quite a precedent. I agreed
to suggest it to the president, though I was sure father would
think it laughable.

Sure enough, when I passed it on to father, he laughed so

hard he almost toppled from his wheelchair. Catching his breath, he shook his head and said he was sorry, but that, too, was out. Before I could relay the bad news to Joe, however, father called me in to tell me he'd been thinking about it and was kind of intrigued with the idea of twisting the lion's tail a little, so to speak. He wanted to talk to Joe about it.

When Joe arrived at the White House, I took him into the president's office. Father said to him, "Joe, would you mind stepping back a bit, by the fireplace perhaps, so I can get a good look at you?" Puzzled, Joe did so. Then father said, "Joe, would you mind taking your pants down?" I was as surprised as Joe was. We couldn't believe our ears. Joe asked father if he'd said what he thought he'd said, and father said he had indeed. I guess it was the power of the presidency, because Joe Kennedy undid his suspenders and dropped his pants and stood there in his shorts, looking silly and embarrassed.

Father said, "Someone who saw you in a bathing suit once told me something I now know to be true. Joe, just look at your legs. You are just about the most bowlegged man I have ever seen. Don't you know that the ambassador to the Court of Saint James's has to go through an induction ceremony in which he wears knee britches and silk stockings? Can you imagine how you'll look? When photos of our new ambassador appear all over the world we'll be a laughingstock. You're just not right for the job, Joe."

Without batting an eye, Joe looked at him and said, "Mr. President, if I can get the permission of his majesty's government to wear a cutaway coat and striped pants to the ceremony, would you agree to appoint me?"

"Well, Joe," said father, "you know how the British are about tradition. There's no way you are going to get permission, and I must name a new ambassador soon."

"Will you give me two weeks?" Joe asked.

Father agreed to that. Joe pulled up his pants and his dignity and went on his way, leaving father chuckling contentedly.

Within two weeks Joe was back with an official letter from

the British government granting him the tradition-breaking permission. He'd called father's bluff, and father laughed and agreed to name him ambassador to England. Joe and Rose Kennedy and their terrific children spent quite a few years over there.

Years later there were reports that although I had helped Joe get his liquor business started, Joe never made good on an agreement to bring me into the business. I did help him get the business going; I did help him get what he wanted from father. But I did not expect to become part of the business. I have to make it clear that Joe and I never had an agreement to that effect.

I did feel he owed something to the memory of my parents. And after first father, then mother died and we needed money to establish the Eleanor Roosevelt Cancer Foundation at three universities, I went to Joe and asked for his help. He asked how much I expected from him. I told him $50,000. He asked me why he should give that kind of money and pointed out that mother had never especially liked him or been kind to him. I told him father had given him an honor which perhaps was the high point in his career. For father, if not for mother, he might consider helping to make this memorial a reality. He said he'd think it over. A week later I received a check for $50,000 for the foundation.

XIV

We made a home of the White House, but obviously it is no ordinary residence. Our private quarters upstairs, for example, were supposed to be out of bounds to the public, but Anna was once surprised by a tour group walking through her bedroom while she was taking a nap. Nevertheless we made it as much like home as possible by bringing along a lot of our own personal bric-a-brac. I think it's the "junk" that makes a house a home. We put up our own photos. Father hung his naval prints. There was personal evidence of the Roosevelts everywhere.

By the time father became president, Anna, Elliott and I were married, Franklin was at Harvard, and John was at Groton. Before father died and the family left the White House, Franklin and John were married, too. In fact, some of us had been divorced and remarried. The younger members of our family grew up in the White House to some extent, as did some of our children—the grandchildren of the president and First Lady. Father loved to have his grandchildren around, and at one time in his presidency there were thirteen of them to keep him company.

The children of Anna and her first husband, Curtis Dall—Anna Eleanor and Curtis, Jr.—became famous as "First Children" and were the pets of photographers seeking human-interest pictures of the First Family. Nicknamed "Sistie" and "Buzzie," they were active kids and created plenty of commotion in their day, but they became favorites of the White House staff of servants, attendants and guards. Before a formal reception one night, Sistie and Buzzie draped the banister of the grand staircase with toilet paper. Another time, with Anna's help—she was as much a child at heart as they were —they short-sheeted the bed of an unwelcome guest. And when they found out the lady wore long underwear, they stuffed a union suit and parked it outside her door.

Our parents humored their grandchildren. Mother defied the gardener once by hanging a swing from a prominent tree on the White House grounds for their use. Father was also indulgent, though he could not bring himself to part with doo-dads he had handpicked for his cluttered desk, no matter how much my first two—Sara and Kate—pleaded with him. But he did personally order diapers once for John's firstborn, Haven.

What happened was that John and his wife took a trip, leaving Haven behind, and John telephoned father to ask him to order six dozen diapers for the infant. Father was dumbfounded, but decided to place the order himself just for the joy of hearing the surprise of the store clerk on the other end of the telephone when he identified himself: "This is the president of the United States. I would like to order six dozen diapers to be delivered to the White House as soon as possible, please."

The presidential family is expected to maintain a high standard of living. But the president in those days was paid only $75,000 a year, plus $25,000 annual expenses. That seems like a lot, but it didn't go far. The servants and other staff had to be paid and fed, and guests had to be entertained. Father's independent income was around $60,000 to $70,000 a year and he paid $10,000 to $20,000 of it in taxes. After expenses had been met, he was left with little. Granny helped out, though not nearly as much as the $100,000 a year Elliott estimates.

The younger children were in expensive schools. The older

ones, especially Elliott and I, borrowed a little money here and there—to say the least. As increased income taxes cut father's take-home pay by about half during the war, my parents had to tighten up. It may be difficult to believe, but the president's family may have to budget expenses to make ends meet. Ours did.

I have a memorandum mother sent Missy for father's attention. It was attached to a bill and read: "This bill is for Franklin Junior's treatment for piles. He went eleven times, but apparently it does not depend upon how many times you go, it depends entirely on the cure. I know FDR will have a fit!" Missy gave the memo to father, who returned it with the following note handwritten at the bottom: "Pay it. Have had the fit. FDR."

Still, let's not pretend we did not live well. On their twenty-eighth wedding anniversary, father gave mother a $200 check with the following note: "Dearest Babs . . . After a fruitless week of thinking and lying awake to find whether you need or want undies, dresses, hats, shoes, sheets, towels, rouge, soup plates, candy, flowers, lamps, laxative pills, whisky, beer, etchings or caviar, I GIVE UP. And yet I know you lack some necessity of life—so go to it with my love and many happy returns of the day! FDR."

We had to have a full staff of servants, and the one who caused us the most concern was Henrietta Nesbitt. Mother had met her when she was involved in politics at Hyde Park, decided she would make a marvelous housekeeper and brought her to Washington. She was the worst cook I've ever encountered. Mother defended her, but no one else had a kind word to say for her meals.

Actually, Henrietta didn't do the cooking, but she planned the menus and saw to it that the food was prepared her way, which was not the best way. Father sent her memos on how to prepare food ("Do not pluck fowl until just before cooking"), but she paid no attention, so he gave up. He was a gourmet who loved fancy food such as duck, venison, terrapin and oyster crabs. She fed him chicken.

He once wrote mother this memo: "Do you remember that about a month ago I got sick of chicken because I got it at least six times a week? The chicken situation has definitely improved, but 'they' have substituted sweetbreads, and for the past month I have been getting sweetbreads about six times a week. I am getting to the point where my stomach positively rebels and this does not help my relations with foreign powers. I bit two of them today. FDR."

Father sought sympathy from his aides. Once he complained that Mrs. Nesbitt had told him some fancy canned white asparagus he liked was unobtainable. Grace got the girls in the office busy on the telephone. That day they presented him with a case of the stuff.

Mrs. Nesbitt's meals were so bad that guests hated to eat at the White House. Invitations to dinner from the president, normally treasured, were being refused. Father solved the problem by importing an outside chef for special guests. And after granny died, he brought her cook, Mary Campbell, from Hyde Park as his personal chef. He promptly put on a lot of weight, which he didn't need.

Irvin McDuffie was father's personal valet. He took care of father's clothes and dressed him. He'd been a barber in Warm Springs and father brought him to Washington. Later father brought Mrs. McDuffie, too, as a maid. Mac went everywhere with father. He helped him on and off with his braces and was supposed to be available to him at all times. Mac didn't make a lot of money, but he was dedicated to the president.

As Mac got older, his dedication wavered. He started drinking and once failed to show up when father wanted him. Because of his crippled condition, father couldn't tolerate this and he had to fire Mac. But he couldn't bring himself to do it; he made mother do it while he was away, and only after he had found a job for Mac in the Treasury Department. Arthur Prettyman replaced him. He was more reliable but less of a pal to the president. Father and Mac used to kid one another good-naturedly. It hurt father to let Mac go.

Gus Gennerich, father's bodyguard, became a close friend.

He'd been a New York City motorcycle cop who was assigned to look after father when he became governor. Father liked him and had him transferred to the State Police and assigned as his private bodyguard. Later he had him assigned to the Secret Service and took him to Washington as the presidential bodyguard. Gus was a brave guy who had single-handedly arrested several "most wanted" fugitives. After a gun battle in which he was wounded, he was promoted to detective. But after he joined father, Gus never went back to the force.

Father trusted Gus completely and liked him enormously. He regarded him as his "ambassador to the man in the street," tried out ideas on him and called him "my humanizer." Gus sometimes brought interesting saloonkeepers, workingmen, merchants and the like to see father. When we were growing up, Gus also guided us to the right saloons. This was an advantage, especially in the "speakeasy" days. The son of a governor or president had to be careful not to create a scandal by doing what everyone else was doing. Gus and father both were Masons, and I remember Gus took particular pride when father permitted him to be the one to sponsor me into the fraternity.

On our goodwill trip to South America, Gus and I were among those crossing the equator for the first time and were thus subjected to the usual ceremonial initiation by the sailors. Father sat and watched and enjoyed the hijinks. But the roughhousing got a little out of hand and Gus hit his head rather hard. He complained of headaches from then on.

On a night off in Buenos Aires, Gus went to a nightclub and danced till midnight. Then the burly guy who was buying a farm for retirement sat down, slumped over and died on the spot. He'd had a cerebral hemorrhage.

We all took it hard. His body was brought back on the boat with us. I remember father wiring home that the bachelor apartment Gus kept in New York was to be kept sealed until someone close to him could go through it privately to pass on anything of importance to whatever relatives he had. I've always wondered about this. All father would say was, "He was a bachelor and God knows what they'll find there. I wouldn't want mother or anyone else offended or Gus's memory marred."

I found a replacement for Gus in the Boston area—Tommy Qualters, a Massachusetts state policeman. But he never had the relationship with father that Gus had.

Earl Miller, of course, was for a while, mother's bodyguard, maybe much more. She kept him as her friend, but didn't want a bodyguard. She was so adamantly against it, and made it so uncomfortable for those who tried to stay with her, that the Secret Service eventually gave up. They compromised by providing her with a gun and talking her into taking lessons in the handling of it, but she hated it. After she had been sent to the FBI firing range to learn how to use it, J. Edgar Hoover wrote father: "Mr. President, if there is one person in the U.S. who should not carry a gun it's your good wife. She can not hit a barn door." Originally she was supposed to keep it on her at all times in public, but she put it in a dresser drawer and never took it out.

During father's first term, Louis Howe lived at the White House. We were all used to Louis living with us. I remember, when he lived with us back at our Sixty-fifth Street house in New York, I looked in his closet one time and discovered a stack of liquor bottles. It was during Prohibition, and I wrote father that I had discovered that Louis was breaking the law. Although I was just a kid, it was not a nice thing to do. Father didn't even bother to answer me. Before long I realized the booze was as much for father's enjoyment as for Louis's.

After Louis's death, Harry Hopkins took over as father's personal assistant. Father and mother liked and admired Harry. I did, too. He was the one person who didn't seem to mind my entering the picture when Louis died. I remember Harry telling me he thought father was doing the right thing by bringing a trusted son into the White House as his personal aide. I don't think many others felt that way.

Harry was not a well man, and he suffered a great deal during his life. Father could empathize with him, of course. And Harry, though hardly handsome, was something of a ladies' man, which father admired. This was after Harry's wife, Barbara, died, and he moved from his small apartment into the White House. He had a daughter, Diana, who was considered almost a part of our family.

Harry was unsophisticated when he arrived and father delighted in educating him. Father introduced him to his upper-crust pals, and soon Harry was invited to their homes. Father also took Harry with him occasionally when he went sailing on Vincent Astor's yacht, the *Nourmahal*, and rubbed elbows with high society.

Father's enjoyment of these trips illustrates one of the paradoxes of his personality. In public life he was the champion of the little man, but in private life he befriended big men. Father and his pals called themselves "The *Nourmahal* Gang." They were headed by Astor himself, who had a personal fortune of about $150 million. Others included William Rhinelander Stewart, George St. George, Justice Freddie Kernochan, Kermit Roosevelt and Lytle Hull. All were wealthy, and most were Republicans. St. George was married to granny's niece, Kassy Collier, who became a Republican congresswoman. Kermit was Teddy's son and the only member of that family who was not allied against father. Hull had married the first Mrs. Vincent Astor. I guess that gave him a special pass into this curious collection. Astor also married, then divorced, my first sister-in-law, Mary Cushing. Clearly there was a lot of intramarriage on our level.

I once asked mother if she thought father went on these trips to remind himself how high society was thinking. She said, "He didn't have to go on that boat for that. He could get that every day of his life from mama."

I now think he traveled with that group as an escape, back to the world of Groton, Harvard and Hyde Park. These people had everything, so they didn't want anything from father. Most opposed him politically, and knew he couldn't court their favor. In many ways he was more comfortable with them than he was with his political associates, who constantly pestered him with their problems. He could let his hair down and relax with these people, and they in turn enjoyed the prestige of the president's company. They also liked him personally, if not politically, and it amused them to break bread with their bitter rival on the big-business scene. There is not the slightest shred of evidence he ever did any of them a political favor. He didn't have to; they were his friends, as well as his foes. So he sailed with them, and I can still hear the profane wisecracks that accompanied their cutthroat card games.

Perhaps because of his handicap, father was not criticized for being away from the White House as often as he was. When he wasn't sailing, he was at Warm Springs. I think many people remember him in newsreel photos swimming in the pool at Warm Springs. And if he wasn't at Warm Springs, he was at Hyde Park. Then he established a presidential weekend retreat in the Catocin Mountains of Maryland. It was simple and spartan and he called it "Shangri-la." He had a hot line to the White House installed. He could work with aides on the porch, looking out over a beautiful valley. He had his own chef who prepared meals he liked. And mother never visited Shangri-la, not even once.

In the White House, he worked hard. Once settled at his desk, he found it difficult to leave it. With unwelcome guests, or guests with unwelcome ideas, he dominated conversations until their time had expired. They'd leave with the realization that they hadn't gotten a word in. "Well, I can't walk away from them," father once sighed.

XV

When father became president in 1933, he was fifty-one, mother was forty-nine, and they had been married twenty-eight years. Their children were adults or nearly so. Anna was twenty-six, I was twenty-five and Elliott was twenty-two. It was time for us to make our own way in life. Franklin, who was eighteen and at Harvard, and John, who was sixteen and at Groton, were still dependent on our parents.

Franklin enjoyed his share of pranks. He once took a call in the White House from a person who identified himself as Pershing. Knowing Pershing, the World War I general, had gone to his reward, Franklin replied, "There's no one in, but this is Jesus Christ and I'll leave word you called." It turned out to be Warren Pershing, the general's son.

Another time, fraternity brothers of his placed a call in his name to Prime Minister Daladier of France. This almost caused an international crisis. Father couldn't decide whether to be amused or angry.

Once father called Franklin into his office, waved a colorful, perfumed letter at him and started to read it: "Dear Rosy . . ." Franklin snatched the letter and fled. It seems a girl friend had forgotten to add the Jr. to his name on the address and a love letter had gotten to father.

Mostly, when we were young, father was lighthearted in

his dealings with us. He didn't have a lot of time for us, but he enjoyed himself when he was with us. He even tolerated our reckless driving and speeding tickets.

The one who hated the heat the most was Franklin. Elliott was the one least able to tolerate adverse public comments about our parents. He punched a few who were disrespectful. It took awhile for us to realize that anyone in a position such as the presidency has to learn to live with critics. Most people are not put in a situation where they constantly hear their parents praised or condemned. Somehow, you are less pleased by praise than you are displeased by condemnation. As young people we were not as aware that our parents were imperfect as we were to be eventually.

Anna was the first of us to be married—to a stockbroker, Curtis Dall, in the spring of 1926. But by the time father became president, the marriage was on the rocks. Shortly after father moved into the White House, Anna separated from Curtis and moved in with our parents. Anna then met John Boettiger, a reporter for the Hearst press. They were married in 1936 and had a son, John Roosevelt Boettiger. Anna's husband went to work as editor of the Hearst newspaper in Seattle, where she became woman's editor. Later they published their own newspaper in Phoenix, but competition was keen and they had a difficult time and eventually failed with it.

I was the second to get married—to Betsey Cushing, in June 1930. About a year later Elliott married Betty Donner, whose father founded the Donner Steel Company of Pennsylvania. They had a son, Bill.

Elliott, however, was the first to get divorced. No sooner had father moved into the White House than Elliott, turning up his nose at any offer to go into the business with his father-in-law, left his wife behind and took off for the great Southwest, which he had loved since spending time there as a boy. He was headed for the Greenway ranch, owned by Congresswoman Greenway, wife of one of Teddy's Rough Riders and a friend of mother's.

Elliott was the only one of us who did not go to college. He didn't want to go to Harvard because it was expected of him. Under pressure from father, he agreed to go to Princeton. But then he decided he didn't want to do that, either.

After bouncing about from one job to another, he and a pal headed west with a few dollars between them. They were nearly broke by the time they got to Little Rock, but they couldn't cash a check because father had closed the banks. Elliott called home for money, but father said he couldn't help him; he had only a few dollars himself, and he couldn't cash a check because he'd closed the banks.

Then came a stroke of good luck. A Little Rock newspaper reporter chanced on them and wrote a story about the president's son on the road. They were back on the road and on the outskirts of Dallas when a motorcycle policeman flagged them down and took them into town. There Fenton Baker, C. R. Smith and other bigwigs had decided to host a party for the president's son in the presidential suite of a downtown hotel.

They were invited to a similar affair in Fort Worth the next day. And then another in El Paso. They wound up in Mexico. By the time they resumed their journey, they had been wined, dined and bedded down in the lap of luxury for free for about a week.

Along with Baker, Smith and others, Elliott now had new friends such as oilmen Charley Roesser, Sid Richardson and Clint Murchison. He was told they would be happy to help him out with a piece of spare change or a position anytime he wanted anything. Elliott had discovered powerful people courted the sons of kings, and he didn't mind a bit.

During the trip he also met and became enamored of one Ruth Chandler Googins and decided to end his marriage to Betty so he could marry Ruth.

The first "White House child" ever to seek a divorce, his news was splashed in headlines across the country. That was, of course, a conservative time. Our parents would have been upset even had it not been a black mark against father politically. To their credit, they never mentioned this.

Father couldn't or wouldn't go to talk to Elliott. Mother could and did. She agreed to meet him in Los Angeles, where he had taken a job as aviation editor of the Hearst newspaper. He arranged a flight for mother through his airlines pal, Smith.

Air travel was rough then, but she enjoyed it. The press greeted her at the frequent stops and she gave interviews each time. When she got to Los Angeles she spoke to Elliott, but could not talk him into waiting awhile before divorcing Betty to marry Ruth. She couldn't believe he was rushing into another marriage even faster than he had his first.

Elliott went to Reno to get his divorce. As ambassador from the family, Anna met him in Chicago, where he changed planes on his way to his wedding at Ruth's home in Iowa.

Later he went to Washington. E. L. Cord had wrested control of American Airlines from Averell Harriman, Smith had been promoted to president and they had Elliott lobbying with father. Father had canceled government contracts with selected commercial airlines to carry the mail, feeling army planes could do the job cheaper. It was a bad decision, later reversed, but at the time Elliott's efforts went unrewarded. As a lobbyist he lacked diplomacy. "It's probably as big a mistake as you've ever made," raged the new expert on air travel to his presidential father, who shook his head with the wonder of it all.

The next thing father knew, Elliott was criticizing him from his new position as commentator for the Mutual Radio Network. Soon Elliott was heading Hearst's network of radio stations across the country. Then he tried to set up his own station and eventually a network of stations in Texas. In thick with Texas millionaires, he was far from a millionaire himself, and was borrowing money wherever he could. There were times when he'd call up threatening to take his life if he didn't get help. We'd hustle up some help for him, call back and find he was at a party. There was a time when he pressed father so hard that father reluctantly turned to his wealthy secretary of commerce, the Texan Jesse Jones, and asked if he could do something for Elliott.

Jesse did, bailing Elliott out. I don't know if it was unethical, but I know father didn't like doing it. He did it because it was for his son. Father helped Elliott all he could, and he took him to four or five of his summit meetings as an aide during the war in an effort to develop a sense of responsibility in his son. And Elliott did help dad during the war. Elliott had an outstanding record in the war. The truth of the matter is that my brother Elliott was probably the bravest of all the members of our family. He personally flew unarmed planes over the most dangerous enemy territory in spite of a handicap of very poor eyesight. He was never willing to ask any of the men under his command to do anything he had not done himself; and I have had countless hundreds of people come up to me and tell me what an inspirational leader he was. I have also been told, but he will not talk about it, that Elliott performed some other extraordinary heroic feats behind the enemy line in southern Europe. He certainly earned his rank of Brigadier General, and I hope that some of his early critics are compassionate enough to feel a little silly.

Elliott had three children with Ruth Chandler Googins—Ruth Chandler, who came to be called "Chandler"; David Boynton; and Elliott, Jr., who was known as "Tony." By the end of the war years, however, this second marriage had also ended in divorce and Elliott had married television actress Faye Emerson. By then, by 1940 in fact, my ten-year first marriage to Betsey had ended, too.

With the third one of their children's marriages on the rocks, our parents couldn't help being concerned. In my case, father may have been more concerned than mother. She did not totally approve of Betsey, who got carried away by her position in the presidential family. She moved into the White House and practically took over, assuming many of the functions that normally would have been mother's. Mother disapproved, though she seldom was there to fulfill these functions. Father approved because Betsey delighted him. She was pretty, playful, a teaser. She flattered him, and he adored her.

I'd had an operation and was recovering on a ranch in California when Harry Hopkins turned up as father's emissary to try to talk me out of getting a divorce from Betsey. Harry regretted the assignment and carried it out reluctantly. I resented the fact that father had delegated anyone for such an assignment, even a family friend and trusted aide such as Harry; father should have talked to me himself. I told Harry there was no point in speaking about it. He was relieved. We talked about other things for a few days, then he left. I'm sure he returned to tell father he failed. I never could bring myself to reproach father, but he knew how I felt. It never came up again.

My marriage to Betsey was far from unproductive. We had two children—Sara Delano, born in 1932, and Kate, born in 1936. And in 1941 I was married again, to Romelle Schneider. By then Franklin and John had also married.

Franklin married Ethel du Pont in 1937 after graduating from Harvard and entering the University of Virginia Law School. Father had a terriffic time at Franklin's wedding, a lavish affair with lots of rich food and strong drinks. Father found it funny that Franklin was marrying a du Pont, a member of that fabulously wealthy family that opposed him so fiercely. He delighted in bringing his New Deal cohorts to mix with the du Ponts' big-business buddies. As I remember it, father kissed every bridesmaid in sight.

Franklin graduated and practiced law until summoned to wartime duty. He and Ethel had two sons, Christopher du Pont Roosevelt and Franklin Delano Roosevelt III.

The summer of Franklin's marriage, John took off for Europe. At the Cannes Festival in France, the mayor charged John with getting drunk and beating him over the head with a bouquet, then watering the flowers by pouring a bottle of champagne over him. It made headlines all over the world.

John hurriedly wrote home to explain. He did not deny he had "presented" the mayor with some flowers and perhaps spilled a bit of bubbly on him, but denied he had "attacked" him. As for being drunk, how could he have been drunk, he asked, when this had happened at eleven at night and he had gone on until three in the morning? If he'd been drunk at eleven, would he have been conscious by three?

Mother believed him. "He is one of the most dignified of my children," she announced. Father laughed it off. He wanted to write him, "You seem to be having a good time. Wish I could be there."

By the following summer, 1941, good old dignified John took a bride, Anne Clark, from a respected New England family. And he, too, had to go into the service.

Before father died, each of his five children had been married—two of them twice, one of them three times. No presidential parents have ever had to deal with something like this before or since.

After the first couple of times, they didn't try to interfere. Perhaps because Sara had meddled so much in their lives, our father and mother didn't want to meddle in ours. They worried, rightfully, that we married too young and too hastily, and they worried, rightfully, that we divorced and remarried too hastily, but they not only never tried to dictate to us, they never reproached us. Asked if she ever gave advice to her children, mother said, "I am not good at giving advice. I believe in letting them work out their own plans." She did add, "It would be better if people did not marry too young, and if they waited until they had more experience. Unfortunately, most people have to learn by experience."

Frankly, I feel my parents had made a deal to continue their own marriage, never were completely content with it and didn't want their children to do the same. Probably aware they had not presented a picture of a contented marriage when we were children, and that they had in addition moved us about and neglected us, they may have felt partly responsible that we found it difficult to settle down ourselves. Mother did not approve of divorce, but she had come close to consenting to one herself, and did not feel entitled to disapprove of our divorces.

Mother also never sided with us or turned against those we divorced. She did not like all of the people we married, but she did not like them less because we divorced them. She kept in touch with all of them and remained close to some of them. Even after Elliott divorced Faye Emerson, for example—and much to Elliott's discomfort—mother continued to invite Faye to the house. She did this partly to stay close to the grandchildren, but only partly.

Mother did go out of her way to stay close to her grandchildren and make them feel they were members of our family and a part of the presidency and the Roosevelt tradition, whether or not their parents remained married. And father adored all of them.

For the most part, father did not display a great deal of interest in our marriages and divorces. His interests were elsewhere, but he always said he would be there if we needed him, and he always was. It was mother who did the dutiful things, perhaps making up for not having been more of a mother to us when we were younger.

I will never forget father coming to spend time with me when I had to have an operation at the Mayo Clinic in Rochester, Minnesota. I had ulcers and needed serious surgery, and it was touch-and-go for a few days as to how well I would recover. Father flew in from Washington, visited with me several times a day and stayed several days until I was out of danger.

Usually, though, it was mother who came to us when we were sick or in need of help. She joined Franklin's fiancée, Ethel, in tending him at a Boston hospital during Christmas week of 1936 when he required surgery on his sinuses. She came back to Boston the following fall when John underwent dental surgery, and she flew to Seattle that Christmas to take care of Anna's family when Anna had to have an operation. It was mother who responded to a predawn call from Franklin when he and Ethel crashed on an icy road and were hospitalized, though, as it turned out, without serious injuries.

Maybe she was stiffly formal in her ways, even with her

children, but a warm flame burned within her. You could count on her.

In many obvious ways it was difficult for father to respond to our calls, and thus it is unfair to fault him for seeming so far from us at times of crisis. He had a soft heart, too. For example, when granny was suddenly, but not seriously, stricken with an illness in Europe in 1931, a year or so before he became president, he made a hurried trip to be with her, just as she would always have been with him at such a time.

Elliott accompanied father on that trip, and of course met a young lady and enjoyed a shipboard romance. Father teased him unmercifully. Finally, one night, father assigned him to dance with Rosa Ponselle, the ponderous opera star, who nearly broke Elliott's back when the ship lurched and she fell on him.

I also recall that Elliott fell in love with a bronze statue of a mare and colt that he saw in a Paris shop. Father said it was too bad he couldn't afford it, but father gave it to Elliott for his birthday months later.

Once, when asked if his children's problems had hurt him politically, father said, "I believe a politician should be judged on his politics." For the most part, father did not interfere when we went our ways. On the other hand, he didn't help us either.

When I told granny I wanted no more of her money and found a part-time job in a small insurance business to see me through law school, I considered myself lucky. The owner, Victor de Gerard, offered me $50 a week, provided I learned the business. That was good part-time pay in those days, especially for an inexperienced person.

Mother was delighted. "Jimmy's got a job," she wrote father. Miracle of miracles! Father, however, who was governor of New York at the time, was not delighted. Louis Howe had de Gerard checked out. He passed muster, but father still felt I might better have joined a bigger, better-known firm. In an excellent example of snobbery, father grumbled, "I've asked around and no one's ever heard of him."

Well, maybe not, but father never offered to set me up with one of the big houses. When I wrote him about the possibility —suggested by mother—that Van Lear Black might find a place for me, father did not respond. He never even offered to give me an introduction to a top firm, where I could start at the bottom and work my way up. In fact, he never talked to me about my future.

So I took de Gerard's offer. And I worked hard at it. I studied nights and learned the fundamentals of general insurance and passed my exams to become a broker.

Father cautioned me about not letting de Gerard use my name to get business. Of course I realized that it had to be my name that had gotten me my job, but in fairness to de Gerard, he never tried to capitalize on my name and never asked me to do so. Father's other concern was that once I got established in business I'd give up law school. And on that score he was right. I was doing well with my studies but within a year I gave them up to devote myself full-time to my new job. And I don't know that the lack of a law degree ever handicapped me professionally.

De Gerard was a Russian immigrant, a kind of rough-textured man, but decent and able. However, he had only one account of consequence—Shell Oil Company. By itself, Shell Oil was not enough to insure his small firm's future. He had to broaden the base of his business and in my view the only way he could do it would be to cash in on my name. This would have been unacceptable to me, so when a good opportunity came to get out, I grabbed it.

John Sargent worked for a company de Gerard did some business with, and we hit it off right away. We both felt group insurance was the coming thing, and we decided to form a partnership and open our own Boston office, Roosevelt and Sargent. He had the money, I had the name.

Yes, I was going to use my name. I didn't feel guilty about it. It would give me a start. If I followed through by doing a good job, I'd deserve success. And we were a success. We sold a group policy to the Columbia Broadcasting System that endured for fifteen years and is still considered a pioneer program in the field. We devised an innovative group policy for National Distillers. We did work for the New England Power Company. And we landed a lot of small, lucrative accounts.

John Sargent was a typical stingy New Englander, but he was brilliant. I lacked his brilliance, but I had learned a lot under de Gerard and had the daring Sargent needed. He had the ideas and I sold them. We complemented one another. I took him to meet father, and father approved of him. In fact he was so impressed, he later brought John to Washington so he could pick his brain on some private insurance matters.

Incidentally, we also developed a connection with an old Boston firm, John C. Paige and Company, whose principal shareholder, interestingly enough, was Hamilton Fish. He was one of father's opponents and the object of his ridicule in the famous "Batton, Barton and Fish" speech.

Well, when you were FDR's son and in business, you couldn't totally avoid all political conflicts.

Before father became president, I was active in politics in Boston. I met the mayor, old Jim Curley, and he wasn't about to let a Roosevelt get away from him. While most of his party in that part of the country preferred Al Smith, Curley was convinced father was the man of the future. He took me under his wing, taught me a lot about big-city politics and put me to work in the political jungle.

I recall clearly an incident that I think explains Jim Curley. We were driving through the streets of the city during the St. Patrick's Day parade of 1932, and as we passed a modern, massive public bathhouse in the middle of the slums, Curley pointed it out to me. "Look at that," he said. "Isn't it beautiful?"

I smiled and agreed it was.

He went on: "I had it built because there are a lot of poor people in this area who do not have toilet facilities in their homes. If it wasn't for me, the poor people in this area would have no place to wash or relieve themselves. They would have only the streets. I am the only one who cares enough to provide the poor people such a place."

He paused, then chuckled. "Of course," he added, "it did cost an extra million dollars to build, because if you're going to look after the poor people you have to look after yourself."

I looked at him and laughed. He knew I liked him. He was a rascal, but he had reduced big-city politics to its essentials and had explained it to me the way it was, openly and without the slightest embarrassment.

Curley was kicked out of the Massachusetts delegation to the 1932 Democratic National Convention so that his crowd could support Smith. Undaunted, Curley bought the seat of a delegate from Puerto Rico and got himself elected chairman of the Puerto Rican delegation. He was pictured marching proudly down the street beneath a big banner that read, "Delegation from Puerto Rico. James M. Curley, Chairman." Every vote he could control he swung to father. When father was nominated, Curley went back to Boston as the big man in Massachusetts politics again.

Curley carried the state for father. But like a lot of politicians who were fooled at first, Curley learned that his support would not get him what he wanted. Father reserved the right to make appointments as he saw fit, no matter what he owed others.

Curley had grown up around the Boston shipyards and he wanted to be secretary of the navy. But father loved the navy and wouldn't think of having a crook like Curley head it. Instead he offered to make Curley ambassador to Poland.

The Boston Irishman was infuriated, as I relaxed earlier. I tried to help Curley, but father wouldn't listen. Consequently, Curley dropped me.

Along the way I became friendly with George Sweeney, a prominent politician in Boston who became one of the outstanding judges in the state. John Sargent and I had just started in insurance, and I thought it would be a long time before I made decent money. I was looking for something to see me through, and I mentioned this to Sweeney, who referred me to Frank Hale.

Hale had a company in New Jersey called National Grain and Yeast, and he needed someone to help him run it. He offered me the position of president, and I took it. He admitted he wanted me for my name, but insisted he also wanted me to do the job. I bought that. And the salary of $25,000 a year was acceptable, to say the least.

I opened an office of Roosevelt and Sargent in New York, and every day I drove through the Holland Tunnel to New Jersey and worked for National Grain and Yeast. Frank Hale was the sort of man who really ran his company, but I did a good job for him. There wasn't much to learn. We were in competition with Fleishmann's Yeast at a time when yeast was selling well. All I had to do was sell our yeast. My name helped, of course; by then, father was president. On the side I contributed considerably to my insurance firm, which was flourishing. Soon I was making $25,000 a year from that, too. Betsey and I were living the good life.

It was Henry Morgenthau who went to father and pointed out that Frank Hale had some rather unsavory associates. He said it was obvious that the grain was going into bootleg alcohol, the yeast company was just a front, and I was a front for all of it. He made it clear that as the president's son I was doing the president a disservice.

I told him that I had seen nothing illegal going on. And when I subsequently asked Hale about it, he said nothing illegal was going on. But how much could I kid myself? If I hadn't seen the operation for what it was, it was only because I hadn't wanted to. Now I couldn't ignore it. And anyway I was making enough money from the insurance business that I didn't need the yeast money. So, having enjoyed about eighteen fat months, I quit yeast to concentrate on insurance. I owed that much to father. And I really didn't want to be a bootlegger.

I had been spending quite a bit of time in Washington— whenever father asked me to help him out. These were never matters of great consequence. In fact, right after he was elected I was a sort of flunky, a glorified errand boy. I remember the night he closed the banks. He and his aides put in an all-night session and I saw to it that sandwiches were brought up and they had coffee. I didn't mind because it gave me a chance to see what was happening. I knew I was in on the making of a bit of history.

Little by little, father began to trust me with more responsibility. Instead of carrying a written message and waiting for a written response, he'd tell me what he wanted and I'd go and talk to whoever was involved and report back. After a while I was given assignments that only a trusted aide would get. Occasionally there were confidential things to be done—someone to be spoken to privately, perhaps—and father felt he could trust his son.

If he'd had the use of his legs, he would not have needed me as much as he did. But he didn't, and he came to call on me more and more. I always was flattered when he asked for me, and I went wherever he sent me. It simply was more important and interesting and exciting to me than my business outside the White House. I did not have an official position, nor was I paid. And I didn't play a part in any decision-making of consequence. About this time, however, during the 1936 campaign, father was under tremendous pressure and he approached me about my accepting a paid position on his official staff. Again, I was flattered. I also felt he needed help, even if only for the comfort of having family near him. Louis Howe had died, and father said he needed someone close to him, someone he could confide in and who could handle confidential assignments.

I was twenty-eight years old and was being offered an opportunity to play a part in the shaping of history. I wanted to contribute something of consequence to my father in the presidency. My insurance business with John Sargent was on solid footing. He could run it without my day-to-day help. So I went off to work with father.

XVI

At father's suggestion, my new position was to be kept confidential until after the election of 1936. He was confident of winning, but considered it wise to wait, so no charges of nepotism would be raised. He warned me, "We're going to be smeared some, old man. There are people who will think it wrong for a father to take his son into the presidency." I told him, "If you don't care what people say, I don't." He answered, "I don't."

After the election, he had arranged a trip on the cruiser *Indianapolis* to the Pan-American Peace Conference in Argentina. He wanted it to be a combination vacation trip and "Good Neighbor" tour of South America. We were to make several stops, and father wanted me along to help him—personally more than politically. Mother was a rotten sailor, and besides, she hated ceremonial trips. Father thought it would look better if at least one member of his family accompanied him. I agreed to go.

The campaign had taken a lot out of him, but the sea always restored him. He frequently took cruises up and down the Potomac aboard the presidential yacht, the *Potomac*, and entertained visiting royalty there, too. Now we were off to visit South American "royalty" on the *Indianapolis*.

I was aware that war was possibly ahead for the United

States, and I had discussed with father the wisdom of my entering a reserve service program so I could work toward going on active duty as an officer. The marines were my first choice—possibly because of their uniqueness.

Father said, "Well, if you're going to go with me, you should have some official status, so I'll have you appointed an officer in the Marine Reserve and assigned as my aide on this trip."

I said that was fine with me.

It was ridiculous, really, but my papers came through and he made me a lieutenant colonel. It was just that easy. Overnight I became Lt. Col. James Roosevelt, Marine Corps Reserve. No one complained at the time. I think everyone understood that this was only a temporary assignment.

Everyone except me. I thought I should justify my rank by going on maneuvers and things like that, and of course I was totally out of my depth. I didn't know what I was doing. So I eventually resigned my commission. Later I went back in as a captain, but that time I went into training and worked for it. In time I even earned my rank.

The trip to Argentina was one of the most memorable times of my life. Not because it was so vital, though it was eventful, but because it was the longest stretch of time I had ever spent with my father. We were together day and night, at work and at play. We talked to one another. We joked with one another. We laughed together. We were sad together. At official ceremonies we whispered private asides to each other. Not only were we father and son, we were friends. I was proud he was president, but aware he also was my father. I was a grown man, but I was like a boy who got to go fishing with his father. We did fish, as a matter of fact, several times on the trip.

It has been almost forty years now, and I still remember him as he was and as we were on that trip. I can remember the feel of him when I touched him, the smell of him when I was close to him, the sound of his voice, the look of him. He has been gone thirty years now. I hold on to the memory of that month. If it goes from me, I am gone.

It's strange, but when I first started to put together the pieces of that trip I had to stop to think if we took it before or after the election. Then I remembered we were away over Thanksgiving and we listened to the Army-Navy football game on the wireless, and it started to come back to me.

I remember in Rio President Vargas laid it on thick with a lavish reception and party. He put us up at a private mansion that had been vacated for the occasion and was the most luxurious place I'd ever seen.

Before dinner father wanted to take a bath and he asked me to fill the tub for him. The "tub" was the size of a small swimming pool and in the center of the room. I could not find either a faucet or any sign of plumbing fixtures.

"Gee," I said to father, "I'm sorry, but I can't figure out how to turn the darn thing on."

He laughed and said, "Just sit in it, son." I looked at him like he was crazy, but he repeated, "Sit in it."

So I sat down, and to my surprise, warm water began to bubble up. My surprise was increased by the fact that I still had some of my clothes on. I sat there dumbfounded and soggy as the water rose. I began to worry about how to turn it off, but when it got to a decent height it just stopped.

Father said, "Hey, it's supposed to be my bath, not yours." So I got out and helped him in. The water started to recede when I stepped out, but rose when he got in.

"How the heck does the darn thing work?" I asked him.

He laughed and said, "Don't all tubs work this way?"

It was a wonderful trip. We sailed in and out of beautiful harbors and were escorted in caravans of cars through streets lined with cheering crowds. I can't help contrasting our trip with the reception Richard Nixon received in South America years later when he was booed and taunted and had garbage thrown at him. But I can't pin the blame on Mr. Nixon. Our relations with our neighbors had deteriorated by then.

Father was pleased, back in 1936, that relations between our country and the South American countries were good and the trip was successful from the standpoint of creating goodwill. There were lavish receptions wherever we went, officials treated us with tremendous respect, and we received many gifts and decorations.

I remember in Rio father told me I was going to be decorated that night. I asked him what for, and he smiled and said, "For being my aide and my son." For that I was given something called "The Southern Cross," which I still have. Father got an enormous semiprecious stone as a gift for mother, which is on display today at the Roosevelt Museum in Hyde Park. I recall we had to clear the gifts with Congress before we could keep them.

In Montevideo, as I mentioned earlier, I rode in my gleaming white marine dress uniform directly in front of President Terra to protect him from any assassin's bullet. That was great fun, of course.

In Buenos Aires father addressed a peace conference. A young man in the audience jumped up and started to wave a red flag, screaming, "Down with imperialism!" Army officers dragged him out while father finished his speech. Afterward, the president of Argentina admitted sadly that the demonstrator was his son, who opposed his regime. Father turned to me and whispered, "Don't wave any flags."

Later, when we were alone, he said, "Son, I want you to know how much I appreciate what you and the others have done for me, and that you all have been loyal to me."

I said, "Well, old man, you know, we're proud of you. We're sorry when we cause you concern, but we're just trying to lead our own lives. I think we all know your life is not and has not been easy and we're really terrifically proud of the way you've lived it."

We embraced briefly. I guess that was the closest we ever came to exchanging the words "I love you."

Later Elliott opposed father publicly and rather strongly. It was his right, but it was sort of sad, too, remembering what father had said about the loyalty of his children. Still later, John became a Republican, but he was attracted to the Republican party and policies long before he admitted to it or announced it, and he deliberately was inactive politically as long as father was alive.

In Rio, McDuffie, father's valet, disappeared the morning of the day we were to leave and did not return when he was supposed to. He had still not shown up when the time came for us to go. The authorities were looking for him, but couldn't find him. Finally the ship had to leave. Father told the authorities to send Mac on to our next stop if they ever found him.

We felt terrible about it. But we had not yet cleared the harbor when a little boat came racing up. Father said, "I bet that's McDuffie."

Sure enough, it was. Looking somewhat the worse for wear after what must have been a great liberty, McDuffie climbed sheepishly aboard. Father had him brought to his room. There he told him, "McDuffie, when you are serving on a naval ship you are subject to naval command and regulations. You were absent over leave and you have to stand court-martial. I'm afraid you are going to be put in the brig for Lord knows how long."

McDuffie apologized and pleaded for mercy, and father laughed and said he would forgive him this time, but that McDuffie was not to forget the experience. I know Irvin never did. In Buenos Aires, Gus Gennerich keeled over dead one night at a café. Father was asleep when word came to me about it. It was a shock and I decided to handle it myself and not to awaken him. It was suggested that perhaps Gus had been poisoned, but I didn't think father would have wanted an international incident, so father's doctor, Captain Ross McIntire, and I had to talk the officials out of performing an autopsy. We signed some papers and got the body delivered to a local funeral home and from there to the American Embassy. When I told father the next morning he was shaken, but he said I had done what should have been done. No autopsy was ever performed and as I said earlier, we always thought his death was the result of hitting his head on board the ship. We took part in a simple service at the embassy, and later there was a second ceremony in Washington, where Gus was laid to rest. Father wrote mother from South America, ". . . good old Gus was the kind of a loyal friend who simply cannot be replaced."

Back in Washington, father told me he definitely wanted me to serve as one of his secretaries and asked if I was still agreeable. I told him I was.

Mother was opposed to my working for father, anticipating that he would be charged with nepotism—which he was. His favorite uncle, Fred Delano, argued against it too, on the same grounds. So did several of his aides, who felt I would step right over them and take on responsibilities for which I was not suited. This did not happen at any time.

Nevertheless, it might have been wise to have heeded the danger signs and said, "Look, old man, it's nice of you to want me with you, and I want to be with you, but it just won't work, so let's pass on it." But I didn't. And he said, "Why should I be deprived of my eldest son's help and of the pleasure of having him with me just because I am president?"

So I went to work for him. We kept it low-key at first, but after a while he moved me front and center and announced I was an aide, officially, and he was criticized for it.

I was a help to him, however, and I enjoyed the two or three years I spent in his service. By then he wanted someone like me near him. His life had ceased to be his own. Because he was crippled, he was alone a lot less than other men. Unless he was asleep, he was seldom alone, even in his bedroom. Gus Gennerich and, later, Tommy Qualters were always nearby. So were Irvin McDuffie and Arthur Prettyman. Louis Howe would often get excited and barge in to talk to father.

Father once said, sort of wistfully, "You know, son, it would be nice to be able to shut my own door and to keep it shut if I wanted." He didn't want to hurt Louis's feelings, so he never let on how he felt.

Louis was an egotist and he never let father forget that he'd put him where he was. He didn't always talk to father with the respect due a president; he often sounded like a boss addressing an employee, or a father talking to a son. And father let him get away with it. I think that after Louis died, father needed someone he could speak to as a son. And that's where I fitted in. I was always respectful, and I certainly never told him anything he said was stupid. For that matter, he never accused me of saying anything stupid either. He always defended my right to speak my mind, even when I wound up saying something other than what I intended.

Once, when the banking activities of the House of Morgan were being investigated, I was accused of defending J. P. Morgan and attacking father's banking policies. At his next press conference, father was asked about it. He said, "I will have to make it clear that Jim is more than twenty-one, and I have not seen him for ten days."

Another time, when I denied having made the statement that the NRA might not have long to live, father said, "You pays your money and you takes your choice. Being his father, I prefer to believe him."

Father gave all of us the right to speak up. When Elliott knocked the New Deal over the airwaves and angered faithful members of the press in the process, father instructed Steve Early to tell them, "Mr. Elliott Roosevelt is an American citizen—free and of adult age. He therefore enjoys, among other things, the right of free speech. . . ."

However, father did not favor the family to the extent that he took our advice very often—though we were rather free about offering it to him. For example, Johnny, while at Harvard, once wrote, "Why don't you tell Congress to go home and the Supreme Court to go to hell?" Father advised John that might be too blunt an approach.

A distant cousin, Mary Willis Roosevelt, of the Oyster Bay Republican Roosevelts, once wrote him, pompously, and misspelled his name, "My Dear Franklyn . . . I shall not sail under any false colors, but tell you that, because of your running mate and all the rest . . . your very bad political strategy . . . bad form in politics . . . I am unreservedly against you. . . . I know many people who have decided they will not vote for you. . . ."

Father replied, misspelling her name, "Dear Marye . . . Thank you very much for writing to me. It is good to hear from you. I am sorry that you feel as you do, but I must tell you quite frankly that it really never occurred to me that you would vote for me. . . ."

He favored short replies. His favorite was a two-word answer to a sizzling letter on "cheap gutter politics" from Mayor LaGuardia of New York, normally an ally. Father wrote him, simply, "Ho-hum!"

Granny was the family member who wrote him most often with advice. Her letters always bore the legend "To the President—Personal—S.D.R." Father called her his "assistant secretary of state" and paid no attention whatsoever to her advice. However, her activities sometimes disturbed him. For example, in 1937 she wrote from Italy, "The Duce sent me a grand bunch of flowers. . . . All seems very flourishing and peaceful." She also wrote that she had met a Spanish countess and "there is great hope that the rebels under Franco will win, as they are the only hope for poor Spain."

It was harder for father to disregard mother's advice. She usually had plenty of it to offer, and it generally came by wire or mail, since she usually was off somewhere. I'll never forget granny writing father and saying, "I hope Eleanor has come out of that coal mine by now."

During the Spanish Civil War mother wired father in Warm Springs: "Just received wire signed Einstein, Dorothy Thompson, etc., about important leaders trapped in Madrid. Are you or State Department doing anything?"

With his sense of humor, father wired back: "State Department doing everything possible in Spain. Had successful dedication of Medical and Education Buildings. Lovely weather. Much love to all of you."

When air hero Charles Lindbergh and army hero Hugh Johnson adopted their isolationist stances and attacked his "warlike" policies, father labeled Lindy an "appeaser" and refused to reappoint Johnson as a brigadier general in the reserves. Mother wrote, "I wish I knew more of what really led to your refusal to renew Johnson's appointment. . . . I suppose there is some valid reason, but to a great many people it looks as though you had simply indulged in annoyance because Johnson has been attacking the administration. . . . A lot of people think Lindbergh has a right to say what he chooses. . . ."

Father didn't even answer that one.

Actually, mother was an admitted pacifist, but she at least did not actively oppose father. In time, circumstances convinced her of the inevitability of the impending war and the need to prepare for it. The isolationists killed the World Court and hurt this country badly because we were not prepared for war.

Father Coughlin led the isolationists, to whom Lindbergh lent his personal popularity. Coughlin attacked communism and internationalism before father became president. At first he favored the New Deal, then he turned against father because he didn't think father went far enough with his war on wealth. Coughlin had a radio program, a magazine and an enormous number of supporters. He raved against "Red atheists," "godless capitalists," "international plutocrats" and father. Coughlin joined forces with Huey Long, "The Kingfish" from Louisiana, who became a senator in 1932 and wanted to be president on a "Share the Wealth" program that promised to liquidate the larger personal fortunes and provide every family a home, a radio, a car, college educations for the young and pensions for the old.

Father fought Coughlin, partly by enlisting Missy's support in rounding up Catholic leaders who would oppose the priest. This got easier when it became clear that Coughlin was amassing a personal fortune and was sponsoring an anti-Semitic crusade, supported by Westbrook Pegler and other Hearst columnists and editorial writers.

Once, when I asked father if he minded being accused of

having Jewish blood, he said he had searched his genealogy in the futile hope of finding some, and added, "I wish I was."

Father had no religious bigotry in him and he hated fighting this war of religion. But he won it. Coughlin's superiors pulled him from the airwaves, and father's administrator canceled his magazine's mailing rights. Coughlin's audiences shrank, and he disappeared into a parish in Michigan, where he remained into the 1960s. Coughlin's power was that he was a persuasive speaker who could inflame audiences the way Hitler did. Huey Long, too, was a clever speaker and might have been a tough rival had he not been shot and killed in September 1935 by Dr. Carl Weiss, the son-in-law of a political rival. Weiss, in turn, was gunned down by The Kingfish's bodyguards. There are still those who think that Long could have blocked father's renomination in 1936, and that father was involved in a conspiracy against him. There has never been the slightest shred of evidence of such a plot. This was not father's style.

The Kingfish, whose son Russell sits in the Senate today, was a fascinating fellow. I recall the first time I met him. Up on the Hill, I punched the wrong elevator button and stepped into one of the Senate's private cars, occupied by Long and a number of other senators. When I began to back out, Huey said, "Oh, come on in, Jim, there's plenty of room. It's time you met the only honest U.S. senator." And he stuck out his hand for me to shake.

I had a split second to think that over. I didn't want to insult him by refusing his hand, but if I shook it I was insulting the others.

I stuck out my hand and said, "I'm happy to meet an honest senator, and I'd be happy to meet all the rest of these honest senators and shake their hands, too."

We all laughed.

That was Long's style. He reminded me of Jim Curley. He really thought he was the only one who was helping the little people. And if he helped himself in the process, why not? That's the way he saw it.

Mother was a rather serious young girl, which prompted her mother to nickname her "Granny."

Father was about eight years old when this picture was taken. WIDE WORLD

Mother and her brother Elliott, "little Ellie."
THE BETTMANN ARCHIVE

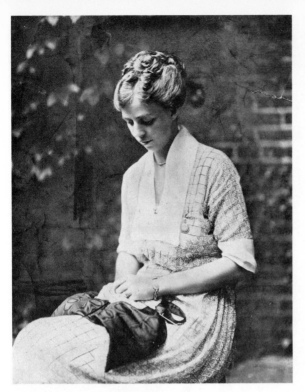

Mother at Campobello in 1920. Father had just been nominated for Vice President.

The house at Hyde Park where my father was born.

Father campaigning in Chicago in the summer of 1932. The man on the left is Chicago Mayor Anton Cermak. Cermak was killed during an attempt to assassinate my father in February 1933. WIDE WORLD

This picture was taken right after we learned that father had won the election in 1932. Jim Farley's on the left. WIDE WORLD

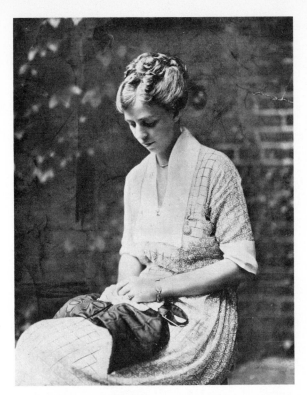

Mother at Campobello in 1920.
Father had just been nominated
for Vice President.

The house at Hyde Park where my father was born.

Mother in her wedding gown.

My parents and my grandmother, Sara Delano Roosevelt, in 1920.

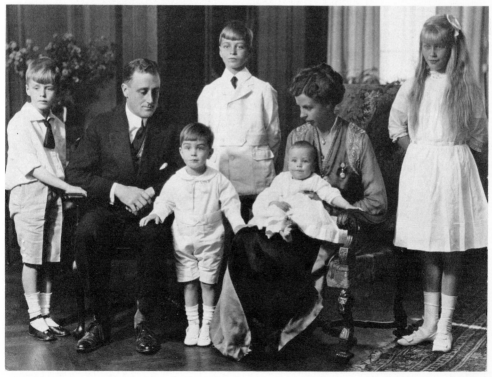

Our family in 1916. Left to right: Elliott, father, Franklin, Jr., myself, my mother holding John, Anna.

My father in 1928, on his way to the convention in Houston where he nominated Al Smith for president.

Father and I arriving in Buffalo, New York, during the presidential campaign of 1932. WIDE WORLD

Father discussing campaign plans with (l. to r.) Louis Howe, Jim Farley and Edward Flynn, Secretary of State. WIDE WORLD

Father campaigning in Chicago in the summer of 1932. The man on the left is Chicago Mayor Anton Cermak. Cermak was killed during an attempt to assassinate my father in February 1933.   WIDE WORLD

This picture was taken right after we learned that father had won the election in 1932. Jim Farley's on the left.   WIDE WORLD

My father's first inauguration, in 1933. He is being sworn in by Chief Justice Charles Evans Hughes. To the right, in back of me, is Herbert Hoover.

This photo was taken in 1933. In the back row (l. to r): Frances Keller, Mary Dreier, Marion Dickerman, Antonia Hatvany. Middle row: Nancy Cook, Franklin, Jr. and John. Front row: mother, father and me.

My grandmother, Sara Delano Roosevelt, greeting my parents on their arrival at Hyde Park in the summer of 1933.   WIDE WORLD

Father greeting mother on her return from a trip in March 1934.   WIDE WORLD

I accompanied father on a trip to Rio de Janeiro in 1933. Seated next to father is Brazilian president Getulio Vargas. We were on our way to the Inter-American Peace Conference in Buenos Aires. WIDE WORLD

This photo was taken under the South Portico of the White House as father and I were leaving for special services at St. John's Episcopal Church preceding the inauguration ceremony on January 1, 1941.

WIDE WORLD

My favorite picture of my father, reviewing the fleet in 1938.

In August 1942, I was second in command of the Marine contingent that struck the Japanese on Makin Island in the South Pacific.

Father visiting Camp Pendleton in 1944.

Conference at Yalta, 1945, draws to a close as leaders dine at the Lavadia Palace. Father is seated between Stalin and Churchill. On the left is Secretary of State Edward R. Stettinius, Jr.; on the right is Soviet Foreign Minister Molotov.

This is my favorite photograph of my mother. She's arriving in Washington, weary but carrying her own bag.

This was taken just before the opening of "Sunrise at Campobello" on Broadway in 1958. The play dealt with father's fight against polio following his attack. To the best of my knowledge it's the only photo of mother and her four sons as adults.

When I became part of father's official family, I was assisted by Jimmy Rowe, a former law clerk to Justice Oliver Wendell Holmes, and Margaret "Rabbit" Durand, the freckle-faced and peppy former secretary to Louis Howe. Rabbit was delightfully irreverent. I remember when one fidgety congressman stopped by while I was out, she left me a memo: "Nervous Nellie was in today."

We worked long hours. Our workday began in father's bedroom. Father had his breakfast and read the morning newspapers in bed. He sometimes was still there when his secretaries—Steve Early, Marvin McIntyre and I, and sometimes Pa Watson—arrived to discuss the day's order of business. Usually he was being dressed or was dressed and ready to go. Occasionally we talked by hollering back and forth while he shaved in his bathroom.

He'd be helped into his wheelchair and ride the elevator to the ground floor, then was wheeled outside past the rose garden and into the executive offices, bells sounding all the while to warn that he was on his way. Once in his office he was a captive, protected from unwanted visitors by McIntyre, Missy and Grace, but hosting a stream of visitors nevertheless. He had lunch on a tray in his office. Sometimes he was annoyed when there was no one to summon, since we often ate out, or in the executive cafeteria. At those times he would scribble notes on scraps of paper and stuff them in his pocket.

Late in the afternoon he went through what was left of his mail after Missy had cut the eight to ten thousand daily letters to the less than a hundred he should see. Later, mother turned over letters written her that she thought would be of interest to him.

He tried to spare his family an hour or so by having dinner with those of us who were in residence. But after dinner he often went back to work, either in his study or bedroom, or in the executive office. I often was with him, taking notes and talking things over. He usually was in bed by ten. He was an early-to-bed, early-to-rise guy. Sometimes he'd listen to radio programs or read a mystery novel.

One of the reasons a president needs so much help is that he and his key aides would otherwise be inundated by the petty chores that have to be attended to every day. For instance, thousands of gifts arrived every year. We called these "booby traps" because, though most were well meant, many were intended to gain favor with father. The larger ones were returned immediately, with a note of regret. The smaller ones were kept so as not to insult the giver, but rarely were used. After a while, the basement began to overflow with dreadful paintings of father, recordings of his speeches, homemade wine and so on. I remember one painting that was four times life-size.

People offered him ships ("How would you like a floating White House?"), carloads of prize heifers, lifetime supplies of special shoes. He was also offered the opportunities of several lifetimes to get into everything from oil wells to a candy business. I was included in the invitation to join in the latter, and all that was asked of father and me was an investment of $10 million.

I received many offers, as did his other aides. I remember one man wrote to say he looked so much like me he wondered if I might need a double on occasion. He also wondered would I mind if he accepted a good offer to impersonate me?

Poor father, who had trouble just getting from one room to the other, was besieged with invitations to the Mullins Tobacco Festival in South Carolina, the Malta Rodeo in Montana, the Daniel Roper Watermelon Party in Tennessee, and so on. He was invited to movie premieres and private parties, the Redwine Methodist Reunion of Georgia, and the Citizens of Muscle Shoals Dirt-Breaking Jubilee in North Carolina.

I found these invitations among trivia I kept. Part of my job had been to help sort out the invitations and send the proper regrets. While father hated to have anyone forge his signature, it had to be done. Not only was there too much minor mail to be answered, but far too many "autographed" photos to be sent out.

A more important part of my job was to act as presidential

liaison with Congress, along with Tommy Corcoran. My basic assignment was to coordinate father's dealings with those government agencies not under a cabinet office—the CCC, SEC, etc.

I was his "legs," carrying confidential memos back and forth. I participated in some policy-making meetings, though the decisions were his, of course. I was also a sounding board for some of his speeches, though his favorite for this was Moses Smith, a colorful character, a man of the earth who ran father's Hyde Park farm. I carried father's messages to Congress. I sounded out senators and representatives and counted heads so that we would know where we stood on some issue that was due for a vote.

For the most part the cabinet members were cooperative—though, as I have pointed out, there were those who were suspicious or jealous and resented me. An example was Bill Douglas, who was chairman of the Securities and Exchange Commission at the time.

In a book, Douglas wrote that when he rejected an offer by one Charles Schwartz to act as intermediary between the commission and the major electric power utilities at a fat fee, I entered the Douglas office and raised the roof about denying Democrats the opportunity to make money while they were in power. He said that when he reported the incident to father, offering to resign, the president put his head on his arm and cried like a child for several minutes, then wiped away his tears, talked Douglas out of resigning and spoke of what a problem I was to him.

The facts are, I never spoke on behalf of Schwartz, who was, in fact, a Republican; I never was in Douglas's office; I never in my life saw my father shed even a single tear. I don't think father ever considered me a problem to him. He never wanted me to resign. If Douglas offered to resign because of anything I did, he was not much of a fighter.

Douglas was a man of great talent, but emotionally erratic. Accordingly, father passed on the opportunity to make him his running mate in 1944, for which Douglas never forgave him. In later years Douglas did develop impressively. He was close to John Kennedy and had an illustrious career as a liberal member of the Supreme Court, despite a controversial personal life. More recently, as age and illness ended Douglas's effectiveness, President Ford tried to have him impeached. However, when Douglas finally resigned under pressure, the president praised his career.

Father had his foes in Congress, but he respected many of them—Robert Taft, for example. Bob was opposed to father on almost every issue, but he was a brilliant man and certainly entitled to his views. He never got personal in discussing father's policies, so father never got personal in discussing him. They admired each other's ideals, if not each other's ideas. Had Taft been more personable and a better speaker, he might have been a strong Republican nominee for the presidency, but he was left out in the rush to the popular Eisenhower in the 1950s. As conservative a person as Taft would have had a hard time getting elected, anyway. The able Barry Goldwater couldn't swing it, and the personable Ronald Reagan couldn't either.

Father openly supported the Republican Fiorello LaGuardia in his fight against New York's Tammany Hall and made him his Civil Defense chief when the program needed a strong salesman.

On the other hand, father had no respect for Martin Dies, whose House Committee on Un-American Activities was itself as un-American as the worst offenders it investigated. Seeking to rout communist influence in this country, Dies's group attacked the innocent along with the guilty—if there were any. There were those who, between the wars, associated themselves with groups seeking to better conditions in this country, and it took time to see that many of these groups were misguided. Others simply let their enthusiasms carry them beyond the bounds of reason.

Mother was one of those who, through her friend Joe Lash, associated herself with many members of the "Popular Front," including—despite father's disapproval—the American Youth Congress and the Student Union. She was criti-

cized by Dies's committee, as were father and Frances Perkins
for refusing to deport the leader of the longshoremen's union.
"Without legal grounds for acting against Bridges, I will not
act," father declared. Dies spoke of father, Perkins, Hopkins,
Ickes and others as dupes of the Communists.

The Dies drive died of its own indefensible tactics—as did
a similar drive mounted later by Joe McCarthy, though not
before building a following and doing dreadful damage to
many good Americans and the American way of life.

I think father failed to deal firmly enough with J. Edgar
Hoover when he, too, started to take his FBI down this road.
Appointed by a previous administration, Hoover was reap-
pointed during father's administration and those following,
despite evidence that he was misusing his power. The fact is
that father, like other presidents, misused it too. Apparently
father had Hoover tap the telephones of Hopkins and Corcoran at one time when he wanted to check up on them. So he
could hardly damn the man. And we forget how popular
Hoover and his FBI were at the time of father's presidency.

Father had his troubles with labor leaders. He and John L.
Lewis were friends for a long time, but they split when Lewis
was swept up in his own importance and started to ask for
things that were not in the national interest.

Because of his resonant speaking voice and biblical manner,
the miners' boss became the most dramatic of the labor leaders who rose to power on the provisions of father's NRA. But
father's neutrality between management and labor at the time
of the sit-down strikes, as evidenced by his "a plague on both
your houses" speech, angered Lewis.

Many powerful labor leaders of the period allied against
father. Others sided with him—Sidney Hillman, for example,
and Bill Green. Eventually, the war ended the Depression,
everyone rolled up their sleeves and went to work and, for the
time being, the big labor leaders had no cause for concern. In
the end, I think labor came to see father had been a friend
whose acts and policies did more for them than any other
president had done.

My role was meant to be an anonymous one, but, because

of who I was, this was impossible. I never called attention to myself, but the spotlight sought me out.

I remember the time when father sent mother and me as his representatives to Calvin Coolidge's funeral. In order to go I had to take a detour from another trip, and the proper formal attire was to be sent to me. When I opened my suitcase, however, I found a full-dress suit and opera hat. I wore the hat and hoped my heavy overcoat would conceal my other attire.

It was so hot in the church that I started to perspire. Mother thought the whole thing was very funny, and when I mopped myself with a large handkerchief she began to giggle. This made me laugh, too. It was contagious and we couldn't quit, even though we were getting dirty looks from mourners.

Reporters took note and sent wire reports to the newspapers suggesting we had found the funeral funny. When we got back to Washington, we suggested to father that he not send us to any more funerals. He agreed.

Most of the time I did not have to make any mistakes in order to be reproached. Some newspapers started calling me the "crown prince." Someone changed it to "clown prince." *Time* magazine featured me on its cover over the title "Assistant President." And then the *Saturday Evening Post* published a story, "Jimmy's Got It," by Alva Johnson, who reported that by feathering my insurance business with golden eggs obtained in my father's office, I had an income that approached $2 million a year.

At the time I was in the Mayo Clinic for ulcer surgery, and it was difficult to defend myself. Father had to talk mother out of rushing into print in my defense. But when *Collier's* offered to run my reply in a story to be written with Walter Davenport, father approved the plan. He suggested, however, that I adopt a light tone and not lay too heavy a hand on my critics.

I did so, turning over my income tax returns for the period in question, showing that between 1933 and 1941 my income ranged from $21,714 to $49,167. I did not have a dime of unreported income and I paid my taxes in full. I knew my name had helped my business, but I did not deliberately use any influence I might have had in my position as father's aide to land any new business. In fact I neglected my business interests while I was working in the White House.

I think Alva Johnson simply created a story out of thin air, based on the most irresponsible of rumors. Even my worst enemies within the White House considered the story irresponsible and totally inaccurate. It simply wasn't true. But I was burned by it, as was father.

I have made mistakes in my lifetime; I have done things I regret. But I did not do any disservice to my father while I was in the White House—except by allowing myself to be there. The accusations tore me apart, and left me with severe stomach problems. And it hurt my father. So I resigned.

Elliott has written that father was angry at me for divorcing Betsey, that he accepted my resignation without reservation and did not invite me to Hyde Park for Christmas.

This is not true. Neither Elliott nor I, nor, for that matter, Franklin or Anna had any reason to be proud of our marital misadventures, and there were a few times when mother or father tried to talk us out of acting hastily. However, they never to my knowledge reproached any of us or cut us out of their lives for even an instant.

None of us served father as did Howe or Hopkins, but we did what we could do, and he was happy with our help and content when we were with him. I did not need an invitation to Hyde Park for Christmas of 1939 and would have been welcomed had I decided to make the trip home. I was busy in business, as at times was Elliott in Texas.

I love Elliott as a brother, and I respect him, but we have differing views on the lives we have led. We have had disagreements before, and I suppose we shall have them again.

Father did not want to accept my resignation. He didn't need me, but he wanted me. He didn't care about the critics. But he did care about my health. He refused my resignation at first, but when it became clear it would take time for me to recuperate, he reluctantly, and with some sadness, let me go.

I went on to other interests for a while, falling into something I did not deserve, just as Elliott did, and then Franklin, because of who we were, not what we were. Later father called me back, when I was in a position to help him. I don't know how much help I was, but I certainly was not at any time an "assistant president."

"One of the worst things in the world is being the child of a president," father once said. "It's a terrible life they lead."

XVII

The presidency is a lonely job for any man, but in some ways father seemed especially lonely, and I didn't like leaving him. Perhaps if father and mother had been together more they could have recaptured the closeness they once shared. Maybe that would have helped them to get through their difficult days.

I have always thought that there was a deeper, more enduring bond between them than others realize. I have seen their letters, and there are hints of regret in them. Father writes mother: "The Lord only knows when this will catch up with my Will o' the Wisp wife. . . ." And she writes him: "We are really very dependent on each other though we do see so little of each other. . . ." She concludes: "Dear love to you. I miss you and hate to feel you so far away. . . ." He writes: "I feel just as far away as if it were Europe. . . ."

But they seldom discussed their life in depth. Mother once told me, "He would never discuss an intimate family problem unless it was something that had reached the stage where it just had to be discussed. Then we would talk it over, he would tell me what he wanted done and I would do it."

I think they both wanted to close the gap between them, but neither knew how to do it.

Father came closer to taking his children into his confidence about personal matters than he did his wife, but he was too private a person to bare his soul. He took comfort in having his children close to him. That is why he wanted me with him in the White House in the first place, later brought me back to undertake a secret mission overseas for him, always brought me back for his inaugurations. In spite of his problems with Elliott—even after Elliott opposed his third-term bid—father had Elliott accompany him to five major wartime meetings overseas, and Anna to another. And Anna stayed with him in the White House while his sons were serving in the armed forces.

When I left my post beside father, I entered the Mayo Clinic. There I met a man named Murphy who had invented the coupling for railroad cars and made a fortune. He knew father, and he invited me to recuperate at his ranch in California, which was staffed but otherwise unoccupied at the time. I accepted the invitation, as well as the offer to ride out in his private railroad car. And it changed my life because I fell in love with California. I have lived here on and off ever since.

I rested at the ranch and regained my strength. While there, I was invited to a Hollywood dinner where I met Sam Goldwyn, Louis B. Mayer, Joe Schenk and other movie executives, as well as Joan Crawford and other stars. After I had talked to Mr. Goldwyn awhile, he asked me to come to his office to talk with him further. I did, and he offered me a job. He said I was bright and could learn the business fast, that I had administrative experience that would be useful to him.

You and I know that the average outsider does not receive such an offer. I was willing to take advantage of the fact that I was not the average outsider. I have always felt that, even if I accepted an undeserved opportunity, if I worked hard to make the most of it on my own, any success I had would be deserved. I couldn't see how Goldwyn could take advantage of the fact that I was the president's son. It looked like an interesting job. The money was attractive—$500 a week. Not a lot of money for Hollywood, but a lot for me. Later I was raised to $750 a week, which came to almost $40,000 a year.

Being Goldwyn's administrative assistant was an interesting job. There were times when he was busy and I operated the studio on a day-to-day basis. There were no disasters, and we made money. I met the most prominent movie people and stars of the day, and I enjoyed the experience. Although there was plenty of studio politics, it was a change from political life.

I did not date many stars. Although my marriage to Betsey had ended, I had met the girl I was going to marry next, Romelle Schneider. She'd nursed me at Mayo, I'd fallen in love with her, and had brought her to California to nurse me when I was told I needed nursing care for a while. Like a couple of my brothers, I fell in and out of love far too fast and too easily, but I was young and foolish. Well, okay, I was in my early thirties, but still foolish about life and love.

Goldwyn was a fascinating fellow. He was famous for misusing the English language, but I was never sure that his famous malapropisms weren't strictly for effect. He had a feel for what would sell, a flair for show business. Through Sam I met some fascinating people, including Howard Hughes.

I sat in on a session once when Sam and Howard were discussing the possibility of Hughes operating out of Goldwyn's studios. I wish I could reproduce it, but I can't. All I remember is that it was funny. Whenever Sam got stuck on some point, he'd mumble one of those malapropisms that didn't mean anything to anyone. Hughes, who had a hearing problem, would cup his ear and ask, "What'd you say, Sam?" But when Sam said something Howard wanted to hear, Howard heard him loud and clear.

Another memory that comes to mind concerns a luncheon date I had at the studio with David Niven and Loretta Young. In the course of our conversation, Niven said we Americans were the most gullible people on earth. To prove it, he pointed to a ten-gallon hat a cowboy actor had hung on the wall and said, "I'll bet you the price of this lunch that I can take that hat and go from door to door in the offices of this studio and mumble some mumbo-jumbo about taking up a collection to care for children or something and I can come back here in ten to twenty minutes with a hundred dollars."

I bet him he wouldn't pick up ten dollars, and off he went, with Loretta going along to make sure he played it straight.

In about twenty minutes he was back with, believe it or not, more than a thousand dollars. Loretta offered testimony that he had made up a different, more meaningless story at each stop.

I've never forgotten it. I told father later, and he roared. I guess we *are* gullible.

So many people were making so much money so fast in films in those days that I decided to leave Goldwyn to go into film production on my own. I had run into a man who financed films for the Bank of America, and he liked an idea of mine. It had to do with the "Pot of Gold" gimmick Horace Heidt was using in his radio show and in tours with his band. The contestant would spin a wheel and answer questions and could win a lot of money.

We called the picture *Pot of Gold*. Horace was in it along with top stars Jimmy Stewart and Paulette Goddard, and it was directed by a leading director, George Marshall. It wasn't a bad picture, but it wasn't good, either. And while it wasn't a flop, it wasn't a pot of gold.

I had borrowed half a million dollars from the bank to finance it, and for months I had trouble sleeping, worrying about my investment. Clearly, I have some of father's blood in me. Also, it seemed like everyone who had walked past the set was cut in for a piece of the profits. Still, we paid everything off, and, as I remember it, I came out of it with a small profit.

Then a Hollywood veteran named Henry Hennigson introduced me to some fellows from Chicago named the Mills Brothers. Not the singing group, but the guys who supplied slot machines to Las Vegas and other Nevada gambling houses.

They had a terrific idea. Jukeboxes were big at that time,

and they had come up with a superjukebox. Instead of just playing records, it projected onto a screen on top of the box a picture of the artist performing while the sound track played the song.

We had to get top stars signed up and filmed and machines placed all over the country, and we had a lot of trouble with record and jukebox companies. Still, the company was beginning to go and would have succeeded if fate hadn't stepped in. We couldn't get production on the machines because of the war. After the war, television took over and our machine was a dead duck.

I'd lost the money I'd made from the movie. I had some bad publicity, too. Stories appeared that I was mixed up with Mafia mobsters. Then there were stories that I was involved in the production of dirty movies. By the time the machines came out and it was clear that I was connected with the cleanest sort of entertainment, my reputation and father's had already been hurt.

While I was in Hollywood, a friend of Joe Schenk's called to ask if I could help Joe. He'd been indicted on charges of income tax evasion and faced a long jail term. I looked into it and felt that at most he was guilty of minor infractions. He'd been a longtime Democrat, an ardent supporter of father, and he was an old man who might be killed by imprisonment. I decided to plead his case with father.

Father told me he'd consider the case. But a few days later he told me Morgenthau was angry about it and had threatened to resign. I said I thought that was just too bad, that I saw nothing wrong with trying to help a friend by bringing his case to the one man who might pardon him or who might see that he was put on probation. Father agreed that there was nothing wrong with my pleading a person's case, but in this instance he said he had looked into it and decided he could not take Schenk off the hook.

I thanked him for having heard me out, and that was that. Joe served a term and it didn't kill him. Maybe he deserved it, but I didn't think so. I thought if he hadn't been rich at a time father was cutting down the rich, the Treasury Department never would have pressed the case.

Morgenthau later wrote in his book that I had been wrong. Maybe I was, but I didn't think so then and I don't now. If I hadn't been the son of the president, no one would have thought anything of it. People plead for their friends every day in government and in every area of business, too. I began to think there wasn't any business I could go into without creating some sort of fuss. I told father that perhaps he'd better put me on the WPA. He laughed and said they'd raise hell about that, too.

The war was coming. As the battle in Europe and Asia intensified, all of us waited for developments from day to day.

I'd learned to fly, along with Jimmy Stewart, Brian Aherne and others of the Hollywood community. However, I was a member of the Marine Corps Reserve and decided not to try for an air force commission. I started to take extensive officer's training. Soon I would have to go on active duty.

Early in 1940, Elliott was telling his Texas radio listeners that father would not break tradition and run for a third term. Elliott was nominating John Garner as the ideal candidate. Anna and her husband John Boettiger were editorializing in the *Seattle Post-Intelligencer* that Elliott was out of line, and that in this time of crisis the country needed FDR. Meanwhile, mother was pumping for Cordell Hull. Jim Farley was pumping for himself. With Louis Howe dead and Harry Hopkins dying, father was waging a lonely fight, surrounded by men who were not close to him.

Hitler's Nazi blitzkrieg stormed into Scandinavia, Belgium, the Netherlands. Neville Chamberlain was disgraced and he was replaced as prime minister of Great Britain by Winston Churchill, who promised blood, sweat and tears and pleaded for help from father as England went to war. British forces evacuated almost a quarter of a million men from the beaches at Dunkirk. Nazi U-boats roamed the seas, sinking

British ships. The bombing of Britain began. The British reeled. Mussolini's Italy declared war on France, and the Germans marched into Paris. Involvement was inevitable, but some could not see what they did not want to see. Led by the isolationists, Congress was reluctant to aid our allies and risk our involvement in another world war.

As father had been paralyzed by polio, Harry Hopkins was almost crippled by cancer. But Hopkins rallied from a near fatal bout to stand by his old friend as father declared he would seek that controversial third term, over the opposition of many members of his own family. Although it was politically unpopular, father pushed for selective service—the drafting of American men to give us a respectable standing force of trained soldiers.

Elliott recalls the nominating convention and election as close calls, but they weren't close. Father overwhelmed minimal opposition in the convention balloting and, with Wallace replacing Garner as his running mate, routed the respected Willkie at the polls.

One week before the election, the Selective Service Act had gone into effect. The first peacetime lottery of numbers drawn to turn civilians into soldiers was held. Nevertheless, in the last week of what was a grueling campaign for him, father, seeking to reassure the electorate, again promised, "I have said this before, but I shall say it again and again—your boys are not going to be sent into any foreign war." But the first week after his election he began to push for an extensive Lend-Lease Act to supply our allies. His foes fought him on this, but the tide was turning.

In an address to Congress in January 1941, father called for us to act as an "arsenal of democracy." He asked for a deficit budget above $17 billion, most of which was for "defense." Father called for Willkie's help and the Hoosier responded patriotically. Early in 1941 Willkie visited England to confer with Churchill. He returned to voice support for the Lend-Lease bill, which passed in March. Meanwhile, Hopkins visited England, then Russia. And planes were being turned out at the rate of a thousand or more a month in our defense plants, to say nothing of tanks and guns. Ships were being built in the shipyards. Yet we maintained a pretense of peace. Our men were not yet fighting.

In the spring father summoned me for a secret mission. I was to accompany Major Gerald Thomas on a trip to the Philippines, China, Burma, India, Iraq, Egypt, Crete, Palestine and Africa. On the surface, Major Thomas was to observe and report back to the president on the military buildup and the success of our supply lines in these areas. Beneath the surface, I was to speak privately to the heads of state or governing officials to assure them in father's name that, although we ourselves were not at war with Germany, Italy or Japan, he would do everything he could to help those who were at war. I was to suggest that we might well be at war before long and that we then would pitch in with both hands to help them. In effect, I was to tell them, "Hang on until we get there."

Major Thomas knew nothing of this. Only father and I and his closest advisers knew. I presume I was selected because as the president's son I would be believed and because father felt he could trust me to keep the mission confidential. I would present the leaders of these nations with ceremonial gifts, then take them aside for secret discussions.

Father said, "This must be completely confidential. The Congress, the press and the public would never approve my message, but I consider it critical to the morale of countries we must support. If you speak publicly of it, I'll deny it and disown you. If you get in any trouble, you'll have to get out of it on your own. There will be times when you will leave Major Thomas and go off on your own to see who I want you to see. I can't provide you government planes or anything like that. As an officer you can hitch rides on military aircraft, but you'll have to make your own arrangements as you go along. We can't take the chance of having you communicate with me formally while you're gone, but report to me the moment you return."

His final words to me were, "You're going to go into some areas where there is shooting. Take care."

I grinned and said, "Don't worry, I'll keep my head down." Which of course was just talk. I'd never been where there was shooting. I'd never had to keep my head down, except on marine maneuvers. I had no idea what war was really like.

I wanted to settle things with Romelle before I left, and so we were married in April. I left on my trip in May. While I was gone, the world continued to turn upside down. A U.S. freighter was sunk by a German sub, and father declared an unlimited state of national emergency. He froze German and Italian assets in the United States, and these nations in turn seized our assets in their countries. Our respective embassies were closed. We stopped shipments of oil to Japan. Germany attacked Russia, and against the advice of the isolationists we granted the Soviet Union $40 million in credit and started to supply her with defense materials. Harry Hopkins flew to Russia to assure Stalin of our support. Japan sank a U.S. gunboat, but apologized. We moved forces into Iceland, German U-boats attacked some of our ships off the coast, and our ships were ordered to attack any German or Italian ships that entered our waters.

Father secretly sailed to meet with Churchill at sea off the coast of Newfoundland. Here, with Elliott at his side, he worked out the Atlantic Charter with the British prime minister. Devised as a treaty that Congress would not have to approve, it was an agreement by these national leaders to act together against nations who use force to impose their will on others or to seize territories. Although others subscribed to it and Stalin approved it, copies were not available.

Congress barely passed an extension of the Selective Service Act by a single vote, 203–202. Senator Burton Wheeler pointed out that father would never win a vote to go to war. Charles Lindbergh charged that three groups were pressuring our country into war—the British, the Jews and the Roosevelt administration. Such was the mood of this country as I pursued my mission.

The mission was a success. I met and passed father's message on to the leaders of the nations in the part of the world I visited. While some were resentful that we had not jumped into the fighting with both feet, all were grateful to be assured of our interest and support. They were, I think, bucked up by it.

My experiences ranged from the serious to slapstick. We went from Hong Kong to Kowloon on the coast of China, and from there were to fly inland to Chungking to meet with the Chiang Kai-sheks. The weather was terrible. There was a thunder-and-lightning storm. I told Major Thomas there was no way we could fly out that night. However, our Chinese pilot told us we would take off in ten minutes. I was startled and asked how we dared try it in such bad weather. He said it was good weather—the best for our purposes. "No Japanese air action tonight," he smiled. I hadn't thought about that, but could see the sense of it. So we took off, and, though it was a rough flight, we made it to Chungking. There was Japanese air action the morning we arrived. A Chinese servant, a young boy, was assigned to us, and when I heard the air-raid siren, I asked him to direct us to the shelter. He smiled and said, "No hurry, no hurry."

"What do you mean no hurry?" I exclaimed. "My God, didn't you hear the siren?"

He said, "Heard the siren. Is OK. Only first warning."

So we waited around rather nervously. An hour later the siren sounded again. We rushed to him, asking, "All right, now, where is the air-raid shelter?"

"Not worry," he assured us again. "Wait another hour. Then third warning."

So we waited. And sure enough, after another hour came the sound of the siren again.

"Now," he said, and took us to a shelter built into the side of the hill. A few minutes later we could hear bombs exploding all around us. It was an unsettling experience, to say the least. After a while the bombing stopped and the all clear sounded.

That evening, I asked a local official about the three sirens. He said, "This is a civilized war. Neither nation has effective antiaircraft guns. Nor do we want to kill civilians. We are aiming at military targets. So we have observers at each other's airfields. And by mutual agreement we have arranged to provide one another with a three-hour notice before the bombers take off. At one-hour intervals we sound warnings to the population to prepare for the raid that day."

Outside of Chungking I saw what seemed like ten thousand men and women hauling heavy rollers up and down a field to prepare a runway for B-17 bombers. I inquired and was told the officials had more people than equipment and had to do this work by hand. When I asked how they could afford to pay ten thousand people to build airfields by hand, I was told they did not have to pay them, that work was so scarce in the country that people were happy to work in exchange for room and board. They built inexpensive housing and had an unlimited supply of cheap labor. At this time father was being plagued by strikes back home, and I couldn't help comparing the two situations. I remember that women with babes on their backs crushed and carried rock.

In Chungking we were given the new house of a dignitary in which to stay. It was palatial and had the most magnificent gold plumbing fixtures I've ever seen. But, as it turned out, there was no water. When you turned one of those gorgeous gold handles, nothing happened. Instead an aging coolie was provided to serve us. He lugged jugs of water on his shoulders so we could take baths and flush the toilet. Coolies pulled us about in rickshas, and one pair almost dumped us into a ditch. What a contrast between rich and poor in China.

We had dinner with the Chiang Kai-sheks at their retreat in the hills. They were very kind. Somehow they knew I'd had ulcer surgery a few years before. Somehow they knew everything. Madame Chiang had cows driven across the hills from Peking and I was fed a milk-and-egg diet. She was charming. So was he, though dictatorial in manner. Beneath their charm one sensed steel. She joined with him to form a firm bond. They knew what they wanted.

As I was leaving Hong Kong, I saw a little Chinese boy fall overboard in a great crush on the ferry. No one raised a finger to help him and he drowned. Life there is cheap, I suppose. But later I wondered why I had not helped. Was it fear? Would anyone have helped me? But at the time it did not occur to me. Was it because he was not one of mine? Yet my heart went out to the boy, and I was angry that his people did not rescue him. I had no right to be angry. I had not helped him, either.

In Egypt, I was presented to King Farouk as he was returning from a duck hunt. When I gave him a shotgun as a gift of the U.S. government, I was told he and his party had shot two thousand ducks that day. Hunt? That's what I call slaughter! Clearly, he did not need our gift.

Crete was next on our itinerary, and although the British argued against it, we flew there. The Nazis had already begun their aerial assault on the island and the British feared for the safety of the American president's son. I feared for my life, too, when our slow Sunderland flying boat took a few shots at a Nazi patrol vessel, and then had to dodge Luftwaffe fighters as we landed on Suda Bay.

Gallantly, King George of Greece, in uniform, directed the defense. He greeted us, and I conveyed my father's message. But it was too late. We were hustled out the following day, under bombardment, and shortly after our departure Crete was enveloped by the enemy, arriving in gliders and by parachute.

Dickie Mountbatten left Crete with us. He had been rescued when his ship was sunk. Mountbatten is a marvelous man, and we began what has turned into a lifelong friendship. Since he had no way to get home, he decided to hitch flights across Africa with us until we could make our way to Lisbon. From Lisbon he would head for England while I headed home. So I had a member of the royal family in my party as I made my calls on heads of state.

As I look back, one stop merges into another in my mind.

One incident I remember was being routed out of our rooms by air-raid sirens just as Major Thomas was changing from his uniform into his pajamas. We heard the planes even as we heard the sirens. At such a time one does not bother with the amenities. The major fled for the shelter in his birthday suit.

Another time, in the Persian Gulf, we were in a truck when we heard aircraft coming, and we were told to scramble out and hit the ditch. We did so just before three German planes swooped low, strafing and bombing the road. Our truck was hit and exploded into a ball of fire. I don't remember feeling fear; I remember feeling helpless. There was nothing you could do, no way to strike back.

In one community in Africa there was a small British colony of about fifty souls and they decided to get up a game of polo, of all things, in honor of Mountbatten. So they rounded up some horses, staked out a field and brought out mallets and a ball. Well, the horses weren't trained polo ponies, and the field was a bombed-out stretch of rubble. Mountbatten admitted he feared more for his life in that game than he did under fire. But, he said, "What could I do but play, old chap, after they had gone to such trouble for me?"

We weren't too welcome in Gambia, because there simply was not enough food to go around. A few distinguished guests meant a few more mouths to feed. Dickie suggested we should try to do something to help out. I agreed, but wondered what. Pointing to a large flock of pigeons that had gathered on the roof of the governor general's house in which we were quartered, he suggested we borrow some shotguns and shoot some pigeons. We did. One of us would fire to put the birds in flight, the other would try to pick some off. We bagged seven or eight, presented them to our host and ate pigeon till we were sick of it.

After leaving Gambia, we had to go to twelve or thirteen thousand feet flying over Dakar because of antiaircraft fire. Besides the fact that we had no pressure or heat in our plane at that height, one of the engines began to act up and we had to turn back. We were about twenty minutes out of Gambia when the pilot, a Briton, came back and presented us with a bottle of Scotch.

"Kind of you, old chap, but why?" Dickie asked.

"Well, I'll be truthful with you," the pilot told us. "The plane is behaving rather badly. There's no wind. The moon is bright and glaring off the water. I've never made this sort of night water landing and I'm not sure I'm going to make a good one here. You might have to do a bit of swimming, so I thought it would warm you to have a bit of Scotch inside you."

Thus encouraged, we put a bit of Scotch inside us and awaited his landing. It was perfect.

We had to wait four or five days for a replacement before we flew out again. I recall that on the flight Dickie was scratching fiercely, and I asked if he had neglected to bathe. He laughed and said, "Oh, I bathed, but the chameleons are scratching me something dreadful. You see, Edwina, my wife, adores chameleons. I picked up a pair for her, but figured they'd freeze to death in the freight compartment, so I put the beggars inside my shirt."

Some time after we got home, father called me to his office and announced that he had a bill of about $2800 for me from the British government. I said I didn't owe the British a penny. He waved a piece of paper at me and said that indeed I did; that apparently I had shot up the roof of a government-owned house in Gambia on some sort of fool pigeon-hunt. I had caused leaks they could not repair, which had damaged furniture and rugs during the rainy season.

I was really dismayed—until I saw the twinkle in his eyes. "Dickie Mountbatten isn't by any chance behind this?" I asked. Father acknowledged that Mountbatten had been the complainant. And we both started to laugh.

Mountbatten and I went to war our separate ways after that. While I played a minor role on our side, he played a major one on his. After the war I raised some money for one of his pet projects out of the Investors Overseas Service project. When I am in England I sometimes visit him at his country estate where he lives in retirement. Often, we talk of that trip.

For me, the important thing was that I carried the president's message to many of our allies in that part of the world, and father was pleased with the feedback from it. It was not long before we were in the war, of course, and no such assurances had to be given our allies.

XVIII

By December 7, 1941, all FDR's sons were in the service, either in the active reserve or on active duty. Franklin was in the naval reserve, John had been commissioned an ensign in the navy early in the year, Elliott was in the army air force and I was in the marines. I was working as a liaison officer between marine headquarters and what was to become the Office of War Information on that "day that will live in infamy."

I was off duty and napping at my suburban home when I was awakened by a telephone call from the White House. I was told that the Japanese had attacked Pearl Harbor and that my father wanted me with him.

The attack was totally unexpected, and it shook me. I hurried to father's office. I remember noticing he was wearing an old sweater of mine. I had given it to him when he admired it. He said, simply, "Hello, Jimmy. It's happened." He had been working on his stamp collection when Secretary of the Navy Frank Knox telephoned him the terrible news. Father asked me to stand by as he conferred with his civilian and military aides who passed through his office in a continuous flow on that sad Sunday.

I was present at the conference he held with his key aides to plot the Declaration of War against Japan he was to deliver to a joint session of Congress the following morning. I watched him write the speech himself in longhand, then turn it over to Bob Sherwood, Harry Hopkins and others for review. With the exception of a single sentence near the end of the speech, suggested by Harry, his words were allowed to stand and were delivered the next day. Thus, almost all of it, including the memorable phrase ". . . a day that will live in infamy . . ." was father's.

(Incidentally, father handed me the text of this speech after it was delivered the next day. I laid it down. Remembering it later, I went back for it, but it had disappeared. It never was found.)

I stayed with father through the long day and evening as one dreadful report after another reached us. All eight battleships at Pearl Harbor were hit, five sunk and destroyed. Some two hundred aircraft were also destroyed, and 2300 servicemen and civilians were killed. It had begun, and before it would end almost 300,000 Americans would be killed, almost 250,000 Britons and hundreds of thousands of others, including literally millions of Russians. Germany would lose more than three million men, Japan more than a million, Italy close to a hundred thousand.

That night, after I helped father into bed, we talked of the long, dark tunnel we had entered, one which had no end in sight at that time. I had been after him to have me reassigned to field duty. Now I said I wanted combat duty. But he was worried about my health. He pointed out that I'd had two-thirds of my stomach cut out. I said I felt fine.

I felt I had to fight. I was being no braver than millions of other Americans at the time. We were swept up in a surge of patriotism such as we in this country may never know again. Although I did not say it to him, I felt that as the son of the president I had to seek combat. I'd had only the slightest taste of it. I did not yet know what it was to feel fear.

On Monday we declared war on Japan. On Thursday Germany and Italy declared war on us. Thanks to father, we were better prepared than we otherwise would have been, but we were far from ready. By Friday, Japanese forces had occupied Guam. A couple of weeks after that, they captured Wake Island. Early in January, Manila fell and, on orders, General Douglas MacArthur withdrew his small contingent of troops to Bataan. By mid-March he'd had to depart for Australia to reorganize American forces, vowing he would return to reclaim the Philippine Islands. Captured American troops were forced into the infamous Bataan "death march" across the island, thousands dying of starvation or gunned down.

Thus, although by April we had begun to bomb the enemy, we were on the defensive for most of that year, and there were, of course, times when the Allies were close to collapse.

Father has spoken of how lonely he was during the war years. Granny had died in September. His sons were far from him. Missy suffered a stroke in 1941. Mother often was away. Still, with the imposing power of his personality, that marvelous man who was my father rallied this nation to a tremendous war effort, driving himself hard despite his deteriorating health. There can be no question that the years between the beginning of the war in December 1941 and his death near the end of the war in April 1945 were the hardest of his life, but they were also the most memorable. He was our inspirational leader as surely as Churchill was Britain's.

I know he was deeply proud of his sons, who served this nation as well as the sons of other men. And I know he was terribly hurt when a Republican representative from Kansas, William Lambertson, took the floor of Congress to attack our war records with the implication that we were protected. When Elliott wrote him in response to the attack, "Sometimes I really hope that one of us gets killed so maybe they'll stop picking on the rest of the family," mother recalled that all the color drained from father's face and he started to shake.

Father's chief act of favoritism toward us during the war was to summon us when he was at a conference within any of our war zones. He caught up with Elliott and Franklin a couple of times and had Elliott with him at several overseas conferences.

Elliott was originally assigned as an air intelligence officer in Newfoundland. With the coming of the war, he signed waivers so that he could fly in the combat zone despite poor eyesight. Soon he was flying reconnaissance missions in unarmed photographic planes under heavy fire over theaters of war from Europe to North Africa. Impartial press observers praised him as one of the bravest men they saw. He rose on merit to the rank of brigadier general, commanding a wing of more than 250 planes and 5000 men in North Africa. Among other decorations, he won the Distinguished Flying Cross.

Yet, what is remembered about his service is that an overzealous officer bumped an enlisted man from a military transport traveling to the West Coast to make room for Blaze, a dog that belonged to my brother. It was, of course, inexcusable, but my brother was not to blame. He had simply asked that the dog be shipped home when possible, never dreaming a soldier would be bumped because of the animal.

Franklin served on a destroyer that dodged torpedoes from Iceland to Minsk. He became executive officer of the destroyer *Mayrant*, which was bombed at Palermo in the Sicilian invasion. The famed war correspondent Quentin Reynolds went out of his way to write mother how bravely Franklin performed in that bloody ordeal, in which he won the Silver Star for exposing himself under fire to carry a critically wounded sailor to safety.

Later, as a lieutenant commander, Franklin was in charge of his own destroyer escort in the war zones. Known as "Big Moose" to the men who served under him, he did a tremendous job.

John was the only one of us who had no opportunity to lead a fighting unit, yet he, too, served under fire. Assigned as a lieutenant in the Navy Supply Corps, he persuaded father to get him transferred from shore to sea duty. He served aboard the aircraft carrier *Hornet* in the war zone, winning the Bronze Star and promotion to lieutenant commander for his actions while his ship was being gunned.

I served with a group called "Carlson's Raiders." I had met Evans Carlson in Washington, and we went together to Camp Elliott in California. At the time, we were losing so many ships in the Pacific that we had little chance of recapturing islands we had lost there. Carlson, however, developed an idea for a special kind of outfit that would be trained to make swift, surprise attacks on these islands in order to weaken their defenses before our massed might moved in.

I asked in on it and was accepted. The plan was rather revolutionary, but father bought it and helped sell Admiral Nimitz on the idea. We were given a free hand to recruit volunteers from the San Diego Naval Base.

I remember the first time a group was called together to hear us out, Carlson made a stirring plea for volunteers, but one in which he stressed the hazards involved in this sort of raiding action. When, in conclusion, he asked those interested to step forward, no one budged. It was embarrassing, to say the least, the low point of our program. But finally one man moved forward. Then another.

In subsequent talks, Carlson placed less stress on the dangers, and more men joined us until we had recruited a group. I was able to use my influence to get "Carlson's Raiders" the special equipment we needed, such as boots which would hold up under the rigors of wet landings on coral reefs. And of course there was some resentment at our getting equipment others could not get. But by May of 1942 we were ready. To prove it, we "captured" Admiral Nimitz and his party while they were at a picnic on a beach in Honolulu, without arousing the military in Hawaii.

Convinced, Nimitz sent us from Pearl Harbor in two submarines to mount a sneak attack on the Japanese-held Makin Island three thousand miles away. To make room for our 240-man party, the torpedoes were removed from the tubes, in which some of us then slept. Traveling underwater most of the way, we maintained contact by tapping on the hulls of our craft. Somehow, we sped safely, side by side, to our distant rendezvous.

We landed after dark on rubber rafts. A couple of the rafts became separated from us in the rough surf and landed on another part of the island. This proved helpful, as the defenders then felt they were under fire from many groups instead of one, and divided their defenses. Actually, a nervous member of our party fired too soon and alerted the enemy long before they otherwise would have become aware of us. When alarms sounded, the surprised defenders rushed into position and resisted our advances.

I remember a walkie-talkie was shot right out of my hands. I simply asked for another one. I didn't have any sensation of fear until later. I was too busy with the battle at the time to be frightened. The awful noise of the gunfire blotted everything else out.

The surprise element of our attack worked well for us. Carlson had properly anticipated most of the problems we would face and we were prepared to deal with them. We destroyed the airfield, burned hundreds of thousands of gallons of fuel and killed hundreds of the enemy. But before we could get away, an enemy gunboat sped into the harbor on the opposite side from our subs. I felt that if I could get a good vantage point I might direct fire from our subs at the enemy craft across the island. With a walkie-talkie, I directed the subs to surface and man their big guns. Then I climbed to the highest point I could find and directed the shooting of shells which struck and crippled the gunboat.

By then, however, the seas were too high and we couldn't get off the reef. We were stranded. We assembled in the thickest jungle growth we could find and voted on our course of action. Carlson ran a democratic show. Back in camp we had passed evenings discussing life and taking votes on our feelings. I remember how surprised he was when the men once voted against his suggestion that all men be limited to $25,000 a year income as a means of spreading the wealth of the nation. Their reason was that if they survived the war, they did not want to return to a world in which they would be denied the opportunity to become one of the wealthy.

This night we voted on survival—whether to surrender or try to survive the night and escape when the tide went out in the morning. We voted to stay and try to escape. That night enemy aircraft bombed and strafed us. We kept moving about the island, leaving signs to confuse the enemy so they would misdirect their fire. Somehow, most of us survived the night.

In the morning I led the first group back to the subs. But there were more men than there was room on the remaining rafts. Many clung to the sides, and some of them slipped into the choppy surf. We rescued those we could. I saved three or four from drowning. Officially I saved three, for which I later received the Navy Cross. Others deserved as much or more and were also honored.

All except one raft in my party reached the subs before enemy aircraft moved in. That one raft was about two hundred yards away when the skipper of the sub said he had to take us under. I pleaded that he wait for the last raft, but he said he couldn't. We went under. And we never saw the men from that raft again.

Below, while planes dropped depth charges all around us, surgeons on our sub operated on those of our wounded that needed it.

Carlson had remained with the second half of our party on the island, planning to leave the next day. They took to their rafts when our subs surfaced again, but he had to leave without nine of his men who had become separated from the main party. Later we learned they had been helped by friendly natives, but were found and executed when the Japanese reoccupied the island.

After Carlson's group reached the subs, we left. The toll was seventeen lost or dead on the island, five in the water.

Victories in war do not come without the loss of life, and ours was a victory. It was the first American offensive in the Pacific and was hailed as a military and psychological victory for our side. We sneaked through the dark water back to Pearl. There we were surprised to find bands playing and the piers lined with cheering people. We had not shaved or bathed or washed our clothes for two weeks, so I sent my men belowdecks to clean up as best they could. It turned out to be a hero's welcome. Ships in the harbor were flying broomsticks, which meant we had cleaned up on the enemy.

I was promoted to lieutenant colonel. Father rejected the promotion at first, but the marine brass finally convinced him it was earned. Our battles had only begun, however. Fifteen months after that daring raid on Makin, I returned with the army to capture that island in three days of bloody battle that brought me the Silver Star.

The army group was the 165th Regiment, successor to the old "Fighting 69th," and it was led by Colonel Jim Conroy. I was assigned to them because of my experience with this sort of raid on this particular island. This time we were accompanied by an aircraft carrier with air support, and used landing boats to reach the beach. But the island had become an important sub base for the Japanese by then, and they had improved their defenses. We were pinned down on the beach, unable to move.

I made a little speech: "Those of you who want to stay on the beach, stay. But those of you with the guts to take this island have got to make a move. We've got to go right to them and I'm going. Any of you who want to come with me, come."

Most came, including the colonel. We kept moving forward on the island, a little at a time, into the teeth of their attack, enabling our support to land supplies behind us. When we had gone as far as we could without help, I suggested it was time to call in the tanks that had been landed. This was done, and the tanks came up behind us. The colonel stood up to wave them on, and at that instant a sniper shot him right between the eyes, killing him instantly. He fell by my side. I had to leave him there as the tanks plowed into the last line of the enemy and we moved up behind them. We broke the back of their resistance and secured the island. Later we went back for the colonel's body.

From time to time I returned to the States to train new groups before returning to action. I was given command of a fourth raider group which I trained at Camp Pendleton near San Diego. These were tough men and I gave them tough training. Stateside life was too tame for us. One night we shot out all the street lights and under the cover of darkness captured the mayor and all the city councilmen at a San Clemente meeting. It was good practice for us, but they didn't approve. Somehow, the news media missed this incident.

Another time we were told that we would not have bread with our meals for a while because some requisitions had gotten lost. The lads didn't like that very much. The food was far from gourmet, and bread and butter was our staple. I simply signed some requisitions for bread from civilian sources, authorizing that the bills be submitted to the army at the base. My quartermaster went into the city with a truck and got bread from every bakery in town. I had no right to authorize this, but by the time the bills came in, my group and I were long gone.

Overseas, I received a cable requesting that I explain my actions, threatening me with court-martial if my explanation was not satisfactory. In essence I replied, "Court-martial me."

They didn't—possibly because I was the president's son, although later father laughed and told me he'd heard nothing of the incident at the time.

Before I left Camp Pendleton, my commanding officer stuck me with a chaplain. His name was Father Redmond, and I was told he'd been assigned to me because he insisted on being sent into action. I had no place for a chaplain in my organization and I tried to talk him out of it, but to no avail. He accompanied us when we sailed on the old *President Polk* for our South Pacific base at Espiritos Santos, south of Guadalcanal.

He turned out to be a great guy, organizing recreation and so forth for the two thousand men who were crowded aboard that ship. The only thing that bothered him was the language. Men in the military lean heavily to obscenities. During the last Sunday services he held on the ship, he stood up and, instead of preaching, he unleashed the longest string of obscenities I've ever heard.

Everyone was shocked. Then he said, "Frankly, fellows, I learned most of these words from you. I know they are only words, but they are offensive to some of us. I don't think saying them has made me any better or braver a man. And I don't think saying them will help make any of you more of a soldier or stop a single Jap from shooting at you. I wish you would think about whether it is important to you to go on talking as you have been."

Incredibly, I heard few obscenities from the men after that, even in battle, and none around the chaplain.

Father Redmond, nevertheless, nearly got me court-martialed.

The men were unloading the ship late one night when the captain of the *Polk* came pounding on my door. Red-faced with rage, he announced he was going to have me court-martialed. When I asked why, he said my men had taken his piano off the ship. I told him I knew nothing about it. He said I'd better find out about it.

On a hunch, I turned to Father Redmond, who had used the piano in his recreational programs. He said he didn't know where the piano was. I asked him if he might find out. He said he'd try.

The next morning I heard a commotion and went outside my cabin in time to see a beaming captain watching his piano being returned to his ship. Later, I confronted the chaplain. He confessed that the men, considering the piano essential to their life on that island, had pressured him until he had agreed to make himself scarce while they removed the piano. Some nuns from a missionary group on the island had hidden the piano behind the altar of the chapel. Reluctantly, the men returned their trophy.

As a chaplain, Father Redmond was most unusual. He went into combat with us to lend spiritual assistance to those brave and frightened boys, ministered to the wounded and dead, and won three or four Navy Crosses. I believe he was the most decorated chaplain in the navy during World War II. I remember him complaining to some men bound for battle that they had not been to confession for some time.

"I'm as serious about the one thing as you are about the other," he said. "If you expect me to have the guts to go into battle with you, I expect you to have the guts to come to confession with me. If I give you respect, I expect you to give me respect. If not, I'm not going to be there when the time comes to give you last rites out on that battlefield."

Right after the incident, I called him aside and said, "Father, I do not know whether or not it is proper in your faith for you to threaten men like that, but it is not proper in my service. I here and now am issuing you an order that you never say such things again and never deny any man religious comfort for any reason. If you do, I will send you home in disgrace."

He was taken aback, but he was a big enough man to say that he was wrong for having spoken that way, that it had been an empty threat, anyway, that he would never repeat it and would not, of course, deny any man religious comfort at any time.

I have in my life been wrong many more times than Father Redmond was on that one occasion. I admire him enormously and still see him from time to time. He is well up in years now, living in retirement in northern California. I still see many of the survivors of the original Raiders, too, for we hold annual reunions. A surprising number of us attend the reunions. The chaplain was at the last one I attended, which drew 350 of us to the *Queen Mary* in Long Beach. We tell our tall war tales and toast one another and our departed comrades.

Carlson is long gone. When the Raiders were regrouped into a regiment, he expected to be named commander. When instead he was named assistant commander, he suffered deep disappointment, but stayed on, going into battle with the new group on Okinawa. Seriously wounded, he was shipped back to the States, but he never fully regained his health.

Carlson's wife leaned far to the left politically. I didn't know that he did, too. He accepted the nomination to run for the U.S. Senate for the Communist party in California after the war. That futile quest finished him with the marines. He retired in failing health to Oregon, where he died.

It was his right to be given a full military funeral and ceremonial burial at Arlington Cemetery, but I found that his widow didn't have the money to make the trip back with his body. The military refused her an allowance. I didn't have the money, either, but I went to friends in Hollywood, who provided it. They were liberals, but not Communists. The man had been a patriot, regardless of his politics. His men loved and respected him and were pleased he received, as he deserved, this burial with honors.

I served with my men in the continuing struggle for Midway. I fought with them at Tarawa, and on Guadalcanal, where we came in as support troops following the original landing. These were still bloody battles, under bombing and sniper fire in the face of the enemy's suicidal soldiers. They were being beaten back now, but battling with a bravery almost beyond reason.

I came down with a severe case of malaria and was sent back to the States to recuperate. I saw father alive for the next to last time in July 1944 in San Diego. He had decided to run for a fourth term and had been renominated. Dropping Wallace, he threw the vice-presidential choice open to the convention. Even as the convention was selecting Harry Truman over Wallace, Jimmy Byrnes and Bill Douglas, I was with father in his private railroad car at rest on a siding as he prepared to observe from a hill a landing exercise to be staged by the Fifth Marine Division.

Jim Bishop, in his book, said that father wrote mother that he suffered "the collywobbles" and stayed on the train that night after reviewing the operation. The fact is, he was stricken before emerging to review the operation. We had been catching up with each other. He was happy to see me recovering from malaria. Although I did not say so, I was sad to see him looking poorly. He had aged a lot, but, after all, which of our fathers does not seem to have aged when we have not seen him for a long time? All the while I had been in the Pacific, there was another war in the Atlantic. Six weeks earlier, D Day had brought the Allies to the beaches of France en route to Germany. As commander in chief, father had agonized through an awful strain. But I did not think he was dying.

That possibility did occur to me, however, when he was stricken. We were talking politics. He explained that he felt he had to run again so as to maintain a continuity of command in a time of continuing crisis. It's easy now to look back and say we had almost won the war and could have afforded a change in leadership. At the time, we did not know the war was won.

Father told me he was tired, but otherwise all right. Who was not tired, worn out by the war? He was running again, but he did not expect to have to run hard. Since he couldn't take time from the war for politics, the vice-presidential candidate could campaign for him. He didn't care who it was— Truman, Wallace, Byrnes—what did it matter? Let them name someone and get on with it, he said. The war was waiting.

Outside, the military waited. It was almost time for him to depart for the exercises.

Suddenly, he began to groan, his face took on an expression of suffering, and all the color seemed to drain from it. I rushed to him where he sat in his bed. He said, "Jimmy, I don't know if I can make it. I have horrible pains." It was a struggle for him to speak. I felt more fear than I ever did under fire. I gripped his hand and said I'd call the doctor. He said no, he didn't need a doctor, it was just stomach pains. He got indigestion from eating too fast at times, he said. It was from not being able to get up and walk around and exercise, he said. He was sure it wasn't his heart and insisted he would be all right if I would help him stretch out for a few minutes. He lay on his back on the floor of that railroad car for perhaps ten minutes (the bed was too short to accommodate him). I said I'd tell them he couldn't make the exercise, but he said I shouldn't, that it would create unnecessary alarm and jeopardize his chances for reelection. It's easy to say now I should have done what I thought was right, disregarding his wishes, but it was hard then. He was not only my father, he was the commander in chief. I was there to help him.

I did what he wanted done. And, minute by minute, as he lay on his back in that train and I kneeled alongside him, he seemed to get better. At first his body shook a little. Then it stilled. At first he closed his eyes. Then they opened. The color seemed to return to his face. He was breathing easier.

"Help me up now, Jimmy," he said. "I feel better." .

I helped him into his wheelchair and he smiled. He looked better. I was relieved.

When you see photos of him that day as he watched the exercise, you see the grin. You have to look closely to see the weariness.

Restored to duty, I spent three months in the Aleutians as a full colonel assigned to Intelligence. We were asked to take Kiska Island from the Japanese. Fed information about their massive armaments there, we plotted a full-scale offensive and blasted the island heavily before landing—only to find that the enemy had long since fled.

In the comedy of errors that was the war, this was a laughable episode. At least no lives were lost. But it is an episode the military still prefers not to talk about. I learned to question all intelligence information after that. What I had not seen with my own eyes became suspect to me.

I had led advance parties on scouting tours of Okinawa and various islands where we landed by dark of night and scouted out appropriate landing sites for the actual attacks. The better reinforced the islands were, the more difficult and costly they were to take. Okinawa was only three hundred and fifty miles from the main islands of Japan and was the closest of those sites from which we proposed to launch an attack on Japan, but we lost thousands of men on Okinawa and twenty thousand men on Iwo Jima. I think it was with these tragic numbers in mind that the decision was made to drop an atom bomb on Japan in the hope of avoiding a manned attack.

During the 1944 political campaign, mother wrote me, "I don't think father would really mind losing the election. If elected he'll do his job well, I feel sure, and I think he can be kept well to do it, but he does get tired so I think if defeated he'll be content. I am only concerned because Dewey seems to me more and more to show no understanding of the job at home or abroad."

I disagree. Father disliked Dewey, and even the thought of a possible defeat by Dewey drove him to campaign a lot harder than he had planned. After he won, father called it "the dirtiest campaign in all history" and wrote me, "The little man made me pretty mad."

I saw my father for the last time at his inauguration in January 1945. I was in the Philippines when I received a letter from him pointing out that I had attended all three of his prior inaugurations and asking me to attend the fourth. I replied that I'd be delighted to, but couldn't unless he, as my commander, ordered me to Washington.

He had special orders cut, signed them personally, sent them to me and I was on my way for a brief stay in Washington. It was during this visit that he told me I had no need to worry about any invasion of Japan, that he had something else in mind.

I had been back in the Philippines for several months when an orderly awakened me at 5:30 in the morning with routine overnight dispatches. I looked them over and lay back down to grab a few more minutes of rest. The orderly returned. He had a piece of paper in his hand. He said he had something for me, but he did not give it to me. I was struck by the strange way he was acting. I asked him if anything was wrong. He started to cry, dropped the piece of paper on my cot and fled.

It was the official communication to the fleet that the president had died.

I just sat there looking at it. It was the twelfth of April back home, and my father was dead.

XIX

The last time I saw my father alive, I said to him, "Old man, you look like hell."

He laughed and replied, "Oh, I'm all right. I'm a little tired, that's all. A few days in Warm Springs will fix me right up."

A few days in Warm Springs always had worked wonders for him. But this time I wondered. He really looked sick. His color was bad. He looked terribly tired. And I noticed that he was short of breath.

I went to Vice Admiral Ross McIntire, who had been father's chief physician for years, and said, "Mac, father looks awful. I'm worried about him."

The admiral said, "Gosh, no need to be, Jim. He's just a little tired. He had a hard campaign. It's been a hard winter and he's working too hard. But a few days will fix him up."

It was as though together they'd written the dialogue.

Dissatisfied, I went to Lieutenant Commander George Fox, an old friend who'd started out as a pharmacist and masseur and worked his way up until he was sort of an assistant medic to father. "George," I said, "I'm not happy with the way father looks."

George said, "I know, Jimmy, but I guess you've got to expect him to show a little wear and tear. I don't think it's anything to worry about. We're none of us getting any younger, you know."

He was evasive and I couldn't pin him down, which concerned me.

They had brought in a bright young doctor, Lieutenant Commander Howard Bruenn, to give father an extensive examination. But they didn't reveal the results, not even to father. Bruenn all but took over father's medical care, but there were always a lot of doctors around him and the addition of a new one was no particular cause for concern.

Thirty years later it was reported that in his last year father was suffering from an enlarged heart, hardening of the arteries, hypertension and chronic fatigue—ailments not uncommon in men in their sixties.

He was not a well man; that was no secret. But if they did not think he could live more than a couple of months, or even a couple of years, why didn't they tell him? They did not. If they had told him he would not live out a fourth term, he might not have run a fourth time. They told him he'd have to take it a little easier. Smoke less. Get more rest. But they'd been telling him that for years.

If the doctors thought he couldn't make it, they should have tried to talk him out of a campaign in which he stood in the rain, making a speech in Brooklyn. They could have taken their case to mother or to any of us to enlist our help in getting father to retire.

Maybe they lacked the guts to go to him or to us. Or maybe they underestimated the severity of his problems. If you read Jim Bishop's book about father's final year, you come to that conclusion. In Jim's book everyone keeps a fearful eye on father, expecting him to keel over at any moment.

I think this is all hindsight. No one realized that father was within months of the end, much less minutes. The people close to father, including his doctors who have survived, look back and say they saw the signs. Obviously, they did not see the signs very clearly at the time. They did not foresee his death.

I attach no special significance to his summoning me to his

side for that fourth inauguration. I was the only one he called, but I was the only one who'd been by his side during the other three, and I was the eldest son.

It was snowing—a grim, cold day for the inauguration. Father said he didn't want to have it up on the Hill; he didn't want a lot of pomp and circumstance; he didn't want a parade because we were at war and he didn't need ceremonial trappings. I'm sure he wanted to spare himself. So the crowd gathered on the lawn outside the South Portico. He stuck his head outside and said, "It's a lousy day," but I couldn't get him to put on a coat or hat. I begged him to wear his cape, but he insisted he didn't need it. In a show of bravado, he appeared without coat or cape, bareheaded, and gave his short speech.

After that, he asked that we be left alone for a while. "You know, Jimmy," he said when the others had gone, "I have to go to a reception now and shake hands with a thousand people, and I don't think I can do it."

"Then don't do it," I said.

He said, "I have to do it. It would look bad to bow out. I don't dare shake the faith of the people. That's why I ran again, Jimmy. The people elected me their leader, and I can't quit in the middle of a war." He sighed and added, "There's a bottle of bourbon up in my room. If you'll go up and sneak it down to me and I can get some inside of me, I think I can get through this."

I went up and got the bottle and smuggled it under my coat, and we drank from it.

That's when we talked about his will. He said, "There may not be time later, so there's something we better go into now while we've got a few minutes." He told me about the provision he'd made in his will to take care of Missy, and that he knew it might be misunderstood, but since Missy had died the provision would not apply. He explained that after all the trouble he'd had ironing out the details of his will with Doc O'Connor the first time, he was not going to go through that a second time. I said I understood.

He also told me that he had selected me as one of three

trustees and executors of his will. I was the one chosen from the family. The other two were Doc O'Connor, his key legal aide, and Henry Hackett, his mother's key legal aide. I said I would be honored, but hoped I would not have to serve for a long time yet. He laughed and said he was sure I wouldn't. "But," he added, "someday that day will come. When it comes, there is a personal letter in my safe that I have addressed to you which contains my instructions for my funeral. Among other things, I want you to have the family ring I wear. I hope you will wear it."

I said I would, and I do.

That conversation, of course, clearly indicates that he was thinking of death, but I took it to mean only that he was thinking of a death which had to come. Now that I look back, I realize why he insisted mother go to the trouble of having all thirteen of his grandchildren at that inauguration, but I did not see that then. I did not suspect, when I left him, that I was embracing him for the last time.

Father had seen us through war, and he wanted to take us on to peace. He was the one man above all others who understood the strategy of our war effort, and he wanted to be the man who dictated the terms of peace. He had wrestled with Churchill and Stalin and thought that a new man entering the picture late in the war would be at a tremendous disadvantage in dealing with these powerful leaders. He was passionate during our last talks when he spoke of his prospective trip to negotiate with Stalin at Yalta, and how determined he was to establish a strong United Nations. So he went to Yalta, and was wasted by the ordeal. That famous photo of father with Stalin and Churchill makes father look like a man at death's door, but how many saw it then? The press protected him all along, but how many columnists commented on his condition as it deteriorated? Even the most critical of the opposition press did not see what so many see so clearly now.

On his return, in his report to Congress, he apologized for delivering his speech sitting rather than standing. By then his body was conspiring against him. But he had done and was

doing what he had to do without the thought that each act
might be his last.

Afterward, he went to Warm Springs to rest. A party was
planned for that evening. He was going over his mail and
other papers, weary from posing for a portrait. The artist,
Elizabeth Shoumantoff, Lucy Rutherfurd, Daisy Suckley and
Cousin Polly were fussing about the room when he was
stricken.

It was 1:15 in the afternoon. He was taken to his room while
Bruenn worked on him. Mother was in Washington, and
Polly called to tell her. Anna was in Washington too. After
Dr. McIntire got the word, he passed it on to Anna. If they
had been waiting for this, why weren't mother and Anna
with father? Anna was working with him in the White
House, taking care of him. They were told father had fainted,
that it didn't seem serious. Mother went on to a meeting.

Two hours and ten minutes after he was stricken, father
expired. Mother and Anna were notified. The news was
flashed around the world. Halfway across the world, I got the
word. In a short while, a personal message reached me
through official communications. Mother sent each of her
sons the same message:

DARLINGS: FATHER SLEPT AWAY THIS AFTERNOON. HE DID HIS JOB
TO THE END AS HE WOULD WANT YOU TO DO. BLESS YOU. ALL OUR
LOVE. MOTHER.

I thought then, as I sat alone awhile in my room, that father
was as much a victim of the war as any soldier who had been
killed in battle. I think now how the Civil War aged Abraham
Lincoln, how World War I wasted Woodrow Wilson, how
World War II exhausted my father, how much the Korean
War took out of Dwight Eisenhower, and how great a toll the
Vietnamese conflict took on Lyndon Johnson. If they out-
lasted the wars, as my father did not, how little was left of
them, and how little time left for them. The presidency makes
brutal demands on men in the best of times. In the worst of
times, it asks more than men have to give.

Admiral Davis came in to see me to ask if there was any-

thing he could do for me. We got word that the official ceremonies were to be held in Washington and the burial at Hyde
Park. I told the admiral I would like to get back for the funeral
if possible. He said he would do everything he could. Within
four hours I was on a plane. But I was nine thousand miles
away, and the complicated travel plan called for me to make
one stop en route to Guam, change planes, stop at Wake en
route to Honolulu, on to San Francisco, then cross-country to
New York, and upstate to Hyde Park. I knew I could not
make the ceremonies, but I hoped to make the burial—until
head winds slowed my schedule.

I had wanted to be with him one last time. I had known all
along I admired him. But I did not realize until then how
much I loved him. I was sorry I had never said it in so many
words, though I think he knew. As father and son we'd not
had the opportunity to be close most of my life, but working
with him and for him the last few years before the war, we
had come close to one another. I was grateful for that at least.
I would like to be able to say that I thought about what
father's death would mean to the world, but I thought only
of what it would mean to mother, to me, to my brothers and
my sister. Our lives had gone down one road for so long that
we knew no other way. Now our lives would be altered, to
follow another course. I thought it would not be so different
for us children since we had already begun to go our own
ways, but it would be different for mother, who had found a
place for herself with people in need and now, I supposed,
would be moved into the background.

I think I saw that father had been the glue that held us
together. Little as most of us had actually lived in the White
House, home was where he was. Mother was seldom home.
With father gone from us, I supposed we would come apart
as a family.

As I ran further and further behind schedule I had word
sent ahead to mother that I would not arrive in time for the
funeral. She got word back to me to wait for her in New York,

meet her at her train at Grand Central Station and go back to Washington with her.

When I got to Grand Central, I found I had a few hours to pass while waiting for mother's train. I checked my bag and began to walk up Park Avenue. It was late afternoon on a sunny April day. I was in uniform and no one noticed me or recognized me as I strolled distractedly along the avenue until I got to Eightieth Street, crossed over and started back.

Suddenly a cab pulled to the curb alongside me, the driver got out, rushed over to me and asked if I was who he thought I was. I said that I was Jimmy Roosevelt if that was who he meant. He said it was, and he started to tell me how much he had admired my father. His passenger leaned out and said he'd hired the driver to take him home, not talk to some son of a bitch about that bastard Roosevelt, who would have been better off dead long ago.

I had long since hardened myself to endure the most unfeeling of insults, but at this time it was too tough to take. I excused myself to the cabbie, shook his hand and thanked him. He had started to cry. As I walked away, I turned back in time to see him haul his passenger, a well-dressed Wall Street type, out of the cab and deposit him on the curb. Then he drove away.

Some loved father, some hated him.

I have, of course, seen films of the ceremonies in Washington and the burial at Hyde Park. I remember in particular the caissons carrying father in his casket through the streets of Washington for the last time—slow-moving, stately and impressive. Many wept. Many shared our sorrow, I know. Many still miss that man. He left his mark on most of us who lived during his day. He left a lot of himself behind with us, which, I suppose, is his true memorial, more than all the museums and all the mansions we can visit.

When I met mother she was composed. I do not know if she had cried, but she was not crying. As always, she carried herself with a sort of stately reserve. We embraced briefly and she said she was glad I'd gotten home safely, but was sorry I'd not been able to get back in time for the ceremonies or the funeral. Anna was there, of course. And Elliott, who'd made it back from England. But Franklin and John had not been able to get back from duty at sea. Our wives were there.

One reason mother was happy to see me was that I could now open a handwritten letter from father addressed to me which she'd taken from his private papers after his death. Although the envelope was marked "funeral instructions," she had not opened it because it was addressed to me. That was her way. When I opened it I found he'd written his instructions in long-hand on long sheets of ruled yellow paper rather than entrust them to the typing of a secretary. While it was too late to follow these instructions, he'd obviously discussed them with mother, because many of the arrangements she'd made were as he'd requested. Some of the arrangements were not as he had wanted them, but I suspect that is the way it is for many of us when we die. We no longer have the final say, and circumstances sometimes dictate the decisions of funerals.

Father had, in essence, wished the simplest of services, with few ceremonial proceedings. He wanted the official service in the East Room of the White House, with a service for friends at Saint James Church in Hyde Park. He did not want to lie in state anywhere but to rest overnight in a sealed, dark wood casket in front of the fireplace in the East Room before going to Hyde Park for burial in the Rose Garden the following morning. He expressed the hope that his "dear wife" consent to a plot alongside his with a common stone simply marked with their names and the dates of their births and deaths.

He got most of his wishes, but he had been president and mother consented to appropriate ceremonies. So he did lie in state, though she prohibited the presence of his grandchildren. She wished them to remember him as he had been in life, not as he was in death.

It is not common knowledge, but father specifically requested that some associates who had turned against him politically not be invited to the ceremonies. I never asked mother if she knew of this wish, but some of these were invited to the service in the Blue Room. Also present were important members of father's official and unofficial family and of the Washington political scene, friend and foe alike. The new president, Harry Truman, attended: The king is dead. Long live the king!

I am told that as the services began, two minutes of silence were observed in my father's memory, not only in Washington, but all across the country. As church bells tolled, trains stopped on their tracks, subway cars ground to a halt, planes paused on airport runways, traffic lights held on yellow. Then, the slow march to the slow train to Hyde Park. I am told Anna passed through the entire train, speaking to each person in the funeral party. At Hyde Park, cadets from West Point fired volleys into the air above the Rose Garden as the metal casket was lowered into the ground.

On the train ride back to Washington, mother worried about what her life would be like. She had contracts for columns and articles and books and appearances. She wondered if she should go on with these projects, whether the people paying her would want her to now. She supposed not. I know that after the funeral she had told reporters, "The story is over."

She was wrong, but she could not have known it then. At the time she didn't know how much money she would have to live on or even where she would live. She knew I was an executor of father's estate and she hoped I could get that business disposed of without too much difficulty. She needed help from me as she had not often needed it in the past. With a feeling of warmth for her rushing over me, I was ready to take care of her.

When we got back to Washington, she had to move out. It was that simple. A new First Family was moving in. There was little time to spare. Life had to move on. Amidst the cruel clatter of collecting our family's possessions and shipping them out, we didn't have a moment to sit down as a family and reminisce. Well, we were always a family that looked ahead, not back. But there wasn't even time for a good cry.

Harry Truman took command decisively. The war was winding down, but our boys were still dying. The generals and admirals had a good grip on the battle, but top-level decisions still had to be made. Truman grabbed the presidency with both hands and made decisions swiftly. He was not a man of great intellect, but one of good common sense. He was not a powerful figure, but he was a battler. He had the ego to do things as he thought they should be done, not as others thought Franklin D. Roosevelt would have done them. And when he encountered an underling with a comparable ego who refused to go along, Harry did him in.

Such was the case when he fired and thus arrested the rise to power of Douglas MacArthur, who would have been president, if not God. And, eventually, when the decision had to be made whether to drop the atom bomb or invade Japan, Harry decided on the bomb, saving our lives at the cost of theirs.

At the time of father's death, Allied forces were well into Germany and Nazi resistance was crumbling. Less than a month after father's death, Hitler committed suicide. In July, Truman met with Churchill and Stalin at Potsdam, near Berlin, to discuss the demilitarization of the beaten Nazi nation. In August the atom bombs fell on Hiroshima and Nagasaki, and Japan was jarred toward defeat. The following month she surrendered.

Back in the Philippines, I requested release from duty so I could return to straighten out the tangled affairs of my father's estate. My request was approved. Many of our men were returning to the States by then, anyway. As that fateful summer of 1945 ran out, I returned.

Although father willed Hyde Park to the government, there was a provision leaving mother about a thousand acres, including Val-Kill cottage. All income from the rest of his estate went to mother for the remainder of her life. After her death it was to be passed on—half to their children and half to their children's natural children. Since he had conservatively invested holdings worth just under $2 million—just under $1 million of which had been willed him by his mother —and since funeral and administrative expenses ate up about a half-million, mother was left with about $25,000 to $30,000 annual income in interest. There was also life insurance, but this was the property of the Warm Springs Foundation.

More than seventeen years later, when mother died, half the principal passed to us and half to our children. By then the holdings had increased in value and amounted again to about $2 million. Since the five living children divided half, we inherited about $200,000 each, with another $200,000 each to be divided among our natural children on our deaths. If one of us has five natural children, for example, each would get $40,000.

You will note that the terms of the will stipulate "natural children." I personally think an adopted or inherited child should mean no less to the parent than a natural child. I myself never even use the term "natural child." But that is the way my grandmother's will, my father's will and my mother's will read, as though to keep pure the Roosevelt family strain. It is not the way my will reads, I assure you. I have an adopted son and he is no less to me than my other children. But my parents and their parents were traditionalists, to whom bloodlines were the wellsprings of their lives.

Mother's doubts about the usefulness of her role without father were soon dispelled. Mother was a marvel. I don't think anyone who ever knew her would dispute that, not even her enemies. And she had enemies. Not because she hurt anyone, but because she espoused some unpopular causes. She fought for the blacks against the bigots. She fought for the workingman against the bigwigs. She was one of the first to fight Joe McCarthy's indiscriminate campaign against anyone who'd ever came in contact with a Communist. She opposed John F. Kennedy as he was gaining in popularity because he did not oppose McCarthy, for whom Jack's brother, Bobby, had worked. For opposing McCarthy, she drew the wrath of

Westbrook Pegler, who castigated her cruelly in column after column.

Mother supported Adlai Stevenson in opposition to Dwight Eisenhower when Ike was at the peak of his popularity. And she supported Governor Herbert Lehman of New York in opposition to Carmine DeSapio at a time when DeSapio ruled Tammany Hall and thus the city with an iron hand. She fought Cardinal Spellman over his quest for federal aid to parochial schools and drew the opposition of the Catholic church, costing her more than two-thirds of the newspapers that carried her column. But she fought on.

She fought with her legs and her tongue. She was the most tireless of travelers, one who may not have missed a country in the world in her journeys after her husband's death when she was supposed to drift into retirement. She became America's "Ambassador to the World," speaking on behalf of the causes she supported. She became, despite her high-pitched tones, a superb speaker who could grab and hold and shake an audience with her powers of persuasion. Harry Truman called her "The First Lady of the World" and named her a delegate to the first assembly of the United Nations in London.

Mother served as a delegate to the United Nations and chairwoman of the Commission on Human Rights until Eisenhower made it clear he would accept her resignation. Ike was bitter because she supposedly had spoken of Mamie Eisenhower's bouts with the bottle at a cocktail party. As mother later explained it, she was asked if she had heard rumors that Mamie was an alcoholic, and she replied that she'd heard the rumors but knew nothing of them. No doubt she should have replied in stronger terms, but she did not. She was given at times to gossip, though she usually confined it to her family and friends. She was, as father was, as we all are, imperfect.

Her public image was damaged when Earl Miller's wife named mother a corespondent in a divorce action, though Earl settled the issue with his wife before it got to court.

Mother had a variety of close friends, including Earl and a professional dancer, "Tiny" Chaney, the writer Joe Lash and his wife Trude, the writer Lorena Hickok, the refugee doctor David Gurewitsch and his wife Edna, mother's secretary, Malvina "Tommy" Thompson, and her successor, Maureen Corr, and many others who were constantly moving in and out of mother's various apartments in Greenwich Village and on the East Side of Manhattan. Tommy actually shared mother's apartment as her roommate until she became too ill to continue. They were wonderful friends to her and a great help to her.

Mother really came to consider Hyde Park home—at least her Val-Kill cottage. She lived there with Elliott for a while. John also lived at the cottage for a while. She always had time for her children. She made time for us whenever we wanted something from her. She really did not get a great deal from us, except perhaps disappointment. Our divorces, one after another, disappointed her deeply. Like any mother, she wanted us to be happy. When she saw we were unhappy, she was unhappy. She felt guilt for not having done more for and with us early in our lives. She felt frustrated that she could not do more for us later in our lives.

She did more for Elliott than for the rest of us. She always felt closest to Elliott, and it is no secret that she always felt he needed the most from her, that he was the one least able to manage on his own. The rest of us felt that, too, and understood.

She formed a partnership with Elliott to purchase that part of Hyde Park that was for sale. She paid most of the purchase price. In what I've called "The Rape of Hyde Park," Elliott sold his part to a Howard Johnson's and other commercial ventures that have turned it into a Forty-second Street. The hilltop cottage father had built as his retreat was part of the property Elliott sold.

In order to help Elliott, mother did radio and television shows that he produced. With her as his star, he was able to sell the shows. She didn't like appearing on radio and TV, but she did it for her son. She also appeared on a radio show produced by Anna.

Mother resented Anna's moving into the White House to take over father's personal affairs after Missy was stricken. I don't know why mother resented it. I don't think she herself knew why. Certainly she would never have taken on the job herself, and father needed to have someone close to him. Missy was dying. She died in 1944 while he was on a trip. Howe was long dead. Hopkins was going. Farley, who had been a friend, was now a foe. Father's sons were away. Mother was always away. Anna became close to father in those last years in the White House. She needed someone, too; her second marriage had ended sorrowfully.

When mother found out that Lucy Mercer Rutherfurd had been with father on his dying day, she was furious. When she found out father had seen Lucy often during his last few years, she was even angrier. She confronted Anna with this information, and an ugly scene ensued. Anna tried to make less of it, but mother wanted to make more of it. She felt as if her own daughter had conspired to betray her. Anna spoke of this scene sadly. And yet when mother was taken sick, it was Anna who hurried to be with her and who took care of her during her last months. Like mother, Anna was always there when you needed her.

In her last years, mother loaned or gave a lot of money to Elliott and Anna, who were deep in debt. She allowed Elliott to manage some of her money for a while, but she took a loss on that. I also managed some of her money for a while, and though I did not do very well with my own money, I'm happy to say that I was able to make a profit on the money I managed for her.

Later, she told me that since father had named me executor of his will, she thought it only fair to name Franklin and John her joint trustees, and she hoped I would understand. I said I certainly would. She was afraid to name Elliott a trustee, she said, but she would leave him property, which she did.

She said, "I've always tried to work things out so no one

feels left out. I've tried to take care of Elliott all my life. You understand, don't you?"

I said, "I understand, darling. I think you've been thoughtful about every family matter and you have no worry about offending me."

Her own money, which only amounted to about $100,000, she left to Anna, in trust for her lifetime, to be passed on to those of us who survived on Anna's death. Well, Anna was her only daughter, and Anna never had much money. She had more debts than assets. Mother made close to $100,000 a year some years, but she gave most of it away.

She never stopped being a mother. Once I was seated next to her on the dais at a dinner and she noticed I wasn't eating very much. Though I was by then in my early fifties, mother leaned over and whispered an order: "James, eat your peas."

So many things about mother were amazing. She never forgot those people close to her. She kept a looseleaf notebook in which she listed the important dates in everyone's life and the gifts she gave them. She had a list of the Christmas presents she had given each of her grandchildren and great-grandchildren since 1935.

She did many thoughtful things. For instance, she always sent Louis Howe's widow flowers on his birthday until Mrs. Howe's death in 1955. On her last Thanksgiving with the family, in 1961, mother read father's 1933 Thanksgiving message to the nation, which she had found somewhere.

She was vigorous almost to the end. She traveled great distances to campaign for Franklin and me when we ran for office, and she took to the road to campaign for Adlai Stevenson in both 1952 and 1956. I suspect she admired Adlai more than she did father. It was she who convinced Adlai to run again in 1956 when he didn't want to, and it was she who almost convinced him to run a third time in 1960.

Although she distrusted John Kennedy at first, she learned to respect him and supported him. She was responsible for his appointing Stevenson American ambassador to the United Nations in 1961, and she herself accepted assignments from

Kennedy and became one of his roving ambassadors, as she had been Truman's.

Those who disliked her thought she did more than a woman should, pressing forward in an "unfeminine" manner. The first president's wife to make an international impact in her own right, she simply was way ahead of her time. On one of her birthdays she said, "Life has got to be lived— that's all there is to it. At seventy I would say the advantage is that you take life more calmly. You know that 'this, too, shall pass.' "

At seventy-five she still was going strong. She wrote, "When you cease to make a contribution, you begin to die. Therefore I think it is a necessity to be doing something which you feel is helpful in order to grow old gracefully and contentedly."

At seventy-seven she began a new career as a lecturer at Brandeis University. She said, "I suppose I should slow down, but I could not, at any age, be content to take my place in a corner by the fireside and simply look on. One must never, for whatever reason, turn his back on life."

Mother had been sick on and off since the late 1950s with what her friend, Dr. David Gurewitsch, diagnosed in 1960 as aplastic anemia, which is a disease of the bone marrow inhibiting its ability to manufacture red blood cells. She suffered from aches and pains, fevers and chills, but she kept going strong until the spring of 1962 when, returning from a trip to Europe, she found she had trouble keeping up with her crowded schedule. Despite the efforts of Anna's third husband, Dr. James Halsted, to provide her with specialists, she would only let Dr. Gurewitsch tend her and refused all other physicians when he was away. Accordingly, some of us felt and still feel she did not get the best possible treatment.

She was in the midst of writing another book when Dr. Gurewitsch returned from a month on the hospital ship *Hope* in Peru. He found her "burning up" and in bed. Another doctor had given her a blood transfusion, but it hadn't helped. Dr. Gurewitsch had her taken by ambulance to a hosptial. As soon as I was notified, I flew at once to be by her bedside, but she was so sick she didn't even recognize me. This was July of 1962.

She recovered sufficiently to submit to a series of tests that so depressed her she confided, "I wish I was dead. It's my time." So sure was she that it was her time that she sent out cards and gifts for the holiday season six months early. But she bounced back sufficiently to leave the hospital, against doctor's orders, and attend the dedication of the FDR Memorial Bridge linking the United States with Campobello Island. She vacationed at Campobello a last time.

She was weak, her voice so faint, we could hardly hear her when she spoke. She went to her Hyde Park cottage for a rest, told the housekeeper there would be no more big parties, but then added that there would be "fourteen for breakfast." She rejected an offer by telephone from New York Congressman Emannuel Celler, who wanted to nominate her as a candidate for the U.S. Senate.

Even those close to her simply could not accept the notion that she was sick, much less dying. It was difficult for her, but she went to great pains to describe her sickness in detail to others so that they would excuse her for not coming to their assistance when they sought her help.

Early in September she attended a special affair at the United Nations and she was busy there throughout the month. Somehow she summoned the strength, but she was failing, and late in the month she had to be hospitalized again. She hated the hosptial and dreaded dying there. She begged David Gurewitsch to promise he would put her out of her misery the moment all hope was gone, but he could not in good conscience grant her this.

I believe by this time she had lost her will to live. If she no longer could do the things she had been doing, she did not want to live. She told me over and over again whenever I saw her, "I do not want to be a burden to anyone." She hated it as she weakened and she could barely speak, much less write. Her handwriting, bad at best, became completely illegible.

For her seventy-eighth birthdy present she asked that a party be given at her home—an apartment on Seventy-fourth Street in Manhattan—for her grandchildren and the children of friends who lived nearby. And so in her honor a children's party was held in her absence, complete with cake and ice cream, gifts and favors.

Mother begged her doctors to permit her to go home to die. They relented later in the month. The publicity she disliked pursued her to the end, however. The press was tipped off, and photographers and reporters were present as she was carried, looking awful, on a stretcher up the stairs to her apartment. It was her final embarrassment. And yet when she was settled in her bed, her first thought was that she had forgotten to thank the stretcher-bearers and she wanted to be sure that someone did that for her. Then she asked for her checkbook and in an unsteady hand began to write out checks to make sure everyone got what was due them.

There remains considerable controversy over her illness. It was not until near the end of the month that doctors decided she did not have aplastic anemia, specifically, but a rare sort of tuberculosis of the bone marrow. Scars had been found from an old, unnoticed affliction of her lungs, but she did not seem to have emphysema. Some thought she must have cancer, but of course the word "cancer" covers many diseases. I don't suppose it matters much. I doubt she could have been given much more time, whatever the treatment. And she refused treatment. She hid her pills, instead of swallowing them.

Her children were with her on and off throughout the last weeks. Adlai Stevenson was also allowed to visit her. Dr. Gurewitsch had refused him admission to the hospital, but he wrote mother, asking to see her, and we arranged it, knowing it would please her. He was, I believe, the last person outside her family to see her alive, but she did not recognize anyone at the end. Her heart seemed strong, but it failed finally on the seventh of November.

John and Jacqueline Kennedy, Lyndon and Lady Bird

Johnson and Harry and Bess Truman were among the mourners at her funeral. I do not believe Mamie Eisenhower went, though Ike was there. It was quite a turnout and quite a tribute to that remarkable woman who was my mother. She was buried alongside father at Hyde Park, as he had wanted.

Incidentally, Fala is buried nearby, too. After father's death, Fala went to live with Aunt Polly for a while, but at mother's request I arranged for him to be returned to mother. He was happy enough with her, and she with him, though Fala lost some of his spirit and lived only four or five more years after father died.

When I think of my mother, I do not think of her as she was when she was dying, but as she was when she was living. The one picture that best captured her spirit, I think, was one that showed her striding across a deserted train station, suitcase in hand, on the move, so briskly that a younger person could not keep up, carrying her own luggage, pulling her own weight, a sort of lonely warrior fighting for those things she believed in.

From the narrowest sort of sheltered background she emerged to the broadest public service possible. And yet, for all the satisfaction she felt in the work she learned to do, I do not think she ever was a truly happy person. I think of her as a lonely person, in the midst of crowds of admirers. All of this is not to say that I have come to fully realize what a truly great human being she really was, and how genuine were her deep feelings for people, resulting in an affection for her personally. As an illustration, this little story: One afternoon about 5:00 I was standing on the corner of Fifth Avenue and Forty-second Street in New York City trying to catch a taxi cab. At that hour empty ones were few and far between. All of a sudden to my delight, a taxi pulled up to the curb. The door flew open and out stepped a tall lady—my mother. I gave her a quick kiss and before I knew it, she was halfway down the block. I got into the cab and the driver, with a disapproving look, turned around to me and said, "Hey, young fellow, do you know who that lady was?" I said, "Yes, sir, she is my mother." He did a sort of double take and peered at me even more closely. After a second or two, he smiled and said, "You know, I'm not going home and tell my old lady this story. She will think I stopped on the way and had too much to drink." Even to this day many a taxi cab driver in New York City will take the trouble to tell me how much they liked my mother. I wish I had been closer to her, but I never felt I could talk to her as I could to father.

And yet, how often did I speak intimately to father? Both of them were not nearly as much a part of their children's lives as they might have been. They did more for others than for themselves and their own.

And so, shaped by their public lives, shadowed by their towering images, we were, finally, left to live our own lives as best we could.

XX

Children of fame, we grew up seeking our own individual identities. We did not know then that as the children of Franklin and Eleanor Roosevelt we would, to our deaths, be overshadowed by them. We knew simply that we would have to create identities for ourselves, and that it would be difficult because more would be expected of us.

Now we were on our own. We could make our own opportunities, direct our own destinies—except that circumstances thrust opportunites at us too tempting for us to resist, too much for us to handle. Because of who we were, not what we were, Elliott and I, and Franklin and John, and Anna, too, were handed positions we could not handle and did not deserve. We never set goals and grew into them.

Thus Elliott went to Texas and all of a sudden found himself in radio. And I went to California and all of a sudden found myself in the movie business. And so it has gone all of our lives. Anna went to Arizona and found herself so out of her depth in the newspaper business that her marriage failed and her husband took his life. I landed in Switzerland in a company named IOS and ended up in hot water.

There are also things we did that we can justifiably take pride in. I feel, for example, that I contributed to my country as a congressman and as a member of the United Nations, though I know my name helped me make it to Congress and the U.N. If the name sometimes served us badly, it sometimes served us well. Because of his name, Franklin landed an automobile dealership that made him a great deal of money. He is the only one of us who is really well off. Of the rest of us, only John has had a stable financial life.

All my life there have been those who have told me how lucky I was to be born a Roosevelt. In many ways I was. Through my parents, I became a part of history, as did my brothers and sister. We were there while history was being made, witness to the ways a world was shaped. There even were times when we could contribute to shaping it. We met many of the most important people of our day, and at times we could even exert a small influence on some of them. When we were able, we learned from them. Experiences were ours which were denied to others. Doors were opened to us that were closed to others.

Certainly, life was not nearly as hard for us as it is for most people. If we were not as wealthy as has been assumed, we certainly were not poor. While we were growing up, none of us had to work to help out. We were given the best educations. We had the opportunity to make as much of ourselves as there was to be made. If we did not, it is our fault. We could better have been shown the value of a dollar. We could better have been shown the strength one draws from one's own sweat, from sacrificing and working in quest of some goal. Father tried to show us the value of work, such as the time he sent me to the north woods.

At first, each of us married into moneyed families. Not because we needed money, but because we were exposed to moneyed people. We moved among the rich and famous, so we met the rich and famous. I married a Cushing, Franklin married a Du Pont, Elliott and John married rich girls, Anna married a successful stockbroker. Our mates were used to luxury, and they assumed a wealth we did not have. They married into a glamorous family, and if we turned out to be dull, they were bound to be disappointed.

I assume there was a feeling of love when each of these marriages began, but that feeling faded under the circumstances. Each of these marriages failed. Eventually, we made other marriages. Some of us married outside the social register, but most of these marriages failed, too. Undoubtedly we did not give enough to them. We were used to receiving, rather than to giving. Hopeless romantics, we Roosevelt children remarried again and again. Some marriages ended messily. In the end, some have endured.

We have had happiness, but few of us have found serenity.

Aside from the ill-fated infant, first Franklin, who was born and died within one year, Anna was the first born and first to die. When I began this book all of us were alive. She died on December 1, 1975, at the age of sixty-nine. Each of us has enjoyed reasonable longevity.

Less than two years apart in age, Anna and I were close as kids, but drifted apart as adults. We never had any arguments, we merely took different paths and wound up in different parts of the country. I don't think any of us were close to Anna over the last thirty or thirty-five years, but then few of us have been close to one another during this period. That is the kind of family we became. There was always great warmth when we were together, but those times were few and far between. There were so many marriages that few of us attended each other's weddings after the first one or two. I remember when my youngest, Becky, was christened at Hyde Park in 1971, Anna stood in for my daughter Sara as godmother. Anna and Elliott were the only ones able to make it to father's funeral. We were all at mother's funeral, and all but Elliott at Anna's funeral. He could not come in from England for that sad occasion.

Anna had a full life, if not an entirely satisfactory one. Although Elliott and Franklin frequently flew into rages at the intrusions into their private lives, I think Anna and John liked publicity the least and, more than any of us, sought the shadows. Although she was brought up in "society," Anna disliked the idea of being a debutante. She went to Cornell, studying agriculture, of all things, but gave it up to get married young. She always said she got married too young. Which of us didn't? But she was only twenty when she wed in 1926 and only twenty-one when her first child was born. She really didn't have much of a youth.

Anna and her first husband, Curtis Dall, were mismatched. She shared mother's liberal Democratic philosophies, while he was a conservative Republican. He was Wall Street through and through, a successful stockbroker, but Anna did not find a stockbroker's life as exciting as the life she'd had with father. Curtis was a decent person, but he and Anna just didn't make it together. They parted about the time father was entering the White House in 1932, and she and her two children moved in with mother and father.

In the White House, Sis met and married John Boettiger, a correspondent for the anti-FDR Chicago *Tribune*. Hearst sent them to Seattle, where John became publisher of the *Post-Intelligencer* and Anna the women's editor. But as Hearst became more critical of father and saw that Anna and John were not giving him an "in" with the president, he welcomed their departure.

They borrowed some money, bought a weekly shopping newspaper in Phoenix and turned it into a daily in competition with the Gene Pulliam newspaper there at that time. They had a hard time of it. I think John overestimated his talents; he was an excellent reporter, but not such a good manager. They borrowed more money.

John, who had been a lively, active sort of fellow, became quite depressed, and it disturbed their marriage. During one of the few times Anna and I ever discussed our personal problems, she spoke to me about how worried she was at the way this second marriage was going. She hung on to her husband with both hands, but they had little left between them by the time the war took him away.

He came back in a deep depression. They divorced in 1949, then he committed suicide. The fact that he and Anna were already apart made his violent death no less tragic to Anna and she never could bring herself to discuss it. He left her with a son—John Roosevelt Boettinger—and a lot of debts. I remember before John died she told me she desperately needed money for the newspaper, and I loaned her $25,000 and found a friend to loan them another $25,000. Of course that went down the drain when the newspaper failed. She could not even bring herself to acknowledge the loan later.

I don't think my brothers loaned Anna any money, but I know mother did. *Gave* her money would be more accurate, I suppose. In her early years, Anna was close to mother. She was prettier than mother and more gracefully built, with gorgeous golden hair and a flawless complexion. She was not stuck with mother's high-pitched voice, but neither did she have mother's enormous energy. She said several times she was not about to bounce about the world as mother did while her marriage went to waste, but Anna's first two marriages failed anyway.

When she moved into the White House to serve as a secretary and aide to father, she was estranged from mother. She went with father to Yalta, which mother had wanted to do, belatedly wishing to take a place by her husband's side. And Anna was party to father's affair with Lucy, which further estranged her from mother.

Yet after father's death, mother did much for Anna. She appeared in a radio show for her and gave her money and did what she could to help Anna get out from under her debts. When mother got sick, it was Anna who went to her side. After her death, Anna moved into her apartment and spent six months straightening out mother's affairs.

Anna lived for a while in Los Angeles and Berkeley in California, where she met Dr. James Halsted, who was attached to the Veterans Administration Hospital there. They married in 1952 and moved back to Washington, where he was chief of internal medicine for the VA and worked for the Department of Health, Education and Welfare. They even lived in Iran for a while, where he was a Fulbright exchange professor.

Jim retired to a general practice in upstate New York, a community called Hillside, but retired from that in 1973 as both of them reached their late sixties. They had built a comfortably large ranch-style house on 130 acres of forested hills and seemed content. Some of the furnishings came from mother's factory and cottage. Jim went into Albany a few times a week to consult on a nutritional program he'd started at the medical center there. Anna went to Hyde Park occasionally to care for the FDR Library and Eleanor Roosevelt Museum. She said she had a hard time keeping up with correspondence concerning our late parents. She also served on the boards of the National Committee on Household Employment and the Wiltwyck School for Emotionally Disturbed Children.

Although Anna and Jim had no children together, they both had children from previous marriages. Curtis, Jr., who hates to be called "Buzzie," was with the United Nations awhile, a top man in the refugee program there. He lives in New York now. He married and had a daughter, Juliana. His sister, Anna Eleanor, "Sistie," married a man named Seagraves and they have a daughter, Anna Eleanor, and two sons, David and Nicholas Delano. They live in Washington. John Roosevelt Boettiger lives in South Hadley, Massachusetts, where he teaches and lives a family life.

My sister aged gracefully, but the last time I saw her alive she was dying from throat cancer and the end was near. She and Jim had a happy marriage. He is a wonderful, learned man who made a fine home for Anna. They lived quietly. She did her own housework and cooking, though she complained she was not good at it. She was a good person, who would have been happier if she had not been born into the bright, hot spotlight. She was happier in the quiet semiretirement of her final years than she was at any other time in her life.

My youngest brother, John, has had the smoothest, if least exciting, life of all of us. If you look closely you can see that John is one of FDR's sons, but of all of us he has been the least like father. The youngest, he also was the least close to father. Johnny followed in father's footsteps through Groton and

Harvard, but after that he went his own way. As far as that goes, whereas Franklin and I rowed crew at Harvard, he played polo there.

While at Harvard, he married a North Shore debutante, Anne Sturgess Clark, whose wealthy father was a partner in the prominent financial firm of Scudder, Stevens and Clark. They were Republicans, but John always leaned that way. He was a conservative, while the rest of us were liberals.

John made less use of the Roosevelt name than the rest of us. After graduation from Harvard, he went to work in Filene's department store in Boston, which annoyed granny, to say the least. After the war he went to work for Grayson-Robinson Stores in Los Angeles, then, in 1953, formed a partnership in a financial firm—Roosevelt, Lee, Magee, Incorporated, of Beverly Hills. He lived in Beverly Hills for a while and later in Pasadena, but he missed the East and returned with Anne to live in mother's cottage at Hyde Park for a time. He went to work for Bache & Company and has been with them many years now, primarily handling pension funds. He's a senior vice-president and director of the firm. He's also a director of the Roosevelt and Lee Corporation.

It is a family joke that John always was a wizard of high finance. Many years ago when we were young and I was visiting Betsey's family in Ireland, John and Franklin came for a visit. We attended the dog races in Dublin one night and lost on every race until the last. We each picked a promising prospect with what money we had left, but Johnny picked a hundred-to-one shot with his last half-pound. It was the only all-white dog in the field, I recall, and it was recovering from an illness. We all ridiculed John as his dog fell fifteen to twenty lengths behind, but we were stunned when the two dogs in the lead got into a fight going over the last hurdle, and one after another the others tumbled into it—except for John's dog, which raced past to win. John has continued to do well. I don't think he's wealthy—but I don't think that was ever important to him—but he's certainly well off. He's the only one of FDR's sons who never ran for political office, though he did register as a Republican after father's death, has been a supporter of Nelson Rockefeller and has served as a trustee of the New York State University system. I recall that as a Roosevelt he was welcomed to Toots Shor's one night, but when he was introduced as John Roosevelt the proprietor almost threw him out on his ear. "What're you bringing that Republican bastard in here for?" roared the colorful Toots.

We Roosevelts who are Democrats and our Republican brother tease one another politically when we meet. I see and have a meal with John and his wife Irene whenever I'm in New York and he brings me up to date on Republican doings and I do the same for the Democrats.

The saddest part of John's life was the failure of his first marriage. It lasted a long time, and he took pride in being the only one of us who had not been divorced. He used to laugh and say he was the only stable one. He said that he and Anne would never break up. But eventually they did. They had four children—three daughters, Anna, Joan and Sally, and a son, Haven. Sally died in her teens after a fall from a horse and that hurt them terribly. Anne never really recovered. She went to live with Elliott's second wife, Faye Emerson, in Majorca, after they had both divorced Roosevelts. It certainly was an unusual situation. Anne headed downhill and never got back up. She died a few years ago.

John married Irene Boyd McAlpin in 1965. They have no children but have a happy marriage. She is a lovely lady. They have a nice apartment on East Fifty-seventh Street in Manhattan and a summer place upstate in Tuxedo. John has become a bit of a country gentleman. He rides to the hounds, shoots trap, golfs. The tallest of all the tall Roosevelt sons, he looks and apparently feels fine as he moves into his sixties. Joan lives with them. Haven lives in Chappaqua, New York, with his two children, Sara Delano and Wendy Clark. Anne married a man named Luke and they live in New Albany, Ohio, with their three children, David Russell, Haven Roosevelt and Lindsay.

If John has been the most stable of us, Elliott has been the most traveled. If John's life has run the smoothest, Elliott's has been the roughest. The rest of us have always considered Elliott the maverick of the clan. He's always been that way, right from the beginning: his disappearance out west, his suspension from Groton for roughing up a foe in football, his refusal to go to college like the rest of us. Instead of college he went west and wound up working for father's enemy, Hearst, as did Anna and her husband.

Elliott fell in with some millionaires in Texas who promised him a fortune in radio, used his name and left him deep in debt. Against his best interests, father wound up asking Jesse Jones to bail Elliott out, and Jesse arranged a $2-million loan which saved Elliott's skin. New management took over the radio operation Elliott had put together, but at least Elliott got out of it alive—and wound up opposing father at the convention in 1940 when father went for his third term. I suppose Elliott was entitled to support anyone he chose, even if it meant opposing father. But it never sat right with any of us.

Elliott has been involved in many businesses and has done badly in all of them. He was in Minneapolis for a while and worked for Howard Hughes. He moved to Iowa to go into a fertilizer business, but that failed when the woman who had been treasurer of the company went to jail for fraud. Elliott went to Florida and wound up as mayor of Miami Beach. Which was fine except that Miami Beach has an active and enormous Jewish population, and Elliott's fifth wife, Patty, apparently made some injudicious remarks about Jews. In addition, Elliott and Patty joined the only country club in the community that excluded Jews. The result was that his opponents put up a Jew in the next election and Elliott never came close at the polls.

He moved to another part of Florida and started raising Arabian horses and growing fruit, and that worked well.

His first wife, in 1931, was Betty Donner, heiress to the Pennsylvania steel fortune. I think Elliott felt her family would welcome him, but they disapproved of father and consequently disapproved of Elliott. Betty and Elliott made an attractive couple, but they were very young and totally unprepared for the responsibilities of marriage—Elliott particularly. When he took off for Texas without her, he put her out of his life, though it took some time for him to telephone her to tell her so.

Elliott and Betty had one child, William Donner Roosevelt, who followed Elliott into the aircraft field, wound up on Wall Street and has been generous in helping his father out financially. Bill lives in Connecticut and has three sons—Christopher Kyle, Dana Donner and Nicholas. He inherited a lot of the Donner family fortune and is well off.

In 1933, as I mentioned earlier, Elliott married Ruth Chandler Googins, whom he met in Texas. They had three children—Ruth Chandler, Elliott, Jr., and David Boynton. Chandler and Tony both live in Dallas, Texas. David lives in Jericho, New York. Chandler married a man named Lindsley and they have three children—Ruth Roosevelt, Henry Hays, and Chandler Lindsley.

Although he lives far from them now, overseas, Elliott has kept as close to his children as possible. He loves children. In fact, when he married Patty he adopted her children and gave them his name. Although they have a perfectly fine father, Patty wanted her children to have the Roosevelt name, and the children's father consented to it. One of them even changed his name to James Roosevelt III, which scares me a little. But if Patty thought they would be in line for any inheritance, she was wrong. Because of that stipulation in the wills of our parents that the estate be divided among natural-born Roosevelts only, I'm not sure what, if anything, Elliott will be able to leave them.

After Ruth and before Patty, there were two others—Faye Emerson and Minnewa Bell—which gives Elliott five marriages and the championship in this department, though he's ahead of me by only one. I think Elliott's marriage to Ruth drowned in his sea of debts in Texas. He was in such terrible trouble that there was no way he could work at a shaky marriage.

He married Faye in 1944, right after he returned from his air force adventures a real war hero. She was an actress whose career skyrocketed with the arrival of television. She was a prominent and popular performer in the late Forties and early Fifties, and a super person, too. She tried very hard to make a go of their marriage. But it was a hard go. Elliott was barely making out, and then thanks only to mother, managing her radio and television shows. He did not like the fact that Faye was making more money than he was, and was the center of attention wherever they went.

Mother always liked Faye and maintained their friendship even after the marriage fell apart. When her career faded Faye retired to Majorca, where she teamed up with Johnny's former wife, Anne.

At one time Faye was married to the bandleader Skitch Henderson, but after an incident involving some teen-age girls he was dropped from Johnny Carson's *Tonight* TV show and his career went into eclipse. Faye's marriage to Skitch hit the skids. She didn't have much luck in her married life, but she endures, and we think of her fondly.

In Los Angeles, Elliott met and married, in 1951, Minnewa Bell from the prominent California family that founded Bel Air and made millions in oil. Minnewa's brother, Alfonzo, has had an erratic political career and ran for governor at one time.

Minnewa had a lot of money and bought a ranch for Elliott in Colorado, but he was not a success as a rancher. She and Elliott got to drinking a bit too much, and it contributed to the breakup of their marriage. He wanted to move back to Phoenix and had a real estate agent find him a place there. He found a bride at the same time, because Patty—Patricia Whitehead Peabody—was the real estate agent. She started to see him while he was still married to Minnewa. When he divorced Minnewa, he married Patty in 1960.

In Florida, Elliott wound up as manager of the convention center in Miami Beach. He had a fight with the head of the biggest hotel in town and blew that. He also had a business called Roosevelt International, which promoted dozens of different deals.

The next thing I knew, Elliott was running a ranch near Lisbon, Portugal, and was writing a book about mother and father with James Brough. This was the book that blew the whistle loud and clear on father's "affairs" with Lucy and Missy. Franklin received the galley proofs, which we read. Franklin then called a family meeting at his place and we discussed the book. None of us liked it, and we agreed as a family to denounce it. Nevertheless, the book was a hit. It created considerable commotion—and, of course, helped Elliott financially.

Not long after the book was published Elliott called to tell me he'd had open-heart surgery and been given a pacemaker. Later, the first pacemaker failed and a new one had to be implanted. The crowning blow, however, came when the Communists took over Portugal and impounded all of his money and holdings. Elliott took off for England. He says he decided to go there when he learned that authors of books published in other countries don't have to pay taxes on them in England. He and Patty rent a lovely estate in Gloucester, owned by former Prime Minister Macmillan.

Elliott and Brough subsequently wrote a second book on our parents, which came out in 1975, and have a third one in the works scheduled for 1977. I saw Elliott when I was in England in 1975 and assured him that since I had my own book coming out, in which I would present my side of the story, I wouldn't bother to denounce his second book, no matter how he insulted me. I warned him I might insult him in my book. We agreed, however, that blood was thicker than water and our feelings for one another would endure no matter what we wrote.

Anna and John were not about to write books, but Franklin admits he may have to write one in self-defense. Franklin led the denunciation of Elliott's first book, but after living with that one for a while, we weren't particularly bothered by his second one. Franklin, as the only lawyer among us, has as-

sumed the role of our protector. It was he who negotiated our
interests in Dore Schary's play and movie, *Sunrise at Campobello,* and he did a dreadful job of it, but he meant well.

Schary read the play to us before it was produced. Mother
was alive then. She thought it inaccurate and overly dramatic,
but most of us thought it was all right. Most of its inaccuracies
were unimportant and provided dramatic effect. And the fact
is, that period in our lives when father came down with polio
and began to battle his way back certainly was a dramatic one.
The play was a good piece of fictionalized fact and at the least
a tribute to the spirit of our parents. Ralph Bellamy did a
marvelous job portraying father.

Now, of course, people who never knew my parents are
writing books and television plays about them, and we are not
even advised. If no real disservice is done my parents, I for
one do not expect to make an issue of it.

The televised dramatization of Joseph Lash's *Eleanor and
Franklin,* which ran early in 1976, was a beautifully staged and
well-acted production which at times gave me chills, it struck
so close to home. However, it might better have been titled
Eleanor, for the focus was mainly on mother, with little attention paid to father. She was portrayed mostly as a wronged
and long-suffering wife, which, if true in part, was nevertheless only a small part of what she was. And he was given little
credit for his strength and accomplishments, with none of the
great moments of his career reproduced.

I do not really think it right to invent conversations and
situations when one cannot know what took place between
people. I worry that these increasingly popular "fictionalized
biographies"—we will see more of them based on my parents
in the winter of 1977—provide a view of the subjects that
simply is not accurate. But I do not worry about them as
much as Franklin seems to.

Of all of us Franklin is the one who came closest to being
another FDR. He had father's looks, his speaking voice, his
smile, his charm, his charisma. He came close to continuing
the Roosevelt dynasty in the White House, I think, closer

than the records show. He was named to fill an unexpired term in the House in 1949 and won election to Congress on his own the following two terms.

Unfortunately, he had a dreadful record in Congress. He was smart, but not smart enough. He had good ideas and the power of persuasion, but he did not put them to good use. He coasted instead of working at his job, considering it beneath him, while he aimed for higher positions. He may have had the worst attendance record of any member of those days, and it cost him those higher positions.

He resigned to run for governor of New York, hoping to follow in father's footsteps, but he got into a head-on fight with Averell Harriman over the party's endorsement. Harriman had the horses and Franklin lost the nomination. Harriman had done his homework within the party over a period of many years, while Franklin jumped in without having secured the support of any regulars—and he had no Louis Howe to lay the groundwork and plot strategy for him.

Still, the party did not want to lose an attractive young man with the Roosevelt name and some of FDR's magic, so they talked him into running for attorney general instead. Here, however, Franklin ran into Jacob Javits, one of the premier politicans and one of the most persuasive vote-getters in New York history. Harriman won. Javits won. He ran on Franklin's record—his poor record in Congress. I believe every Democrat won except Franklin.

That just about killed him politically, though he did try again later. He ran in the primary to select a Democratic candidate for mayor of New York City, but his congressional record continued to haunt him and he lost. Desperately, he decided to run as the Labor party's candidate. Without a broad base of support, he lost. He was reduced to campaigning for John Kennedy.

At my suggestion Kennedy sent my brother to campaign for him prior to the primariy in West Virginia, where FDR remained a hero. Franklin campaigned hard for Kennedy, maybe too hard. He may have been hitting below the belt when he brought up the "draft-dodger" issue of Humphrey's failure to serve in World War II. Many feel that he may have been responsible for war hero Kennedy winning this pivotal primary which enabled him to go on to win the nomination and the presidency. But this campaign didn't do Franklin's image any good.

The fact is, Kennedy's campaign manager, Larry O'Brien, anonymously received copies of correspondence between Humphrey and his Minnesota draft board, and turned them over to Franklin rather then let Kennedy act as his own "hatchet man." O'Brien says he intended to use the material only in an emergency, but claims that Franklin used it in a moment of anger. O'Brien regrets today the use of such tainted material, but Franklin said he was led to believe it was authentic and for release.

I don't think Franklin's rewards were what he had hoped for, but he was appointed to positions in JFK's regime. He was undersecretary of commerce and chairman of the Civil Rights Commission. JFK and Franklin were friends and their families were close. Socially, Franklin spent a lot of time in the White House during JFK's reign. But when Kennedy was killed, Franklin fell from power.

He made one last try, as the Liberal party's candidate for governor in 1966. At odds with Democratic regulars, he had no hope, so a promising political career came to a premature end. Having failed to take advantage of his first opportunity, he never again was in the right place at the right time.

Unlucky in politics, unlucky in love: Franklin contributed three marriages to the long list of frustrating failures for the Roosevelt children. His first was to the wealthy and beautiful Ethel du Pont. Her father, Pierre, originally supported our father, but later became a bitter foe. Franklin and Ethel lived on Long Island and enjoyed a gay social whirl in the first few years of their marriage before the war separated them. They never recovered from this separation. After he returned from the service, they tried for three years to make their marriage work before they gave up on it.

The most terrible-tempered of us Roosevelts, Franklin could not have been an easy man to live with. He was and is basically a decent person, but he is given to awful rages at times. I'm sure that Ethel had a hard time of it. She did not try marriage again for many years. Sadly, when she did, the second did not work any better for her than the first one had. She began to suffer from poor health and around 1965 took her own life.

She was the second of the Roosevelt spouses to commit suicide, though Franklin could hardly be held responsible more than fifteen years after their marriage had failed. Still, it is as though we all had a hand in the terrible tragedies of our lives.

Franklin's second wife was Suzanne Perrin. An attractive girl without the Du Pont money, she took an active interest in a farm Franklin had started in upstate New York. While Ethel had given Franklin two sons—Christopher du Pont and Franklin Delano III—Sue gave him two daughters—Laura Delano and Nancy. Franklin's first two children have given him six grandchildren. Franklin III, who lives in New York, has had two daughters—Phoebe Louisa and Amelia—and a son, Nicholas Martin. Chris, who lives in Armonk, New York, also has two daughters—Emily and Kate—and a son, Christopher Havemeyer.

After Franklin's second marriage failed he married Felicia Schiff Warburg Sarnoff—a Warburg, a relative of *New York Post* publisher Dorothy Schiff, and the former wife of RCA's president Robert Sarnoff. Attractive and intellectual, she capably managed his estate in upstate New York, south of Poughkeepsie, two thousand acres with cattle and sheep. But after several years of marriage they separated, and divorced not too long ago. She, too, has written a book, though not about the Roosevelts, bless her heart.

Through the Roosevelt influence, Franklin landed a Fiat distributorship and did so well that he wound up with the national rights. He did so well with the national rights, they wound up buying it back from him for a considerable sum.

While he worked at it effectively, a lot of his success was luck since he hit it at a time when there was a boom market for foreign cars in this country.

Franklin still dreams of political success, but in his sixties he is past the age of hope. I consider it a waste because Franklin had a lot more to offer than he had a chance to give. There has been a lot of waste in all our lives; failure has accompanied success; sadness and tragedy went hand in hand with happiness. If I have been critical of my brothers and sister, now I will be critical of myself.

I seem to have jumped in and out of the fire with each of my marriages, and each marriage has made a difference in the work I have done. After the war I moved from one thing to another, and finally into politics. I was involved in losing campaigns for governor of California and mayor of Los Angeles, a winning campaign for the House of Representatives, five successful reelections, a term with the United Nations and a disastrous tour with a disgraced concern called Investors Overseas Services, prior to my present work with my own consulting company, and teaching at the University of California, Irvine.

When I met Betsey Cushing I fell hard and wanted to marry fast. Betsey was agreeable and we were married in June of 1930, but we were both in our early twenties and didn't know what we wanted to do with our lives. I left law school to concentrate on my insurance business, and we lived in Cambridge until I went to work in New York. Later we bought a farm in Framingham, Massachusetts, which was a lovely interlude. A daughter, Sara Delano, was born in 1932, and another, Kate, in 1936. Things started to fall apart for us after we moved to Washington and I went to work for father. We had our own house in Georgetown, but we spent most of our time in the White House. When Betsey all but took over mother's role in the White House, acting as father's hostess and arguing with the housekeeper about father's meals and things like that, mother wasn't the only one to resent it. I did too, because I wanted more of her for myself. I was selfish. I never thought about what I should do for her, only what she could do for me. I wanted her to do for me, not for father.

We began to move in different circles and make different friends. We didn't like each other's friends, and we began to bicker. After a while I only felt relaxed when I was alone, and by the time I went to Minnesota for surgery I'd decided to end the marriage. We were divorced in 1940.

A few years later Betsey married Jock Whitney and they remain married.

At the Mayo Clinic, as I said earlier, I met a nurse, Romelle Schneider, and I fell for her. Maybe it's easy for a sick man to fall for his nurse. I really was sick, I needed considerable care, and she was very kind. I wanted to be kind to her. Romelle needed help as Betsey never had. Romelle had come from a small town in Wisconsin. Her father died young, and her mother needed assistance, so Romelle went to work early. When I came into her life, I must have seemed a glamorous figure who could do a lot for her. I wanted to be helpful to her. I took her to California to nurse me while I recuperated, married her in May of 1941 after I divorced Betsey, moved her mother to California, made her sister my secretary and put her brother through Notre Dame.

The war was partly responsible for our drifting apart, as it was for so many couples. When I came home on leave, we were strangers. Although we had three children—James, Jr., in 1945, Anthony in 1946 and Anna Eleanor in 1948—they did not help us to hold on to our marriage.

Romelle was not satisfied with a simple life, so we moved into a home in Beverly Hills. When she became discontented again, we moved to a place in Pasadena. She was adamantly against my going into politics. The year I ran for governor was a difficult one for us and I could not concentrate on my campaign. After I lost, matters worsened until finally I moved out of the house and into my own apartment.

I suppose any chance of a reconciliation was lost when I announced my candidacy for Congress. I won the election in what was called a great upset.

We were divorced in 1955 and she received a large settlement and considerable alimony, as well as support for our
children. She was a marvelous mother, and I'm grateful for
that.

I had met a receptionist and cashier in my office, Irene
Kitchenmaster Owens. She liked the excitement of politics
and, I guess, the glamour of going with a prominent political
figure. I liked her and married her in May of 1956.

Irene came from Detroit. Her father, an epileptic, committed suicide by shooting himself in front of her. Her mother
tried to keep the family together, but it was too much for her;
she became mentally disturbed and wound up in a nursing
home in Rosemead, where she remained until her death.

Irene had been unhappily married a couple of times, as had
her sister. Perhaps because Irene and I both had had problems
in our personal lives, we felt sympathy for one another. She
was a beautiful woman and I felt warm toward her. She was
sympathetic during my ordeal with Romelle.

Irene wanted children but could not have any, so in 1959 we
adopted a son we named Hall Delano. We were all right for
a while, when I was in Congress in Washington, but the
marriage began to sour after I joined the U.N. and moved to
New York. Part of the problem was financial. I was paying
Romelle so much that Irene and I had to manage with less.
That is why I grabbed an attractive offer from IOS when it
came along, and we moved to that concern's headquarters in
Switzerland.

Irene, however, was unhappy away from her own country.
She especially disliked the social life imposed on her in Geneva. When trouble developed at IOS and I didn't know what
to do about it, she fell into bad habits which hurt her health.
We argued bitterly, and the hostilities were intensified by the
fact that my boss, Bernie Cornfeld, was notorious for having
women around all the time and she accused me of playing the
same game.

One night when I returned from work—and I truly had
been working—we had our last argument. She stabbed me

with one of my war souvenirs, a marine knife, and that, of course, was the end of our marriage. I recovered from my back wound, but the stabbing was a big story around the world. A dark chapter had been added to my life.

I managed to leave that night and never returned to her. I'm sure she did not want me back, of course. I have seen her since because I wanted to see our son. I was worried about him, but she has taken good care of him. He is a very strong young man who was able to endure with a clear head the bitter things that happened between his parents. He cares for her and for me.

In our divorce, I gave Irene the house in Palm Springs, a large sum of money, and agreed to substantial alimony payments, which added to my already heavy load. She never remarried and lives now in Pacific Palisades with Del, though he is almost a grown man now and often spends time in Newport Beach with Mary and me.

The one blessing of that misadventure was that it brought Mary Winskill and me together. She was Del's former teacher. Immediately after that dark night, Irene was in no condition to care for Del, so I called Mary in New York to ask her help. She was as much Irene's friend as mine, and she and Del really liked one another.

Mary and her mother flew over and spent several weeks near Geneva helping out with Del. I saw a lot of her, and as I came to know her I began to think a lot of her. It took awhile, though, before I began to think of a life for us together. She was thirty years younger than I and had never been married, while I was a three-time loser.

Back in New York I saw more of her, and the more I saw of her the more I wanted her by my side. Despite all of my bad experiences in the past, I was convinced Mary would be good for me. I worried about the difference in our ages, but I worried more about what my life would be without her. I convinced her we could overcome this difference, though I'm not sure it ever really bothered her; she says it didn't. She was a very mature and accomplished person, and if she had an interest in me as a husband it was because of me, not my name or what I seemed to be.

Mary was brought up in the north of England, near Chester, and educated in London. She attended the best schools. Her mother was a teacher and Mary wanted to be a teacher. They wound up teaching at the same school. But when Mary got an offer to teach at the International School in Geneva, she decided it was time to go off on her own. She has been around the world reporting on different international schools and has been the principal of the U.N. Junior House School in New York. In short, Mary's a well-traveled, brilliant and beautiful redhead and I'm proud of her.

When I proposed and was accepted, we went the old-fashioned route and asked approval of her parents. They gave it. They're fine people and we visit together here or in England when we can.

Mary and I were married in 1969. We never talk about my previous marriages except as they touch on our lives today. She wants me just to consider her as my wife, not my first or my fourth. Indeed, she's the only one who has made me behave like a husband. Not by argument, but by reason, though it's clear she will brook no nonsense from me. She feels that we are equals in the marriage, and I am most respectful of her feelings. As a result, we have a sharing such as I've never had with a woman before.

I must say I was very proud and happy when Mary became pregnant and then gave birth to Rebecca Mary in 1971. At that time my eldest child was thirty-nine and I was sixty-three, but Becky has made me feel a lot younger than my years. Her youth rubs off on me. It's a joy to have a child in my home and in my arms again. I only hope my health holds up long enough for me to be the father she needs as long as she needs me.

Mary had problems in her pregnancy. The doctor at the clinic in Geneva believed in natural childbirth and he had me take classes with her so I could help her in the delivery room. I remember in a pre-education class hearing someone behind me say, "Gee, isn't it wonderful the way that father is helping his daughter!"

Because of my age, I've taken extra measures to be sure that

Mary's future is secure. I suggested that she go back to school, which she did, getting straight A's at the University of California in Irvine, near our Orange County home, so that she could acquire American teaching credentials. She has taken a position there supervising student teachers. She is the real professional in our family, although I also teach a course in government there and was honored at being asked to give the commencement address in 1976. Mary's younger, but wiser than I am. We have a lot of laughter in our life. After my failures as a husband, I should worry about my marriage, but I do not worry about this one.

My children are the blessings from my bad marriages. I only wish I were closer to them.

Sara has been married twice. She married Tony Di Bonaventura, a concert pianist, with whom she had five children —Andrea Isabelle, Anthony Peter, Betsey Maria, Peter John and Arina Rosaria. Sadly, Sara and Tony were divorced. She then married Ronald Wilford, who was Tony's agent. I hope they are happy. Kate had been married once, but she, too, is now separated from her husband. (Is it me, the family or life?) She married Bill Haddad, an award-winning reporter for the *New York Post*, who was close to the Kennedys. They had three children—Andrea Whitney, Camilla Cushing and Laura Whitney.

I have lived my own life as best I could, and I suppose they have to do the same. I am not ashamed of the things I have done in my life, because I did not deliberately do anything wrong and I never intended to hurt anyone. But I do very much regret the embarrassment and pain some of the events caused people I loved. I think sometimes how hard it must have been on my children when that bright spotlight caught me in an awkward posture. Whether they wanted to or not, they were dragged down to my lows.

However, in chronicling my days, there were highs, too, though these seldom were as well publicized. Perhaps somewhere in the concluding chapter my children will see some highs. I wish they could have shared them with me. Perhaps there are places where they will be proud of the old man. It's an uneven road most of us walk. A step forward, a step backward, some missteps along the way.

XXI

All of the sons of presidents have not been drawn into politics, but there definitely is a tug in that direction. It is difficult to grow up watching your father's success and not yearn to pursue politics as a profession for yourself. I think I have made it clear that I do not consider life in the limelight entirely enjoyable, but we all consider ourselves capable, and the opportunity to accomplish something in life is tempting to us.

That opportunity is more available to the sons of presidents than it is to others. If you have the name and the inclination, why not play the game? And when you get into the game, you find that the first success massages the ego. You cast off the failures. That's the game—win some, lose some.

My name got me into the game. It was my greatest asset, no doubt of that. But if it was a plus, it was also a minus. I was not my father. Some expected more of me. Some saw him in my face and heard him in my voice. And I did have a lot of him in me: I shared much of his philosophy of life and many of his ideals; we wanted the same sorts of things for people; I admired him and supported most of his stands. But I had to be myself.

A different day had dawned, anyway. While some may have expected too much of me, others expected nothing, feeling I was riding on the coattails of a ghost. I did have a lot to give. I gave a lot. But I never really escaped father's image, which shadowed me wherever I went and whatever I did.

After the war I returned to California. My partner in the insurance business, John Sargent, died during the war. He was the inventive insurance man on our team and I did not want to continue the company without him. I kept my license, but did little new business.

I was looking around for something to do when I met up with a newly formed group of artists, scientists and professional people who were backing liberal political causes. Ronald Reagan was a member. Ronnie was considered a liberal Democrat at the time. Now that he has become a conservative Republican, we kid him about his past. Olivia De Havilland was also a member, as were a number of other actors and artists.

The sculptor Jo Davidson, a great character, whom I'd known for a long time, was behind it, and he offered me the job of organizing on the West Coast for $25,000 a year. I took the job because I considered the aims of the operation admirable and because the money was satisfactory, but I had no business organization behind me on which to build. One serious problem was that the more radical members would remain at meetings long after everyone else left and pass resolutions that the others did not like. In the end the organization fell apart because of its own weaknesses. I was in and out of it in less than a year in 1946.

A year or so later, a man with whom I had served during the war, M. C. Plumley, approached me with an attractive idea for forming a credit union for members of labor unions. We would borrow money from banks at a low rate of interest, and the members of the labor unions would borrow it from us at a higher, but still low, rate of interest for furniture, cars and other such costly items they needed.

The heads of the labor unions were in favor of it, and the banks were willing to back it. We called it Union Service, Inc., and we dealt with the AFL, CIO and all the major labor unions in southern California.

It worked wonderfully well for a while—so well, in fact, that the banks and financial organizations became concerned about the amount of business we were taking away from them. It stopped working when they started to charge us higher rates of interest and we could no longer make loans at low rates to union members and still turn a reasonable profit.

By then, however, I was about to return to a political career —which, until the war, had been limited to the experiences I'd had around Boston with Jim Curley and in Washington and other places with my father. I had gotten to know Melvin and Helen Gahagan Douglas and a number of other powerful political figures in the Democratic party in California, some of whom had persuaded me to join them after the war. They thought I would be an admirable front man for the party, because of who I was, I suppose.

Thus in 1946 I ran for the post of Democratic state chairman in California and was elected. It was an unpaid position, but I spent much of the next two years trying to get a strong party organization together. Earl Warren had been reelected governor, but we got Pat Brown elected attorney general and began to make some inroads into what was primarily a Republican state at the time.

As the 1948 presidential election year neared, I joined with Mrs. Douglas, my brother Franklin, labor leaders and others in an effort to find an attractive national candidate. Dwight Eisenhower had emerged from the war with impeccable credentials, and since he had not established any political preference, we tried to interest him in running as our representative. I did not speak to him personally, but Franklin was one of those who did. It was purely practical politics. The Republicans pursued the same course. As it turned out, he fit the moderately conservative Republican image, but neither the GOP nor we knew it at the time. He was simply someone who, it was felt, could win.

I was associated with a "dump Truman" movement, a term that is not strictly accurate. Harry Truman moved into 1948 in much the same manner as Gerald Ford moved into 1976:

Fate had thrust both of them into the presidency, neither had been elected, and it was not clear whether either could be elected. In 1948, in fact, Truman seemed a lot longer a shot than Ford in 1976. Because father had been elected four times, Democrats had held the presidency sixteen years. It seemed so clearly time for a change that only an unusually attractive campaigner could keep our party in power. I was not alone in thinking Truman was not that man.

I rather liked and respected President Truman and thought he did a good job in a difficult situation following father's death. I just did not think he could be elected, so I looked for someone who could. In Margaret Truman's book about her father, she says that early in 1948 I packed a dinner gathering with goons who would boo when Democratic national chairman J. Howard McGrath spoke in praise of Harry. That is absolutely untrue. If I had done anything as devious as that, I could never have been elected Democratic national committeeman from California after Truman's election. When I spoke on behalf of Eisenhower I received a better response than McGrath did when he spoke on behalf of Truman simply because that was the prevailing party sentiment at the time.

In the end, however, Ike turned both parties down and slid into the nonpolitical position of the presidency of Columbia University, and the Republicans returned to Tom Dewey at their convention in Philadelphia in June. Denied once, Dewey did not seem likely to be denied again. With the liberal Earl Warren as his running mate, the GOP looked unbeatable. I joined other party members in sending out telegrams calling for a caucus two days in advance of our own convention so that we could select the strongest and ablest candidate from our ranks.

I'd had a harsh encounter with Truman in California, where he said he regarded me as ungrateful for trying to pull the rug out from under him while he was following my father's policies. But when no one stronger emerged at the caucus we turned to Truman, who was undeniably able. The question was, could he be elected? In desperation, some members of the party tried to talk mother into running as his vice-presidential candidate, but she refused. She was afraid of it, frankly.

Truman won, and I've always wondered whether, if mother had run, she might not have won as the presidential candidate four years later. I suppose not, since Eisenhower finally ran and really was unbeatable, but it's interesting to ponder the possibility that she just might have made it as our first woman president.

At any rate, when she refused, Truman turned to Bill Douglas. Fearing a debacle, Douglas, too, refused, and thereby lost his best chance for future political power. Alben Barkley was shoved into the breach. With Henry Wallace mounting a "third party" candidacy and Strom Thurmond mounting a "Dixiecrat" ticket, the Democrats seemed divided beyond hope.

However, Harry Truman turned out to be a spirited campaigner who apparently won affection as the underdog. Margaret Truman has said he never forgave me for opposing his nomination, but that is not entirely true. It is true he never endorsed my candidacy in my later campaigns, but neither did he oppose me. He did not endorse my candidacy to become national committeeman from California, but he did not oppose it, either. I campaigned for him, too, often side by side with him, everywhere from dinner platforms to train platforms.

I went to see him in the White House later and said to him, "Mr. President, I know that you must have some unhappy feelings that I initially opposed you in the convention, but I hope that you are happy with the way I campaigned for you in California and a few other places later. I really do respect you and I want your respect." And he said, "Jim, one thing you'll find out about me is that I don't hold grudges. I am sorry some of you felt I couldn't do the job, but I am happy that when you saw how I came back you were big enough to go all out for me. I respect your independence."

MY PARENTS: A Differing View   329

I campaigned for him even if he did not later campaign for me. Mother did not endorse him in advance, did not ever give him an unqualified endorsement, and did not campaign for him, though she "supported" him. She spoke to him on my behalf. A practical politician, he appreciated her popularity and appointed her to positions she deserved, such as at the U.N.

Although I got caught up in his contagious enthusiasm during the campaign, I was one of many who never thought he had a chance until all the returns were in and we were proven wrong. I will remember to the day I die Harry Truman holding up and reading aloud that *Chicago Tribune* headline reporting Dewey had defeated him, and mimicking H. V. Kaltenborn's radio report of Dewey's victory.

I learned a lesson from that. Nine times out of ten the political candidate who appears hopelessly beaten will be beaten, but there is always that tenth time. Politics is not an exact science and the mood of voters is never completely captured by polls. The public can be unpredictable at times.

Accordingly in 1950 when I was asked to oppose Earl Warren in the California gubernatorial election, I accepted the challenge, though it did seem hopeless. At least I was starting near the top. I was flattered. And I was told that it would be good for me, win or lose.

At that time cross-filing was legal in the state, but it did not seem appropriate to our two-party system of politics. Although clearly a Republican, a popular incumbent such as Warren could file as a candidate for both parties. If not strongly opposed by the other party, he could win both nominations and go to the statehouse in a walk.

A man named John Elliott proposed that I could do the state a service by seeking the nomination of my party and speaking out against that improper practice. I agreed, but only an unreasonable optimism led me to believe I might go on to defeat a two-time governor on my first time at bat in the elective arena. Perhaps the source of my optimism was that I felt fame was the name of the game. I knew my name was magic. At the same time that I was considering the race in California, Franklin was considering a comparable one in New York. *Look* magazine featured an article by its Washington bureau chief, headlined:

Two Young Roosevelts Race for the White House
Both Have FDR's Political Charm
Both May Become Governors in 1950
Together They May Upset Dewey and Warren

Mother had warned Elliott, "You are better off out of politics. You will only get in a jam." Now she warned Franklin against running in the gubernatorial race. "Be a good congressman first," she said. He had been elected to fill a vacant congressional seat in 1949 and she suggested he would be better off winning the seat on his own in 1950 instead of rushing off in quest of a higher position. But she didn't try to talk me out of the race I was about to make. Maybe she should have. I lost my race, while Franklin won his.

I did defeat Warren in the Democratic primary. I did not cross-file, and he won the Republican primary, of course. But I think I made my point. The practice of cross-filing was eventually eliminated.

Halfway through the campaign I saw that my cause was hopeless, but I carried on, giving it my best shot. I campaigned from one end of the state to the other, making as many as sixty speeches in a week. Borrowing a leaf from father, we converted the tailgate of a truck to look like the rear platform of a train. I traveled about in that truck, sometimes slept in it, and spoke from it.

I stressed, more than anything else, the need to prepare for a possible atomic attack. It seems silly now, but at that time, shortly after the war, when people were digging and stocking bomb shelters, it seemed that something should be done to plan a statewide evacuation of the automobile-addicted population of our major cities. I also spoke of inefficiencies in our state governement, which was not doing all it could for the people. But there were no exciting issues, there was not that much difference between our political philosophies, and Warren was a much more experienced administrator than I. The people of California showed excellent judgment in returning him to office over me by a wide margin.

I was not discouraged by my defeat. I had learned a lot about my state and about the conduct of a campaign, I had made powerful friends within my party and I had made an impact on the public. If I had lost at a lower level it might have been something else, but a loss to an incumbent governor at the highest level possible in the state hardly disgraced me. I had spent less than a quarter of a million dollars on my campaign, and that money had come from a wide variety of contributors. I was not left with debts. I was considered a political figure with a future.

Heading into 1952, my family was divided on our party's presidential possibilities. Eisenhower had decided to run on the Republican ticket and he looked like a hard man to beat. Truman had removed himself from the running. Mother and I were for Adlai Stevenson, but Franklin was for Averell Harriman.

After I made a seconding speech for Stevenson at the convention in Chicago, Franklin got up to speak for Harriman, but started out by speaking about me. He pointed out that the member of his family who had endorsed another candidate had never been elected to office, while he himself had been elected to the Congress of the United States. This personal and juvenile attack on his brother did him and his candidate a disservice. I was angered by it, as were most members of the convention. It was an embarrassment to them. Later on, I was able to laugh it off. I remember saying to Franklin, "I know I made a good speech, but I didn't think it was good enough to have provoked you that much."

Although Estes Kefauver had dominated the primaries, Stevenson captured the convention. Harriman never was a strong contender. After Eisenhower defeated Stevenson in 1952, I supported Kefauver in 1956. I always admired Stevenson, but I felt he had lost to Eisenhower once and would do so again—which he did, despite mother's support. Mother supported him again in 1960, but by then it was clear he could not win.

I was in John Kennedy's corner from the first, and mother was eventually won over by him. After Kennedy's death, I supported his successor, Lyndon Johnson, when he retained his presidential position at the polls in 1964. I was one of the leaders of the California delegation when Kennedy captured the nomination in 1960, and I remember a demonstrator outside hollering at me, "If Stevenson's good enough for your mother, he ought to be good enough for you." As I entered the arena, I smiled and shouted back, "We are an independent family." Which we were.

By then I had not only been elected to office, but had been elected three of my six times to Congress. When Sam Yorty surrendered his congressional seat to run for the U.S. Senate in 1954, a number of the party people suggested I go after Sam's seat. Ed and Ruth Lybeck, political activists in Los Angeles, were the most persuasive of the people who wanted me, and I wanted to be wanted. Fayga Berkowitz, a lovely lady, also joined my campaign. So I went into the race.

It was run out of the 26th District, which has been pictured as the prime example of a gerrymandered district. It ran a crooked course from Watts to Beverly Hills, from Washington Boulevard to Fairfax Avenue, and on out to the Pacific Ocean. Watts was where the poor blacks lived, Fairfax housed the middle-class Jews, Beverly Hills the rich whites. It had nearly 800,000 voters, about double what a district should have, and they represented an incredible cross section. It was impossible to represent such a cross section properly, but I tried. I'll admit I did not know a lot about it when I began, but I learned a lot as I went along.

My divorce from Romelle was prominent news about this time.

I did not and do not feel a person's personal problems should affect his public life. Years ago, a divorce was enough to destroy a man's political career. My father and mother avoided divorce for that reason, but I can't help wondering if my father might not have been an even better president if he'd permitted himself a happier private life. My marriage had ended, I had to tidy up the messy end, but I hadn't given up on life and I felt I could go on to be a good congressman.

I campaigned hard. I spoke in hundreds of homes. I made no promises except to protect the interests of the people in my district and to try to make their lives better. And to my surprise I won the Democratic nomination by a five-to-one margin over Ned Reddy, and I went on to win the congressional seat by a slim margin over my Republican opponent, Ted Owings.

For five campaigns after that I won my seat back every two years by increasingly large margins. I overcame all sorts of foes in these elections, including at one point a black, Crispus Wright. I remember clearly a group of my black constituents telling me that I had represented them well, but that I was not a black man and they wanted one working on their behalf. They put Wright against me, and I defeated him.

Once I got to Congress, I did the kind of job my people approved of. I'm proud of this. As soon as I was elected, I went to Texas to talk to Sam Rayburn. The Speaker of the House had been father's friend. I had known him a long time, and I felt he would be my friend, too. I respected him and asked his advice.

"Well, Jimmy," he said, "the best advice I can give you is to stick to business. If you want to make a career in politics, begin by busting your butt in Congress. Don't make a damn fool of yourself the way your brother Franklin did. The House of Representatives is a distinguished body and deserves more respect than Franklin gave it. Many of us are happy to spend our political careers there. Whether you are or not, make the most of the time you have there. Franklin wasted his time and our time there and I don't want you to make the same mistake."

After two terms in Congress, Franklin had left to lose bids

for, first, the governor's chair, then the attorney general's spot in New York. So, while his first move may have worked better than mine, he now was on the way down, while I was on the way up.

Sam said he'd be available to me any time I wanted to talk out some situation. As soon as I got to Washington, I went to him to discuss the question of my assignment to a committee, a critical matter which to a great extent determines the course a congressman takes and how effectively he can work. He asked me where I thought I would fit best. I explained about my divided district, but concluded that since most of my constituency consisted of working people who had not had a lot of opportunities in life, I thought I should aim at the labor and educational fields.

He sent me to see his friend Cecil King, the senior leader of my delegation and the regional representative on the Ways and Means Committee, which made the appointments of freshmen. Cecil was sympathetic, and not only saw that I was appointed to the Committee on Education and Labor, but that I was placed at the head of the new members, which put me about in the middle of the group in the critical matter of seniority.

I learned a lot in my more than ten years in Congress. I think the committee system of breaking up responsibilities into workable areas of interest is ideal. I think the seniority system by which these committees are run needs modification, but basically works well. You have to get to know the way the House works before you can be an effective member, and you have to get to know the members and the rules, and who to see and what to do to get things done. This takes time.

But while for the most part the senior members are the ones best qualified to operate on behalf of their committees, I don't think seniority alone makes a man a good and fair representative of the public. I think the committee members get to know the men most qualified to lead them, and they should elect their chairman from the three or four senior members of their group. The chairmanship should be rotated periodically. The younger members must be heard. And the Speaker of the House must be empowered to initiate action to replace a committee head whose work is disapproved of by the majority of his members.

When I joined the Committee on Education and Labor, the committee head was a conservative southerner, Graham Barden from North Carolina. He was not sympathetic to labor and did not think the federal government should interfere with education or anything else on the state level. He effectively stymied any action on the part of his committee. Speaker Rayburn wanted a more active and liberal committee, and when we launched a campaign to retire Barden, Sam encouraged it. Barden resisted, partly because the next in seniority and the man to replace him was Adam Clayton Powell, a black man from Harlem. It took two terms before Barden resigned and Adam took over as our chairman.

It is well known by now that Adam had his faults, and I will go into those, but here and now I want to say that he was an effective chairman. Whatever else he was interested in, he was interested in progressive government and the cause of the inadequately educated and poorly paid workingman. He had good ideas and he was willing to listen to and accept others' good ideas. But he was not interested in hard work. He developed a system of subcommittees to divide much of the work the chairman ordinarily would have done.

Adam's scheme to avoid work actually proved beneficial since it let all of us work. I, for example, became the chairman of the subcommittee on labor, charged with responsibilities in such areas as fair employment practices and minimum wages. I did work which led to a large and justified boost in the minimum wage for workers in this country, which I consider the greatest contribution of my congressional years. I'm also proud of work I did on behalf of the civil rights portion of a fair-employment-practices bill that was passed. Ordinarily, a junior congressman would have had no opportunities to make such contributions as early as I did. We had some eager-beaver young Turks on the committee, and Sam Rayburn held the reins on us, advised us and encouraged us so we could be effective.

If we had a problem, Powell was available to us. If you told him you wanted to talk to him, he'd say something like "Come around to my office at five." When you arrived he'd be mixing drinks. He'd give you one of his famous martinis and you'd sit around sipping socially and chatting. You'd tell him informally what you wanted, and if he approved and was in a good mood, which he usually was, you'd get it. He'd see to it that you got it. He knew how to get things done. You might say that he used us, but we used him, too. He was a fabulous front man, handsome, charming, intelligent and a most persuasive speaker. Perhaps because of his Baptist preacher background, he was an orator of the first order—flamboyant, but effective.

I remember when I was running for reelection one time, he came to speak on my behalf to a gathering of about four or five thousand garment workers packed into a large hall in Los Angeles. The audience was only about half black, but before long he had all of them acting like they were at a revival meeting—amening and hallelujahing and standing on their chairs.

He raised them to a fever pitch and then paused, pulling his tie down, opening his shirt and clutching his heart. Everyone hushed. I thought, "My God, he's having a heart attack." He turned toward me, sort of staggered, smiled and gave me a big wink which the audience could not see. "How'm I doin', Jim?" he whispered.

Then he turned back to the audience and explained that his feeling for me ran so deep it got him where he lived, in his heart. He got the crowd back into its seats and listening to him with total attention as he launched into the sincere, soft-spoken, from-the-heart part of his speech. He used dramatic effects to take an audience and hold it in the palm of his hand. His persuasive power was impressive, even frightening.

Like so many others, Powell abused his power. He was wealthy, so money meant nothing to him and he carelessly misused it. His father had made a fortune in real estate in

New York and Adam grew up a member of the black elite, college-educated and accustomed to a prominent position in black society. He fought tirelessly on behalf of poor blacks, but he himself always wanted to be accepted in white society, or anywhere else he wanted to go. He was entitled to this, of course, but his way of getting it was not especially praiseworthy. He saw himself as a sort of Martin Luther King of his day, and he felt entitled to the spoils of his success.

In contrast to the only other black in Congress at that time —Bill Dawson of Chicago—Powell demanded his due and that of his people. He filled his staff with friends, many of them female, many of them white and most of them attractive. He paid them well, with government funds, and took some of them on trips using government money. When an important vote came up, he was apt to be vacationing in the Bahamas or some such place.

I and other members of his staff simply looked the other way. We felt it was not our responsibility to report improper activities of which we suspected him. Nor was it necessary, since everyone in Congress at the time knew what he was doing. It was the job of the House Administration Committee to act against him if they considered such action necessary.

I'm not absolving myself of blame in this matter. I wasn't blind. I knew he had a home in Puerto Rico, a home here, a home there, a mistress here, a mistress there, a life-style that his salary simply could not cover, and which therefore was obviously paid for at least partly by government funds. But the fact was that under his leadership our committee was one of the most important and effective in Congress. He expedited passage of antipoverty programs called for by Lyndon Johnson in his quest for a "Great Society."

I never accepted a penny from Powell. I never saw him sign a voucher that was uncalled for. The clerk on his committee, a Mrs. Dargens, a large lady in every sense of the word, saw to it that the rest of us were protected from being a part of Adam's misdeeds.

It was difficult to live on my salary. I think I was paid

$15,000 a year at the start and $22,500 at the end, and by the time I settled with Romelle I had to pay her $13,000 a year. I had a small income from my inheritances and the remnants of my insurance business, but I had to appear regularly on the lecture circuit to keep myself afloat financially. I remember mother shopped for bargains for me so that I could save $25 here and $50 there on furniture I needed. It sounds silly, but no one who knew me then ever accused me of living in grandiose style.

As a member of the House you have to seek reelection every two years. Sometimes you seem to be constantly campaigning, which is costly. I had to maintain two residences—one in Washington and one in my home district—and I had to go back regularly to report to my people and to be seen. I did not have any large campaign contributors, but a large list of small contributors. My splendid aides, Ed and Ruth Lybeck, Alvin Meyers and Fayga Berkowitz, kept my accounts scrupulously clean and reported every penny that came in and went out. I was never attacked on that count.

As I mentioned earlier, one of my contributors was Howard Hughes, whom I had met when I worked for Sam Goldwyn. Elliott had worked for Hughes and knew him well. In fact, Elliott and Faye Emerson were married at Howard's home and went off on their honeymoon in Howard's private plane. Later on, Elliott helped Howard with his defense when he had to testify at a Senate hearing about some aircraft contracts that came into question.

The Hughes Aircraft Company in Culver City was within my district, and when I first ran for Congress one of Howard's aides called to ask if I would accept a campaign contribution from him. I said I'd certainly consider it, but I couldn't commit myself to any sort of repayment. The aide asked that I go to a certain corner at a certain time that night to be picked up and brought to Mr. Hughes.

It was all very mysterious, but I agreed. I went to the corner and was picked up in a limousine at precisely the appointed time. The shades in the car were drawn and we drove around in the dark for about a half-hour before I was delivered to what I suppose was Howard's home.

We talked about Elliott for a while, then Howard said he would like to contribute $5000 to my campaign and did not expect any particular commitment to repayment on my part. I agreed, and he handed me a check. We shook hands and I was delivered, in the dark, back to that corner.

Every campaign thereafter, he sent me a check for $5000, but I never saw him in person again. One time I was asked for a favor, but it was the sort I might do and did do for many of my constituents. The Hughes people felt Fairchild Corporation had made an unfair bid in beating them out of some helicopter contracts, and they wanted to talk to the Defense Department people about it. I set up appointments for them, and they succeeded in getting the original decision reversed, but I was not asked to and did not apply pressure of any sort on anyone.

I was active in many areas during my congressional service. I also became a member of the Small Business Committee, which gave me an opportunity to champion the cause of the little guy. I took on AT&T, ASCAP, the savings and loan institutions and the major oil companies, who sometimes have tried to squeeze the small businessman out of business. I introduced the first bill aimed at preventing the major oil companies from controlling the distribution of products their member stations sell. For instance, Standard Oil Company has company-owned Standard stations and individually leased Chevron stations, and my bill was aimed at giving the individual some say in his operation.

The major oil companies opposed me bitterly, but something had to be done to give the independent a fair shake. There is a lot of price-fixing which tends to squeeze the independent pretty hard, but because no one has yet been able to pin down where and what the real costs and profits are between the producer and the consumer, government really has not been effective in straightening out this situation. Wright Patman, a William Jennings Bryan type of Democrat, a dictatorial committee chairman, kept his group pretty much in control, but he fought the Federal Reserve Board and other powerful interests fiercely. He made us effective and he taught me a lot about in-fighting.

I had some successes and some failures in fighting for those things I believed in during my years in the House, but it was an extraordinary experience at the very least. I did not approve of all my fellow congressmen and I fought some of them. I also earned considerable recognition as one of the first to challenge the House Un-American Activities Committee and the abuses they committed under the guise of fighting communism. The end does not always justify the means. Fortunately, the time came when enough members of the House and the public recognized the injustice of this committee's acts and stifled it.

In fighting the Un-American Activities Committee, I struck a blow against Senator Joe McCarthy, the leader of this criminally careless crusade against so-called communist influence in this country. Along the way he ruined many promising careers, including those of many members of the movie industry, some of whom were based at MGM in Culver City or in parts of Beverly Hills that were in my district.

One of the key members of the Un-American Activities Committee was also a key member of the Committee on Immigration, in which I was interested. I had to walk a tightrope in opposing his witch-hunting, while courting him on individual immigration cases I represented. Such conflicts are commonplace in politics. I think the reason Eisenhower did not crack down on McCarthy was that at the time Joe was popular with a large number of Republicans and it was dangerous to oppose him.

Several of us got together in the late 1950s and formed the Democratic Study Group, which was designed as a caucus of liberals who would consider problems we thought important and campaign for them within the House. Frank Thompson of New Jersey was one of the leaders—and remains, in my opinion, one of the outstanding members of Congress. Most of us who were associated with the group from its formation were young, but some were older, such as Tip O'Neill, that interesting fellow from Massachusetts who has become majority leader of the House. He remains more or less a liberal, though more conservative than at one time, and a part of the establishment now.

George McGovern was also a member, and I think that was when my mistrust of him started. He was quite articulate and outspoken when we were discussing causes, but he was silent when it came to carrying them to the House. He always had some excuse for not being a member of the committee that carried our proposal to the Speaker or other leader to argue for action. He stood up when it didn't take guts, and sat down when it did. I think that is the way he conducted his presidential campaign in 1972.

We did have bold people who were not afraid to fight for our causes, and we developed quite a solid organization. We were a help to Sam Rayburn, who had a liberal bent, but, as a southerner, needed help to promote liberal causes with other establishment members.

Along the way we decided we should clarify our philosophy, and that the best way to do it would be to get the leading liberals to write pieces which would become chapters of a book we would distribute. We found a publisher for the book, called *The Liberal Papers*, and we wound up making money on it, though it was not a project designed for profit and the cash that came in was turned over to various charities.

I was one of a dozen Democrats associated with the book. I edited it and wrote the foreword, in which I said I agreed in principle with the basic philosophies expressed within the book, even if I did not agree with everything the contributors had to say. They recommended, among other things, recognition by this country of Red China and total disarmament around the world, save for a U.N. police force, both of which have become popular ideas.

At the time, the book was not popular with many members of the establishment, especially Republicans, and conservatives on both sides. As a matter of fact John Kennedy, who was president at the time, expressed his disapproval, suggesting it made his party look like a leftist organization. When I heard this, I wrote him a letter saying I was disappointed in his attitude because I had believed that it was in the best interest of both the party and the country to have an airing of differing views. He replied that, contrary to what I might have heard, he was not in the least concerned about publication of the papers except that it might politically embarrass some good congressmen. He added: "While I have not agreed for a long period of time with many of the writers, I do think that the more that is written and discussed about foreign policy the more meaningful becomes our use of free speech and the more careful becomes our analysis of present and future policies." He concluded by saying that the "bankruptcy of the Republican party" has been exposed by their attitude.

Later, the Republicans replied with something called *The Conservative Papers*, but it was so badly done that even conservatives disowned it.

I was not immune to attack, of course. In fact one time I was put in my place by one of my own relatives, a distant cousin named Kathryn St. George, who represented the Tuxedo Park district. She was in Congress long before I got there, but when one day she said something on the floor I couldn't accept, I rose to challenge it, asking, "Would the gentlewoman from New York yield to me?" A superb speaker with a biting tongue, she observed, "The gentleman from California knows me well, being related to me, but he does not know me well enough, apparently, to know there is nothing gentle about me. Nevertheless, I yield to him." It didn't matter. I was dead. Everyone was laughing at me.

A lot less funny was an incident in which Manny Rivers, the representative from South Carolina, replied to my comments on a civil rights bill for which I was fighting. He said something to the effect that he understood where his distinguished colleague from California got his ideas, since he was "the son of the greatest nigger-loving woman who ever lived in the White House."

The House hushed. My first instinct was to punch him in the nose and I jumped from my seat, but two or three others grabbed me and sat me back down, giving me a moment to think things over. The Speaker then asked me if I wished my colleague's words removed from the record or wished to reply to them, but I said no on both counts. I realized his comments would hurt him more than they would hurt me, and I did not need to lower myself.

As it happens, there was at the time—and I think there still is—a strange rule that permits members to amend their comments before they appear in the *Congressional Record,* and Rivers's remark does not now appear in that record.

I should make it clear that I admired and made friends with many representatives from the South during my days in the House. Vinson from Georgia, for example, one of the senior members and chairman of the Armed Services Committee, was an admirable man in my eyes, though he and I disagreed on many matters. But he was a decent person. He had no reason whatsoever to do me any favors, but I remember when my third wife, Irene, was in an automobile accident in Georgia and was unable to complete the drive to Washington, I asked him if he could help in any way and he responded immediately. He swiftly arranged for an ambulance plane from the coast guard to fly her to town. I was touched by it.

Another Georgian, Phil Landrom, sat alongside me on the Education and Labor Committee and opposed me on many issues, but when any one of these issues was approved by the majority, he worked hard on its behalf. Accordingly, when he was in a contest against a northerner for a seat on the Ways and Means Committee, I voted for Phil because I knew him to be a fair and conscientious congressman.

Indeed, I found most of the members of the House to be fair and conscientious. Because there are so many of them compared to the one hundred members of the Senate, and because they represent so many splintered districts of this country while those in the Senate represent entire states, two to a state, the House is not as efficient as the Senate. Representatives rarely achieve the fame of senators—except when a Gerry Ford is promoted to prominence—but because they are closer to the people, they may better represent the attitudes and interests of the people of this country.

The two-year term imposes problems on representatives that senators do not face. But I believe that because they are closer to the people, representatives should be more accountable to them. I believe there is balance both in the natures of these bodies of Congress and in the shorter and longer terms they serve.

I believe we must restore the balance of power between the presidency and Congress. It is said that my father did more to promote the power of the presidency than any man before him, and began the pull of power away from Congress. But he did take his issues to Congress—and lost on many of them —and unlike some of his successors, he did not take this country to war without asking the approval of Congress.

I don't care what kind of an action you call it, if it involves fighting in which our soldiers kill and are killed, it is a war. I do not believe we would be out of Vietnam today if our citizens had not demonstrated their wishes to their representatives in Congress, causing them to apply pressure on the presidency. It is sad that it has taken violence for the blacks to impress their cause upon the public, but this was translated into a call to Congress for action, which our presidents might not have initiated on their own.

My father might have been dictatorial at times, but he was not a dictator. In our democracy there is no place for a presidential dictator, even if he is a better man than my father was. We need a strong and active president, but also a strong and active Congress. We need such legislation as is necessary to insure that the executive and legislative branches of our government maintain checks on one another while working in as much harmony as possible.

There always have been and I suppose always will be some

scoundrels in public service, and there really is no room for them, no matter how much good they do for others. Such a scoundrel, of course, was Adam Clayton Powell. And it became clear after a while that the powers-that-be were ready to act against him.

This put me in a peculiar position. I felt he had done good work, and he had put me in a position to do good work. Indeed, as the heat on him increased he came to me and said, "Jimmy, I've been a friend to you and I may need a friend before long. I've given you your chance, and now I may need you to give me a chance. I may need a defender, and I've decided you're just the guy to do it for me."

I don't remember replying to him. I think I just smiled and slapped him on the back. I played the part of a friend, but I could see myself betraying him. I might plead for him, but I could not in good conscience plead his innocence. I was on the spot and I was looking for a way out.

One way out that I considered was a race for the Senate in 1964, but I bowed out when the liberal California Democratic Council endorsed a commendable candidate, Alan Cranston. I decided instead to run for mayor of Los Angeles, which I could do without giving up my House seat. I had little respect for Sam Yorty, the incumbent, but he had an appeal to the common man that defied explanation.

Yorty was, to tell the truth, a very common man. He laughed at intellectuals. He opposed new ideas. He did little for the city. He operated a government of conflict, rather than of progress. Yet he had pretensions of grandeur. He wanted to be governor. He ran for the Senate. He even ran for the presidency.

I believe I could have done a better job as mayor than Sam did, but I was a poor opponent for him. People like the Wymans prevailed on me to give it a try, but I was outmatched. I knew my district, not my city. I had no hold on the local situation, as Sam had. Given a little more time I could have accumulated a staff of advisers and such information as I needed, but I didn't give myself the time, I didn't plan properly. I carried the fight to the finish, but I was beaten badly. And, somehow, Sam got reelected and reelected until finally a man he had beaten, Tom Bradley, came back to beat him.

Maybe I picked my spots poorly, but I was beaten in both my attempts to gain the top posts in my adopted hometown and home state. And though I did not know it then, I had come close to the end of my political career, at least as a candidate or an officeholder.

In July of 1965, Adlai Stevenson died. I was invited by President Johnson to accompany his party on the plane trip to and from Illinois for the funeral. On the trip it became clear that the president was talking Supreme Court Justice Arthur Goldberg into replacing Stevenson as head of the U.S. delegation to the U.N. Lyndon was a whiz at twisting arms, so I was not surprised when a few days later it was announced that Arthur was resigning from the Court to take the U.N. position.

By the sheerest of chances, a week later I found myself on the same plane with Arthur on a flight from New York to Washington. We sat together, and in the course of conversation, to my surprise, he said, "Jim, I'm looking for some good people to take with me to the U.N. and I'd like to have you with me." I asked him what he might want me to do. He said he'd like me to be his assistant and fill the position of U.S. ambassador to the Economic and Social Council.

I was flattered, but I wondered what the president would think of it. Goldberg said, "If I'm for it, the president will be."

Well, it was a godsend, a solution to my difficult situation in the House, but I still said I'd have to think about it.

He said, "If the president approves, you're coming."

I said, "Not until I think it over."

His last words to me were, "Jim, if it was good enough for your mother, it's good enough for you."

I still thought I should take time to think it over. Despite my problem with Powell, I wasn't sure I wanted to walk away from Congress. But the more I thought about my problem, the more I thought this was a solution to it. I wouldn't have to speak either for Powell or against him.

It was not more than a day or two before I got a telephone call from President Johnson saying, "Will you be at the White House in two hours, Jim; I'm announcing your appointment to the U.N."

"But, Mr. President," I said, "I haven't even decided if I'll accept the appointment or not." "Oh, there's no question about your accepting the appointment," he said breezily. "If Justice Goldberg says he has to have you, that's it."

That was the way Johnson was. When he wanted something, he wouldn't take no for an answer. He concluded that conversation by saying, "Look, Jim, the Justice wants to get this show on the road and you're in it. I'll see you shortly." And hung up.

That was at eight in the morning. I was at the White House being introduced as the newest member of the U.N. mission team at ten. I announced I would resign from the House shortly, which I did.

I didn't know I was walking away from politics for good, but I was. Maybe I felt it but didn't want to face it. I didn't want to face Powell either, but I did. I told him I'd accepted the appointment to the U.N., was leaving Congress and was sorry I wouldn't get to serve with him in the future. He smiled and simply wished me well. He was tough. Maybe he could have used the Roosevelt name, but he felt he could win without it. One of his assistants said he was sorry to see me go, that the chief sure could have used my help, but that was the closest anyone came to condemning my move.

I resigned in September of 1965. But it wasn't until 1967 that the House got around to removing Powell from his chairmanship, stripping him of his seniority and refusing to seat him, after rather raucous hearings on the matter. He simply ran for reelection in 1968, won, and when the House refused to seat him, took it to court and won his case. He did lose out in the primary in his home district in 1970. He died in 1972.

Meanwhile, I was appointed to the United Nations Mission by the president. The appointment was approved by the Senate, unanimously I believe. Arthur Goldberg, who in reality was responsible to and working for our State Department, headed up our delegation of ambassadors to the mission and we were responsible to him. However, there was an ambassador to each of the U.N.'s councils, and that ambassador cast his own vote on each issue.

Goldberg was our ambassador to the Security Council, which of course is the key council insofar as international tensions, threats of wars and actual wars are concerned. I was our ambassador to the Economic and Social Council, and we dealt with a wide range of problems in these areas, especially as they affected the new members—the many emerging nations of that time—in their relationships with the old, established member nations. The United Nations has also been active in developing special organizations, such as UNESCO, to which each country appoints a special representative. I would have liked to have been that representative somewhere along the line.

Possibly because my father was sympathetic to the old League of Nations and was behind the United Nations from the beginning, and because my mother worked so hard for and was so enthusiastic about the U.N., I was happy to work for the organization. And I remain enthusiastic about it, though clearly it has its problems. For one thing, the United States is to a great extent supporting it financially, while the Soviet Union and Great Britain pay lesser amounts and some nations pay nothing at all. For another, the proliferation of nations has divided voting power almost past the point of reason.

But even in those areas where the veto power exercised by the major charter members has inhibited action, I think the debates have served a useful purpose in giving wide circulation to the sentiments of the various nations on controversial issues. I think the U.N. has rather more effectively than expected enforced periods of peace from time to time in the Middle East and other areas. And I think the U.N. has contributed enormously to the development of many nations and has helped many people who needed help in nonpolitical matters.

My position with the U.N. was not purely political, but there is no way to deal with the other nations of the world without getting into politics. I remember a rather comical run-in I had with the Russians, for example. In the course of a debate I made a speech critical of the Russian position, and of course the moment I sat down the Russian delegate jumped up to exercise his right of reply. But no sooner had he started, "Mr. Chairman, ladies and gentlemen, the distinguished ambassador from the United States says . . ." than the lights and microphone went out. It was New York's famous blackout, in 1965, and the power did not return until long after everyone had left the chamber.

The next morning I was advised that the Russian planned to protest in stern terms, claiming that the blackout had been designed to silence him and was simply an example of how the United States sought to control debates and a good reason why the U.N. should not be headquartered in this country.

On the pretext of apologizing to the body for the power failure, I got permission to speak first. I addressed my remarks primarily to the Russian and said, "Mr. Ambassador, if you wish, we will welcome an investigation of the power failure, but I can assure you that the workings of Consolidated Edison are beyond even the control of the United States delegation. We were deeply disappointed that we did not get to hear your remarks yesterday, and I assure you we will listen with undivided attention and great interest to what you have to say today."

That effectively blunted any attack he might have made. He saw that, smiled, stood up and limited himself to the mildest of comments.

I had one major controversy during my term in the U.N. It arose when the Russian delegate introduced a resolution that each nation be entitled to control and conserve its own natural resources.

Well, I come from a family of conservationists and the

resolution seemed fair enough to me. In my comments on it I said I supported it. To my surprise this created a stir, and when I left the floor I walked into a hornet's nest. Mr. Goldberg and other members of the U.S. delegation made it clear that the State Department was furious with me. It seems that this had been a subject of argument among nations for years, and the United States had continuously opposed such resolutions. We had valuable holdings in other countries—in oil, for example—and the resolution would support the right of these countries to simply take over these holdings, as they often did anyway.

I had not done my homework before I had spoken. But frankly, after detailed discussions of the problem, I still felt I should support the resolution. The United States does a lot of things in other countries which it would not welcome other countries doing here. Even those who felt that we were right when we intervened in Korea and Vietnam would not have welcomed foreign intervention in our Civil War, for example, or African intervention during our black uprisings, and so on. We expect to be permitted to operate without interference in oil and other industries abroad, but expect complete control over the operations of other countries in the United States.

I had simply said what I believed. The problem was I had no right to do so. We all have our own ideas, but when we are representing our country, we must support its policies. I did not agree with the State Department position, but I had to support it or resign.

I was in an awkward position. I had already expressed an opinion and could not in good conscience retract it. So I offered to resign. Mr. Goldberg refused to accept that, suggesting, instead, that I abstain from the vote. Essentially, in offering this compromise solution, he was supporting me. I accepted and was grateful.

One of the things we developed on the Economic and Social Council was the United Nations Industrial Development Organization. UNIDO was set up to provide help for those nations that needed it, primarily the new, emerging nations. Before it even got started, however, a fight developed over where it would be based. The French wanted it in Paris and we wanted it in the United States.

Mr. Goldberg asked me to carry our case to the General Assembly, where it would be decided, but meanwhile we privately decided to support Vienna as a compromise site. Very quietly, I went to our supporters and asked them to switch their support to Vienna. When the time came, I stood up in the Assembly and announced that, putting the interests of UNIDO ahead of our personal interests, the United States was withdrawing New York from contention, was supporting Vienna and hoped its friends would do likewise.

The French were caught off guard. The Austrian delegation had done a lot of effective campaigning behind closed doors in the meantime, and, with our help, there was nothing the French could do to stop the vote from going to Vienna.

I admired Mr. Goldberg enormously and enjoyed the experience of working in the U.N. I met a cross section of important and interesting personalities from throughout the world, people I could not have encountered in any other activity. I think I did good work in a limited way for a little while.

But as so often was the case in my life, personal problems began to intrude. I was not getting along well with my third wife, Irene. We were living on Manhattan's expensive East Side, on Eighty-first Street, just off Park Avenue, and we had a large house because we had to have one suitable for entertaining. I was paid something like $26,000, and not much was left after we paid our rent. Though we had to entertain at different times delegates from most of the 130 nations represented in the U.N. at that time, we were allowed only a few hundred dollars for entertainment, which barely covered one or two parties.

It is said that in my life I made too many decisions for financial reasons. But when you cannot make ends meet, you are driven to decisions you do not make with enthusiasm. We hear about the crooks, but we do not hear enough about the honest men who make personal sacrifices in public service. I am an honest man, even if I was once foolish enough not to recognize that I had been drawn into a dishonest activity. In my life I made many personal sacrifices to remain in public service, mostly because I wanted to do things for others, and partly for the less noble reason that I also liked the life. But there were times when it became a difficult one.

In the summer of 1966 my U.N. Economic and Social Council met in Switzerland. I had my son Del with me and he wanted to go sailing on Geneva Lake. I inquired about a boat, and a man I knew told me of one that I could borrow. It was a motorboat, and Dell and I had a delightful day on the water.

When we returned, I said I'd like to thank the man who had loaned us the boat. I was told it was a Mr. Bernie Cornfeld, and that he no doubt would like to meet me. An appointment was made and I met this magnetic man at his villa in Geneva.

During our conversation Cornfeld talked of his two primary projects—Investors Overseas Services and the Fund of Funds. He asked me if I had known Adlai Stevenson or Stevenson's campaign manager, Wilson Wyatt. I said I had known them very well indeed. He told me Mr. Wyatt was on the board of the Fund of Funds and that Mr. Stevenson, before his death, had agreed to serve on the board. Later, I checked this out and found it to be true.

I was intrigued by the booming business IOS and the Fund of Funds were doing. Asked about my personal circumstances, I said I enjoyed my work but admitted I was struggling. Mr. Cornfeld then asked me if I might be interested in joining the board. I said I might be, but would have to talk it over with Ambassador Goldberg.

There was nothing illegal about an ambassador being a director of a company. Although I had no doubt my name brought me the offer, I was assured the international experience and contacts I had made might make me a useful member of the team. I was taken to visit the Bella Vista offices and met members of management, who impressed me with their enthusiasm.

I went back to the States by boat, and to my surprise received a call on the ship from a *New York Times* reporter
asking me about my appointment to the board of the Fund of
Funds. When I said I had not yet accepted any appointment,
the reporter told me it had been announced in Geneva.

A little later I learned that IOS was in litigation with the
U.S. government. The *Times* editorialized that it was improper for an ambassador to associate himself with a company
that was in litigation with the government.

I got on the phone and raised the devil with Cornfeld. He
apologized for the announcement, admitting it was premature, but said he very much wanted me with them. In fact, he
would like me to go to work for them full time. He offered
me $100,000 a year, generous expenses and a house in Switzer-
land, which was simply a whale of an attractive offer. He
assured me the litigation was a technical matter, offered to
send over a representative to explain it and the company's
operations to me, and said he would welcome my personal
investigation of him and his company before I made a decision.

That seemed fair enough to me, and I went along with it.

Bernie Cornfeld was the backbone of IOS and the chairman
of the board. Edward Cowett was the general counsel and
became the company's president. Allen Cantor was the sales
chief. Together they headed an impressive staff of executives
and hundreds of salesmen. It was an especially promising
business—essentially, a mutual-fund operation which had the
beauty of being international in scope. It took the funds of
individual investors and invested them in businesses around
the world. With a great deal of money to invest and the ability
to invest it in any business anywhere in the world, IOS could
pick its spots most profitably. It was making investments and
returning profits in the hundreds of millions of dollars, and
my investigation disclosed that it was one of the most admired
young companies in the business world.

The thrust of the U.S. government's case against IOS was
that although it was registered as a nonresident Canadian

corporation, had headquarters in Switzerland and had no U.S. investors, a small percentage of its stock was owned by U.S. citizens. The company had originally applied to be licensed as a broker-dealer and did have some investments in the United States, so the SEC felt it had the right to inspect all of IOS's transactions around the world. Refused this right, the SEC was pressing its case in the courts.

I was told that IOS refused the SEC the right to inspect because banking secrecy was considered sacred in many countries, especially in Europe. Besides, investors wanted their privacy protected when they invested in a company that operated as IOS did.

The case eventually was settled out of court with IOS retaining its right to secrecy by surrendering its U.S. license and agreeing not to take in U.S. investors.

My investigations led me to believe IOS was aboveboard in every respect. I spoke to people at the Bankers Trust in New York, which served as a trustee for them. I spoke to the legal firm of Willkie, Farr and Gallagher, one of the most respected in New York, which represented IOS. One of the top three banks in Switzerland served as the IOS agent in that country. The firm that represents the Bank of England represented them in that country.

Thus, though it is easy now to say I should have seen trouble ahead, there really was no indication of it at the time. In my first few years with the company, a $110-million public offering of IOS common stock was sold out and the stock almost doubled in value from its original listing at $10 a share. One summer the company did almost $500 million in sales. IOS was considered the wonder of the worldwide business community.

Although I exercised an opportunity to purchase shares in the company after resigning from the U.N. and moving to Switzerland to join IOS, I was not personally involved in investments or in the handling of money. My assignment was to supervise a policy shift. Many countries resented the flow of investment dollars outside of their borders, so it was decided that a percentage of every dollar invested would remain within the parent country.

At first, forty cents on every dollar was invested within the parent country. Later, fifty cents—half of every investment dollar—was kept within its country. This stimulated the economy of each country while a flow of fresh money for use in investments was kept flowing into our company. In Italy, France, Spain, England, Holland and other countries, I set up promising programs in which we were associated with some of the finest financial institutions in those countries.

In the late 1960s, however, relations between Bernie and me began to fall apart. A number of our salesmen were getting into legal hassles in their countries because they were smuggling money out of these countries in order to make investments in our fund and thus claim the commissions.

These salesmen were independent agents, and it's not common for companies wishing to operate ethically to have problems with their independent agents. Bernie and the others in IOS management told me they were doing their best to clean up this situation, and I believed them for a while. However, there came a time when Bernie asked me why it was wrong for the little guy to profit by the sort of things big businessmen were doing every day. I began to see that he was not really concerned about how the money got to him.

I never participated in any of Bernie's parties. I did not even see that side of him during the first few years. But after a while, as the money started to roll in, Bernie began neglecting his business in order to party with the profits. I saw him as a super-salesman and an inventive and agreeable guy at first, but after a while I began to see him as an undisciplined person who would do almost anything to have a good time. He liked younger women and he had an amazing number of beauties around him at all times.

Unfortunately he had no one around him sufficiently qualified in high-finance management to keep the ship on course. Those who were not crooks were nevertheless not competent. Pie-in-the-sky promises that they would become millionaires made the key salesmen so greedy that many of them skimmed commissions off the top before they even earned them. Moreover, money was not wisely invested in certain companies, and many fraud cases were pending. The public offering preceded a depression in the stock market which sent shares of IOS plummeting. The bottom began to fall out of our entire operation.

Now, I want to make it clear that many made a lot of money from IOS investments. Many bought shares in the company cheaply and sold them profitably as their value soared.

I was not one of those who made a profit out of IOS, and no one has suggested I was, though some may believe this simply because of my involvement. As soon as I saw the situation for what it was, in 1971, I resigned my position. I remained a member of the board of directors and a director of some of its companies for another year or so because I believed in the sincerity of rescue attempts mounted first by John King, then by Bob Vesco, and felt they needed a liaison between old and new management if they were going to save something for the investors. When I saw that they were interested in their own fortunes, not the company's, I left entirely.

When I finally left, I went to Bob Vesco and said, "I'm no longer a young man, but all I can see to do is to go back to California and start all over again."

IOS is in the hands of liquidators and in limbo. Bob Vesco says he bought protection from the U.S. government by making the largest single contribution, $200,000, as an undeclared contribution to the Committee to Re-elect the President, Richard Nixon. Charges of misuse of funds have been brought against Vesco, but, living in exile in Costa Rica, he has not had to face them.

I myself was burned by IOS and turned no profit in it, but I've somewhat recovered. My consulting company has offices in Newport Beach and Beverly Hills. The various companies I represent wish to place products on the market, open up new areas of activities and purchase properties. Doors still open to me, and once I pass through them I have experience

and expertise to offer which is helpful to my clients. I have
not struck it rich with any of these as yet, but we are in there
pitching and the ball game is far from finished.

I enjoy the business world and I have no interest in a
full-time return to politics. I do have an interest in public
affairs. I am on a number of committees and I also represented
the U.S. government as leader of the delegation to Australia
for the prime minister's funeral.

I make an adequate living from my business, my inheri-
tances and a government pension, but my expenses are considerable and there are some potential liabilities. I admit to
my mistakes, but I still value my name and my reputation.

Seemingly, I am left with little. The truth is I still have a
lot. Not in money, which I have learned does not mean that
much, but in life. Most especially in my wife. If it took all my
bad marriages to bring me to this one, they were worth it.
Mary is tolerant of my mistakes, cares nothing about the past
and looks forward to the future. I also treasure my children
—Kate, Sara, Jim, Mike, Anne, Dell, Becky. Most of them are
adults with lives of their own now, and I hold Becky tight,
hugging her to my heart. When a man of sixty-eight has a
daughter of five, life is far from finished.

It has certainly been an eventful life. I was privileged to
have had parents who made history. If that made our lives
difficult, it was worth it. For all of the problems it imposed
on us, I don't believe any of us would have swapped what we
had for uneventful lives within the shadows. I think we all
feel we contributed at least a little to the life of this country
through much of this century. We may have criticized one
another and clashed at times, but we all have loved one another and felt for one another. Franklin, Elliott and John, Jim
salutes you. And Anna, he mourns you.

The hills outside my splendid home atop a place called
Spyglass Hill seem a little steeper these days. But as I look out
over the ocean I think of another ocean which encircled the
island on which as a boy I spent so many splendid days with
my parents. I do not own my own boat, but I borrow a boat

now and then to sail, and at those times I think of my father sailing with me. I think of him as my father, not my president. I think of her as my mother, not an international figure. Thus, I can think of them as few others can. At twilight, I treasure memories others missed.

Index